COLORADO
BOULDERING

MOUNTAINS

PHILLIP BENNINGFIELD

Sharp End

Colorado Bouldering: Mountains and Western Slope by Phillip Benningfield

©2020 Sharp End Publishing, LLC

Published and distributed by:

Sharp End Publishing, LLC

P.O. Box 1613

Boulder, CO 80306

t. 303-444-2698

www.sharpendbooks.com

ISBN: 978-1-892540-99-7

Cover Photos: Sheyna Button on Boulder E in Redcliff

Graphic Designer: Sarah Nicholson

Proofreaders: Phillip Benningfield, Melissa Lester

Publisher/Editor: Fred Knapp

WARNING

Climbing is a very dangerous activity. Take all precautions and evaluate your ability carefully. Use judgment rather than the opinions represented in this book. The publisher and author assume no responsibility for injury or death resulting from the use of this book. This book is based on opinions. Do not rely on information, descriptions, or difficulty ratings as these are entirely subjective. If you are unwilling to assume complete responsibility for your safety, do not use this guidebook.

THE AUTHOR AND PUBLISHER EXPRESSLY DISCLAIM ALL REPRESENTATIONS AND WARRANTIES REGARDING THIS GUIDE, THE ACCURACY OF THE INFORMATION HEREIN, AND THE RESULTS OF YOUR USE HEREOF, INCLUDING WITHOUT LIMITATION, IMPLIED WARRANTIES OF MERCHANTABILITY, AND FITNESS FOR A PARTICULAR PURPOSE. THE USER ASSUMES ALL RISK ASSOCIATED WITH THE USE OF THIS GUIDE.

It is your responsibility to take care of yourself while climbing. Seek a professional instructor or guide if you are unsure of your ability to handle any circumstances that may arise. This guide is not intended as an instructional manual.

Acknowledgments:

It is impossible to collect quality information without the guidance and knowledge of many people! Without proper direction, historical insight, guidance at new areas, and patience checking the problems, photos and text, a guidebook is only a bunch of jibberish. Lastly, there are people we must thank who are not climbers but who certainly play an important role in giving the support we need to concentrate on the guide—that means time to play in the woods and repeat and put up hundreds of excellent two scoop problems.

More than anyone, we have to thank our regular bouldering partners. Your trite suppositions, sarcasm, mind boggling idiocies, pain-killing remedies, patience with our never-ending questions, and attentive spots helped immensely.

A special thanks goes out to Adam Avery (for his unyielding hospitality and delicious beers), Organic, Cordless, Jamie Emerson, Jay Droeger, John Gill, Chris Goplerud, Five Ten, Mike Freischlag, Justin Jaeger, La Sportiva, Will and Jen Lemaire, Scott Neel, Andy Mann, Metolius Mountain Products, John Sherman, Trixie Tartasky, and Pete Zoller—for their photos, philosophies, attentive eyes, and in-depth knowledge of Colorado's mountain boulders.

Other boulderers I'd like to thank are:

Chad Beckelhymer	Charlie Fowler	Greg Johnson	John Ryan
Jim Belcer	Chuck Fryberger	Eric Johnson	Tim Ryan
Charlie Bentley	Kurt Frye	Colin Lantz	Bennett Scott
Tommy Caldwell	Tom Gage	Charles Lintott	George Sowers
Mike Caldwell	Mike Gash	Craig Luebben	Justin Talbot
John Conant	Naomi Guy	Steve Mammen	Matt Tiwonowski
Bob Couchman	Tyler Handy	Andrew McClure	Brad Tomlin
Cameron Cross	Tom Hanson	Mark Milligan	Tim Toula
Patrick DeCicco	Ned Harris	William Mondragon	Dave Whaley
Josh Deuto	Dawn Heigele	Rob Mordock	Pat Wilde
John Dunn	Jonathan Houck	Tony Nordi	Mark Wilford
Ryan Fields	Haven Iverson	Aaron Quinlisk	And so many more
Herm Feissner	Chris Jones	Chip Ruckgaber	devoted boulderers

Bouldering is the heart of climbing! Going bouldering is often a shared activity (although going out alone and scaring the shit out of oneself has merit), hence it retains a highly personal feel—mentally and physically. Sublime feelings often occur at the exact moment when a spotter's encouragement is deafened by needed concentration: the desire to grasp a distant minute edge, or trying to hold on to fleeting confidence as you get way off the deck. These are some of the experiences—unshared and pure—for which boulders are developed. There is also an undeniably simple pleasure of having so much fun that the woods and canyons echo with unrestrained laughter.

Colorado's mountains are filled to overflowing with spectacular problems. There are so many, in too many places to include in one measly guide (I rarely boulder at any of the listed areas as I am constantly finding new boulders that I can't help but keep to myself and a small contingent of mates for the joy we find in obscurity). The sheer volume of daily development has made it impossible to include each and every new V1 or V14! The mountains (not including wilderness areas) are graced with a plethora of boulders of every shape, size, and type of rock. From the pine-covered hillsides and granite of Sheep's Nose in the South Platte to Penitente's rhyolite and high desert environment to Newlin Creeks splitter granite to Sailing Hawks sandstone, the possibilities for problems are endless. With all the areas covered in the guide, you will have to take a sabbatical from school or work, get a home from Down by the River Vans, have leather grafted to your fingertips, and devote yourself, like a monk, to screwing off.

This guide highlights the best boulders that will bring the widest grins and greatest exclamations. Obscure (not seen in videos and magazine ads), high quality boulders will be included! That is to say that some boulders will not be to everyone's liking because they are not on the Internet machine. Some areas with less than ideal stone have been included to get you and your crash pad away from the rock gym and the masses. It is important to remember that not every boulder will be as perfect as The Nickness at Newlin Creek. Adventure, albeit limited, can be found on the low-traffic remote blocks that require gumption and trust in this guide. Other areas have been included but have no in-depth descriptions due to very little development or possible access problems. Whatever the area or situation you may find yourself in, simply turn the page of this awesome guide and even more superlative areas will be revealed.

Colorado Bouldering is devoted specifically to bouldering. As bouldering relies on an individual's mental and physical tenacity—exclusive of all equipment but shoes and chalk—many problems that were originally done on toprope have been ignored. The safety of the rope inherently destroys the fear factor—an integral part of bouldering. An indistinguishable line exists between a solo and highball problem, therefore all ascents considered boulder problems have been left up to the author's judgment.

Enjoy!

METOLIUS

SUPER
CHALK

METOLIUS
SUPER
CHALK

4.5 ounces
127 grams

America's #1
Climbing Chalk

La magnesie la plus
populaire pour
l'escalade en Amerique

www.metoliusclimbing.com

Jonathan Siegrist flashing the Snail Trail V7 Meadow Camp, Oregon. Photo Brooke Sandahl

TABLE OF CONTENTS

CENTRAL MOUNTAINS

01 Sheep's Nose   13
02 Elevenmile Park   25
03 Newlin Creek   33
04 Guanella Pass   43
05 Red Cliff/Hornsilver   51
06 Redstone   65
07 Chapman Reservoir   73
08 Independence Pass   77
09 Buena Vista   103
10 Hecla Junction   113
11 Agnes Vaille   119

SOUTHERN MOUNTAINS

12 San Luis Valley   125
13 Monte Vista   149
14 Crested Butte/Gunnison   159
15 Telluride   175
16 Durango   181

WESTERN SLOPE

17 New Castle   197
18 Unaweep   201
19 Additional Areas   215

LA SPORTIVA®

PAIGE CLAASSEN

CAGE FREE V11
CASTLE ROCK, BOULDER CANYON, COLORADO
PHOTO: ©ARJAN DE KOCK

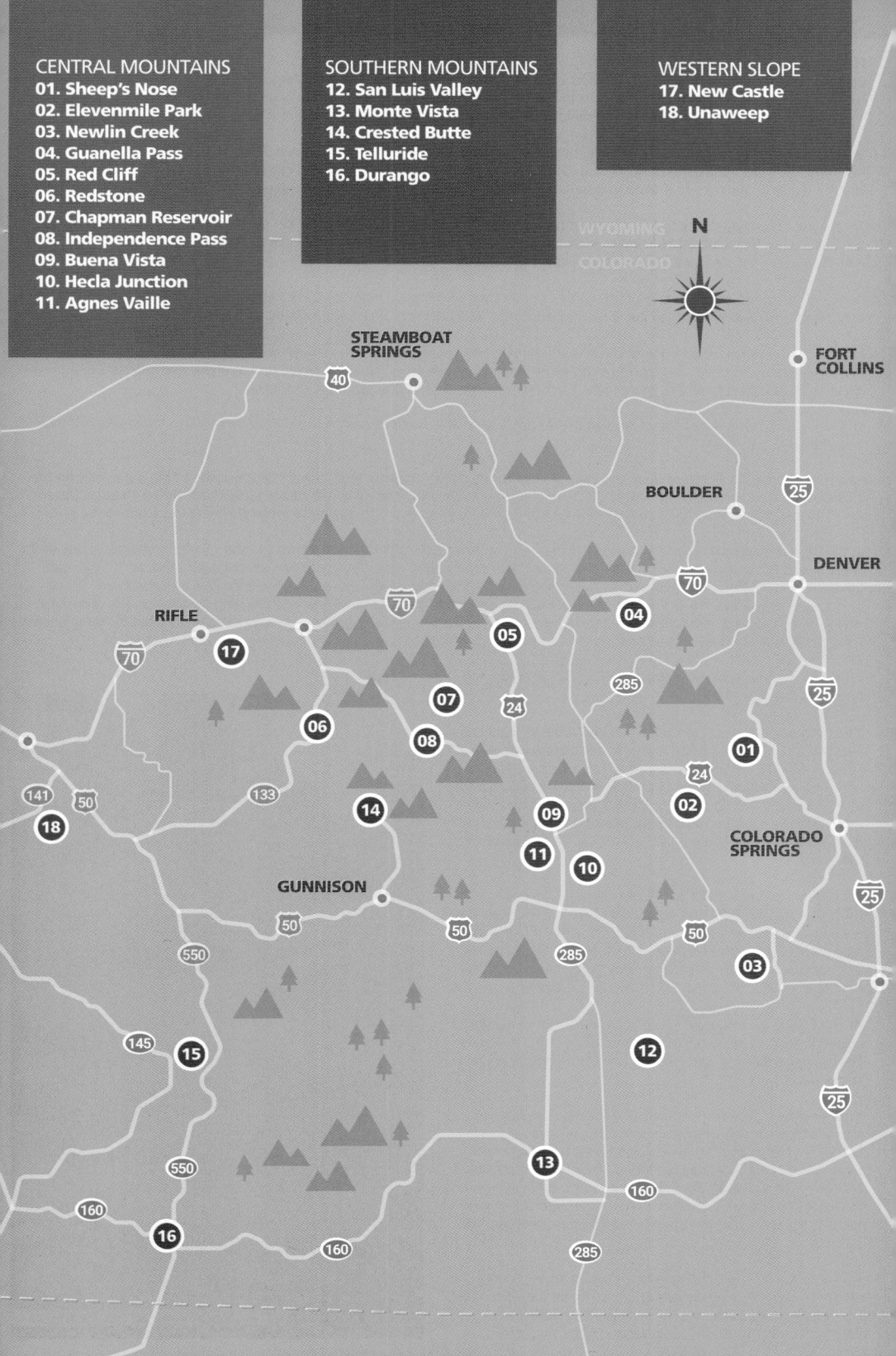

CENTRAL MOUNTAINS
01. Sheep's Nose
02. Elevenmile Park
03. Newlin Creek
04. Guanella Pass
05. Red Cliff
06. Redstone
07. Chapman Reservoir
08. Independence Pass
09. Buena Vista
10. Hecla Junction
11. Agnes Vaille

SOUTHERN MOUNTAINS
12. San Luis Valley
13. Monte Vista
14. Crested Butte
15. Telluride
16. Durango

WESTERN SLOPE
17. New Castle
18. Unaweep

N

WYOMING
COLORADO

FORT COLLINS

STEAMBOAT SPRINGS

BOULDER

DENVER

RIFLE

COLORADO SPRINGS

GUNNISON

History

Bouldering in Colorado—what we now think of as technical bouldering—is seven decades old. Many iconic boulderers cut their teeth at areas close to towns and cities. But the act of scrambling on boulders is certainly not limited to that meager time frame. This guide is devoted to mountain boulderfields and the strong boulderers who have had a lasting influence is massive!

When the technical side of rock scrambling began to be appreciated, climbers like Corwin Simmons and Bob Culp led the way. Not until 1967 did the *Master of Rock*, John Gill, come to Colorado and begin a seemingly systematic routine of ticking ultra-classic boulder problems either close to populated areas or in obscure zones like Lime Kiln near Del Norte.

To this day, John may still be Colorado's most prolific boulderer. In 1967 Gill moved to Fort Collins and promptly began turning the Dakota sandstone boulders lining Horsetooth Reservoir into one of the most famous bouldering areas in America. Rich Borgman helped Gill set standards that are still held in high regard.

As the 60s wore on, more climbers took up this new avenue of climbing. Individuals like Paul Hagan, Bob Poling, Richard Smith, Eric Varney, and Bob Williams all had a hand in creating a vast selection of classic problems.

In the 70s a young kid from Boulder came to the forefront of bouldering. His name was Jim Holloway and his ability went unnoticed by some of his peers as they concentrated on their own endeavors. What has been written about him indicates that he was decades ahead of his time. Another prolific boulderer and friend of Holloway's was Jim Michael.

Througout the 70s many excellent boulderers like Rob Candelaria, Neal Kaptain, Harrison Dekker and Dan Stone also put their strengths to good use.

Farther south on the Front Range at Ute Pass, Harvey Carter, Steve Cheyney, and Stewart Green were picking plum lines on the incipient seams, slabs and sharp cracks of Ute Pass (private). Also down south in one of the state's best mountain areas Eleven-mile Canyon, Bob Murray had a lasting effect putting up difficult lines on the spectacular granite lining the South Platte River.

In the 80s the state got a fresh crop of boulderers with amazing strength and motivation. Christian Griffith repeated many of the classics. Bob Horan was prolific through the 80s and 90s and climbed many new problems at mountain areas across the state. Other noteworthy boulderers include John Sherman, who added many problems on Indpendence Pass and elsewhere. Some of his problems easily rank as the best in the state, with The Ineditable on Independence Pass vying for top honors. Chris Jones was an avid boulderer and repeated many hard problems. In the San Luis Valley many fine blocks were uncovered near Penitente Canyon and Del Norte by Bob Murray, Lew Hoffman, and Bob D'Antonio.

An exceptional boulderer overshadowed by those hungry for fame was Skip Guerin.

Fort Collins boulderers Steve Mammen and Mark Wilford had a lasting influence on bouldering at Horsetooth as well as in Summit County. Wilford also developed problems in Telluride and Naturita throughout the 80s. These areas are but a fraction of the places visited and developed by these two gifted climbers. Surely there are hundreds of problems out in the country that will unfortunately never see repeats by the less adventuresome.

Throughout the years that Gill, Ament, Murray, Mammen, Wilford, Sherman, Griffith, and numerous other first ascentionists were lucky enough to create great classics. Many women were repeating stacks of these established problems. Coral Bowman led the way in the late 70s followed by Carol Black, Beth Bennett, Bobbi Bensman, Hilary Harris and Annie Overlin.

As the 90s came rolling along more and more gifted boulderers arrived on the scene. Rufus Miller, Jim Karn, Chris Hill, Wallace Stasick, Dave Twinam, Jim Surrette, and Calvin Fiddler pushed standards.

With bouldering gaining popularity by the day, the 90s was a time of blossoming energy and boldness. Jim Belcer, Dean Potter, Jim Hurst ,and Tommy Caldwell redefined the boulders around Estes Park as a top bouldering destination. Matt Samet, Pete Zoller, and Charley Bentley climbed many difficult highballs and desperate power problems going farther into the mountains. In the Colorado Springs area Ian Spencer-Green pushed standards.

As the century turned, the number of avid climbers skyrocketed. This cannot be understated! Climbers like Daniel Woods, Bennett Scott, Will Lemaire, Jay Droeger, Ryan Fields, Paul Robinson, Jamie Emerson, Justin Jaeger, Kevin Jorgenson,

The author enjoying Newlin Creek

Mike Freischlag, Dave Graham, Cameron Cross, Peter Beal, Ryan Olson, Chuck Fryberger, Austin Geiman, Chris Schulte, Andrew McClure, and Nick Anderson—to name but a mere fraction of badasses— developed outstanding boulders and spearheaded a jump in grades. Beautiful and impressive lines like The Wilder Arête at Skyland, William Shatner at Newlin Creek, Mind Matters at Guanella Pass, the White Face on Independence Pass, Mikodin Cocktail at the Rock Garden, Immortality at Red Cliff are all byproducts of these fine climbers.

The future of Colorado mountain bouldering is growing by leaps and bounds as more areas are discovered or rediscovered. In the past year, many intrepid boulderers have found numerous new blocks far away from the hustle and bustle of the popular mountain areas. Find your own by simply not being satisfied with going to the cool place or the YouTube documented problem. The sheer fun and unbridled motivation of standing below virgin stone and eagerly trying to figure out the puzzle has grabbed the hearts and minds of devoted boulderers and left them hungry for more.

Access
Access is a touchy subject in the climbing community. As our numbers swell, impact becomes more readily visible. Some areas were omitted from this guide because locals politely asked me not to include them, or because climbing was already an endangered activity.

No private-property bouldering areas are included in this book. Trespassing endangers everyone's access to climbing areas. Other areas with access issues fall under the guise of environmental closures (Lightner Creek). Never go to an area during the time of a closure!

Certain areas in this guide are on National Forest or Bureau of Land Management land but have private access on dirt roads or trails. I have avoided directions to boulders that pass through private land, instead describing alternate directions that may have a longer, less convenient approach. Please follow these directions so as not to threaten our access to the boulders. It may be a little bothersome, but live with it.

Private areas or delicate access spots are not included: Beulah, Ute Pass (Colorado Springs), Split Boulders, Arthur's Rock (Horsetooth Reservoir), Hagermeister and Nicky's Boulders (Estes Park), Red Feather Lakes, Rainbow Rock (Nathrop), etc.. There are many more too obscure to list.

There are two immediate ways you can help with access issues: Don't trespass and join the Access Fund, (www.accessfund.org. Remember, while out bouldering do your best to reduce impact on the land and other people's psyches.

Problem Names
Boulder problems have existed so long in Colorado that the names have been changed for a multitude of reasons: the most rampant and common is that is YOU AND YOUR BROS WERE NOT THE FIRST TO DO IT! Others include: the name was lost to obscurity as an area lost its popularity, the supposed first ascentionist was a liar, or the name was so bad no one in his right mind could announce it in a public place. One of the most common reasons a name may sound wrong is the prolific first ascentionist forgot what he called a problem. Whenever a name does not sound right or exactly match what has been used for the last couple of months, since seeing an inter-web video, is to keep in mind that memories get washed away by too much spray, booze, pills, boredom, work, or mental neglect. Probably that atrociously loose or lichen-covered face that you are sure is called My Opus was ascended by some guy in tennis shoes well before you were wearing a diaper or buying shares in IOT. Any vulgar or displeasing name (and there are quite a few) has not been censured to protect the easily offended. Many areas, boulders and problems will have more than one name to assist in finding a problem. This only goes to show how the true first ascentionists name is mistakenly given a new #tag that is so popular on IG and Twitter and Facebook.

Area / Boulder Names
I have taken the liberty of naming areas and boulders in places where no information was to be found or conflicting or local boulderers had no consensus. The reason I have done this is to help the reader find boulders and problems. Hence the boring, although useful names like Boulder 1, Orange Face and South Boulders. If individuals had given the correct names that I asked for at the boulders, in local climbing shops or through correspondence with local climbers, I would have certainly used the information. Consider the names only in helping locate problems and feel free to inform me of correct names for future editions. We would rather have the correct name given by a first ascentionist rather than some nubile gym climber's mistaken declaration.

Star Ratings:
No stars	Dirty or not especially interesting.
★	A pretty good boulder problem. Better than average.
★★	Puts a smile on your face if you send, it but upsets you if you don't.
★★★	An exceptional boulder problem, well worth the effort. Two scoops please!
★★★★	One of Colorado's best, an irrefutable classic.

Symbols and Abbreviations:

Bad Landing, Highball, Sit-down-start: Bad landings are indicated by a broken ankle emblem. We have used this icon for problems on uneven talus, logs, or a sloping hillside. Also if the fall can be unbalanced due to the body's movement during a dyno, heel hook or slippage. For a highball problem an ambulance symbol is used. This designation is used for problems 15 feet or higher—although a few problems may only be a mere 14 feet, 2 inches. Sit-down-start is sds in problem descriptions.

 Highball: You might need alternative transportation from the crag if you crater.

 Bad Landing: Roots, rocks, uneven terrain, or other factors create a dangerous landing.

  Both: Forgettaboutit. Don't bother falling.

Compass Directions:

Problems are described using compass direction. If a problem indicates the southwest arête that means the arête somewhere within the area of the south and west faces. If unsure, read the problem description and check the photo or topo to narrow down the correct problem. Carrying a compass is highly recommended in remote or newly developed areas.

Orientation:

For problems using left and right descriptions, the orientation is always as one faces the boulder or cliff. Orientation can be difficult to ascertain in gaps and chasms so look carefully at the photo, topo, and other problem descriptions on the same boulder.

Measurements:

Distances and height are given in yards or feet. When exact distance is given, it has been measured with a tape measure. I have gone to great lengths to be as specific as possible when describing problems that are obscure or need extra information (variations, problems starting close to others, etc.). Nonetheless, use your best judgement if something seems awry.

Approximations:

Approximate means exactly that! The distance indicated in finding boulders and areas is a careful, oftentimes exacting process and is roughly accurate (a few yards shorter or longer). Keep in mind that the distance is approximate when using the directions (it is my experience that 50, 75, and 100 yards does not appear the same to two boulderers).

Photo/Topo Numbers:

Problem numbers and lines on photos and topos are not always directly in front of a problem due to trees, bushes, or other boulders blocking a clear view or placement of the line or number. In this instance use the photo or topo to find the boulder, then use the problem's description to locate the correct problem. When a photo or topo is not used for a boulder, use the closest photographed boulder. Orient yourself, then read the boulder's description to locate the problems.

Topo Diagrams:

Topos are not to scale. All topos are drawn from a bird's eye view. The boulders are drawn as precisely as possible (many from standing on top of the boulder). Keep in mind a boulder may not appear as the shape drawn. If it does not look right stand on top—if possible—and locate the problems.

Precautions

Bouldering can be extremely dangerous! Flakes break, feet skid off jugs, fingers melt from holds, spotters are too stoned, drunk, or self-absorbed to pay attention. Bruises, large bloody flappers, broken ankles, twisted knees, scraped elbows, lacerated hands, torn tendons, and sprained wrists are commonplace. Death is possible.

• Always use a crash pad—borrow, buy, or make your own.

• Learn how to spot correctly. Protect your skull; ask for multiple spotters, if needed.

• Use a spotter or two or three anytime you risk a bad fall. The use of a spotter can not be overemphasized. A one-foot drop on uneven talus can easily tear ligaments or rip flesh.

• By using crash pads and attentive spotters regularly, a bouldering session can be far more challenging and rewarding than you ever thought.

Grades

The grading scale used for problems is the Vermin Scale (V Scale). A comparison chart is included to better assist those boulderers who are stuck in the obsolete B Scale or in love with the Fountainebleau Scale. More climbers than we can remember, in more areas than we can remember, have compiled grades. Use the grade as a reference; if it does not seem appropriate (after ascending the problem, which is the only time you will have a clue to the correct grade) then go with your assessment. More than likely the grade will only differ by one insignificant number. Some problems are not given grades but question marks. This was necessary for problems that have not been repeated and were graded on an old scale, problems that have changed significantly and have not seen a recent known ascent, problems that no one does anymore, and problems that probably had toprope ascents but were given an obsolete bouldering grade. These problems are few and far between.

As is the nature of grades, when a problem has two conflicting grades I have ALWAYS chosen the lower grade. There are no slash grades (V6/7) or plus and minus grades (V4+). This keeps grades solid. It is not done to sandbag (ok sometimes)! . As for the plus and minus grades non-inclusion, it helps to lend an entertaining, albeit limited sense of adventure.

Grade Color-Coding

The grades in this guide have been color-coded to help one quickly glance through the book and determine if an area has suitable problems.

VERMIN	GILL	FONTAINEBLEAU
V0	B1-	
V1	B1	5c
V2	B1	
V3	B1	6a
V4	B1+	6b
V5	B1+	6c/6c+
V6	B2-	7a
V7	B2	7a+/7b
V8	B2	7b+
V9	B2+	7c
V10	B2+	7c+
V11	B2+	8a
V12	B2+	8a+
V13	B2+	8b
V14	B2+	8b+
V15	B2+	8c

Ethics

Stand up for the ones you have! Otherwise they are not worth having in the first place.

When it comes to bouldering, the rock is your friend. Would you poke, hit and prod at your friend with a sharp, metal object? The idea behind bouldering is to enjoy the rock on its own terms, appreciating its natural state. If you're fortunate enough to find a pristine boulder, take a moment to consider what the process of putting up new problems involves.

What to do/What not to do

• Chiseling/Chipping: Don't! Don't even think about it! Enough has already taken place. The bottom line is to leave the rock alone. Leave it for someone with far superior technique, power, and genetic make-up. Any problem that would go with a little work is certainly best left in its natural state.

• Cleaning: You have to be able to see and feel the holds. Don't go crazy and clean until you enlarge the hold. Brush the lichen, moss, spider webs, and dirt off the problem…not the surrounding swath of rock or entire face. The most important considerations are to respect both the rock and other boulderers who are far more gifted and motivated.

• Be discreet with chalk, avoid using tick marks, and don't project an overbearing verbal presence in areas with other users. In other words, use common sense. If you don't have any common sense then bring a friend who is more in touch with their humanity to help you out.

• Do not cut trees, limbs, or shrubs to gain access to one measly problem!

• Avoid placing crash pads or gear on vegetation.

• Stay on signed designated trails; use only designated areas where impact has already occurred. Never build your own trails, stairs or platforms.

• Be considerate of wildlife and other users. Respect all wildlife closures. Know and abide by all regulations!

• Pack out all litter AND your crash pads.

• Leave dogs at home.

Luke Parady on Badmouth V8

SHEEP'S NOSE

At the base of the south face of Sheep's Nose lies an immense granite boulderfield called Sleeping Rock. This concentrated area has dozens of worthwhile boulders with cracks, thin faces, and slightly overhanging problems. A number of the boulders have bolts on top to protect the most difficult lines with bad landings. For the bold boulderer these toprope problems without a rope would certainly keep the juices flowing.

The wealth of bouldering at Sheep's Nose is easy to locate thanks to a climber's trail meandering through the area. At an altitude close to 8000 feet, summer temperatures remain reasonable and crowds are nonexistent. Problems not to be missed are Boulder A's V3 and V4 and all of the west face problems on the Air Boulder.

Directions: From Douglas County 73 turn into Westcreek. Drive 0.2 mile until reaching a stop sign. Turn left on Westcreek Road and drive 0.6 mile to Stump Road (Douglas County 68). Turn right and drive 1.8 miles to a dirt pull-out on the left side of the road. Cross the road and walk north past a fence that crosses a washed-out road for approximately 150 yards to a big stone on the right. Take the trail uphill for approximately 175 yards until reaching a round boulder with a couple of white crystals set as teeth in a horizontal crack (Sleeping Rock aka Dinosaur Boulder). This is where the boulderfield begins.

Note: The boulders included here are but a fraction of the problems on the hillside below Sheep's Nose. Many of the blocks have toprope problems.

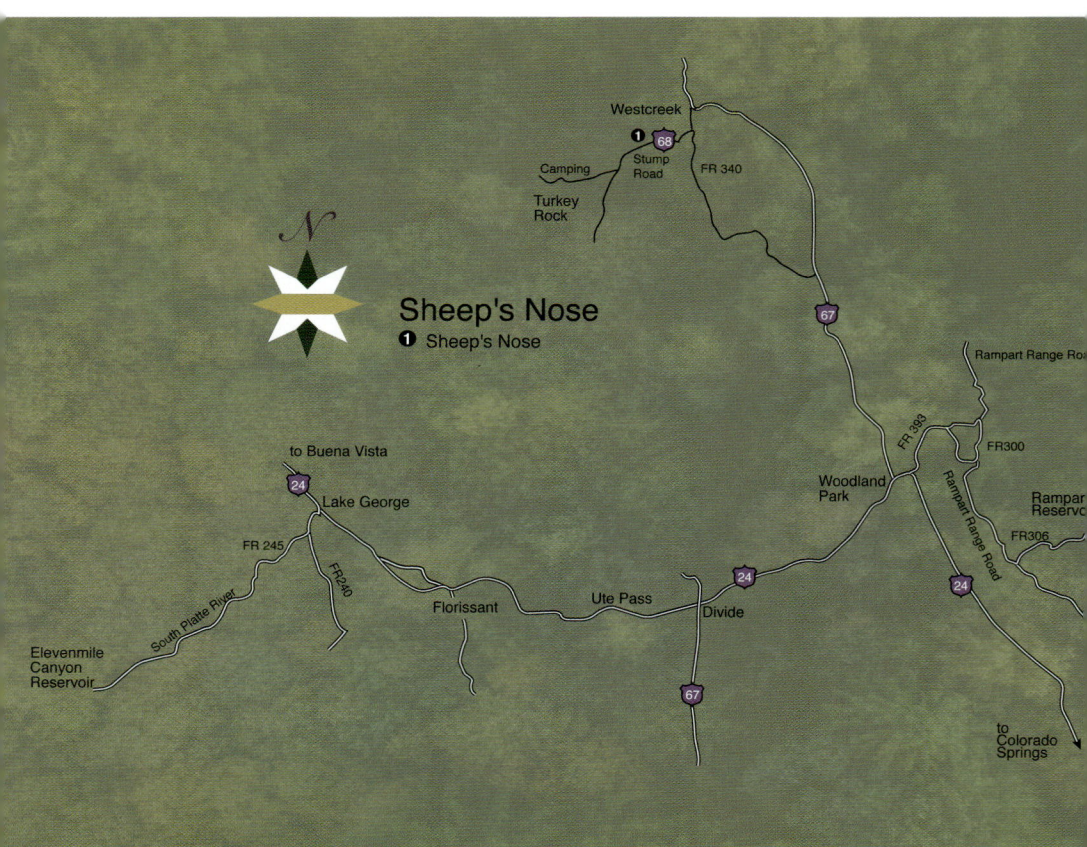

SOUTH FACE HILLSIDE:

The Sleeping Rock Boulders under Sheep's Nose are extensive and seem to go on and on, especially after the Hayman Fire. Boulders are now far more visible and easier to find. The quality of rock differs as much as opinions of a boulder problem's rating. You will find pebble pulling with an excruciating pain factor next to problems so perfect you will giggle and drool like a baby.

Not every boulder problem is included. An old toprope competition topo showing over 150 problems was un-discernable so problem and boulder names may not match history. There are literally dozens of blocks varying from super short safe affairs to extra tall pebble-covered slabs to dozen pad fright-fests.

The Hayman Fire has left snags and downed trees all over the hillside. Be cautious of continually falling trees.

BOULDER A

This is one of the lowest boulders. From the Dinosaur Boulder walk approximately 45 yards up the trail. On the right is a big boulder with a dead tree next to its east face. There are problems on the north face.

☐ 1. **V3** ★★★
The left problem off the flake then straight up. The top-out is dirty.

☐ 2. **V4** ★★★
Start two feet right of #1 and climb secure edges to the same top-out.

☐ 3. **V2**
The hand crack on the north face. Not pictured.

☐ 4. **V4**
A layback problem on the right side of the east face. Not pictured.

SHORT CHANGE BOULDER

☐ 1. **Short Change V1**
A gorgeous short slab facing east and located 40 yards east from Boulder A and downhill from the Warm Up Slabs.

☐ 2. **V0–V2**
Continue downhill from Short Change for 80 yards (50 yards northeast from the Dinosaur Boulder) to a boulder with short north and east faces and super tall easy slabs on the south face. Bolts are on top.

BOULDER B

Just up the hill to the north from Boulder A (approximately 25 yards) is a short block with a couple of V0 slab problems on its east and north faces.

BOULDER C

Approximately 25 feet to the west of Boulder A is a round block with a gray scoop on the north face. Not pictured.

☐ 1. **V0** ★★
The slab problem that follows the seam on the gray scoop. Also the downclimb.

☐ 2. **V3**
On the left side of the block is a problem starting off a layback to minute crystals.

Boulder A

Boulder B

Mike Freischlag on Short Change V1

Boulder D

Continue up the main trail past Boulder A for approximately 120 yards. The trail fizzles out slightly and a small cluster of blocks is on the right. Boulder D has two cracks on its south face.

❏ **1. V4**
The left crack from the high layback. A sds is significantly harder.

❏ **2. V2** ★★
The big crack on the southeast face. A sds to this makes it much more difficult.

Boulder D

Boulder E

This small block 15 yards is due south from Boulder D. Pines stand on two of its sides.

❏ **1. V1** ★
Start on the left side of the crack and traverse right to an undercling, then up.

❏ **2. V1** ★
Just right of #1 is a low crack. Climb the crack.

❏ **3. V0** ★★
On the west face is a triangle-shaped flake. Reach either left or straight up to top out.

Boulder F

This boulder is less than 10 yards south and slightly east of Boulder E. A curving crack moves from the south face up and around the west face. Not pictured.

❏ **1. V0** ★
Climb the curving crack.

❏ **2. V2** ★★
The pebble-strewn face just left of the tree.

Boulder E

The Fire Pit Area

This cluster of boulders is located due west of Boulder D. Take a faint trail past Boulder D for approximately 70 yards headed west, skirting the hillside below the giant talus field. No photo.

Boulder G

This boulder sits next to an old fire pit. It has an unpleasant V4 on the right side of the south face. The potential for thin, gross problems on this boulder is unpleasantly astonishing.

Boulder H

This nice block is located 25 feet west of Boulder G and has an overhanging northeast face.

❏ **1. V4** ★★ 🕷
Climb the seam and crystal edges on the southeast face.

❏ **2. V0** ★★
An easy problem on the northeast face.

Trixie T on Boulder H's V0

Boulder I

Located northeast from Boulder G approximately 10 yards. A difficult V4 ascends the southwest arête with terrible feet and a tough top-out. Not pictured.

Warm-Up #1

From Boulder D (with two obvious southeast face cracks), on the main trail, take a sharp right on a faint footpath for 60 yards to a low-angle slab with pebbles. This is the first Warm Up Slab boulder. A couple more are found 20-odd yards along the trail.

Warm Up Slab 1

Warm Up Slab 2

WARM-UP SLABS

The numerous shorter slab boulders on the hillside are easy to locate and offer casual climbing to get the juices flowing. Problems range from V0 to V4. A couple of ultra-thin lines could be done if you like to tear your tips into bloody masses.

Small But Big with TR Boulder #1 behind it

❒ **1. Squeeze Job V2** 🚗🌊

On a lone boulder between the Warm Up Slabs and TR#1 is a nondescript block with an excellent layback problem on the south face. You can not see the problem from the trail. The landing warrants the phrase "no fall zone" and might make you feel the line is a bit tougher, as you waffle above the leg-breaker fall.

TR BOULDER #1

Continue east from the Warm Up Slabs for 50 yards (visible from the Warm Up Slabs) to a beautiful tall lichen face with an open corner on the lower left (northeast) face. The downclimb consists of carefully making your way down the dark northeast slab (above the White Corner).

*The downclimb is on the northeast face next to the corner/dihedral. You will have to jump off!

Chul Lee on West Arête V3 TR Boulder #1

❒ **1. White Corner V7** ★★

The northeast corner/dihedral. Exactly how to muckle on this bear hug (it might be impossible if you are tiny), one-move wonderfest is up to your arm length and ability to high step at your ear. If you can pull on, place your right boot on the obvious big foothold, throw with all your might to a good right-hand layback and that's about the whole deal.

❒ **2. V2** ★★★ 🚗🌊

Start this classic, fairly dangerous affair on the supporting block under the tall north face. Traverse slightly left on numerous edges. As you venture up you will move left and away from the ankle-twisting support block and a flat landing zone. A straight-up problem can be done at the same grade.

❒ **3. V3** ★★★ 🚗🌊

The classic west arête/face. The landing is safe with six pads and the holds are quite suitable for a classic cruiser. The top-out will invariably scare the poo poo out of you.

SMALL BUT BIG

A short block is found a couple yards northwest (on the trail before reaching TR#1) and offers a handful of safe problems ranging from V0 to V5.

THE BULB

❐ 1. **The Bulb V1** ★★★
A short affair located 15 yards uphill from the north face of TR#1. The problem faces TR#1 and utilizes big jugs to an awkward top-out.

TR BOULDER #2/TOOTH BOULDER
From TR#1 head east on a faint trail for approximately 100 yards keeping an eye out for The Scoop (the problem faces uphill). You'll know you hit the right boulder when you're standing under a gorgeous, golden/burnt orange vertical scoop found on the block's north face. A bolt is on top from the bygone days when toproping was the only safe way to climb up a big boulder. Once again, the downclimb consists of jumping off The Scoop with your feet as low as possible (about six, maybe eight feet from the pads) or down climbing the west face. Bring lots of pads!

❐ 1. **V3** ★★★ 🪨💧
Climb the northeast arête immediately around the corner from The Scoop.

❐ 2. **North Face aka The Scoop V1** ★★★ 🪨💧
This gem looks waaaaay harder than it is. Start on the left side of the north face on a good high edge and stem up the scoop to humungous jugs at the top.

❐ 3. **The Arête V3** 🪨💧
Climb the left-angling northwest arête to the top of The Scoop. Bad feet and good handholds define this outing.

❐ 4. **The Downclimb V0**
On the west face you can climb up about anywhere on mungy pebbles and little dirty scoops. It ain't that hard.

❐ 5. **V3** 🪨💧
On the downhill side of the block start with a left-hand under-cling and move up and left on sadistically small pebbles. Have your spotter(s) at full attention.

CORNER

❐ 1. **Corner V3** ★★★ 🪨
A lone boulder downhill (and between the TR Boulders). The easiest way to find this block is go to TR Boulder #2 then traverse the hillside for 65 yards back the way you came, headed just a little downhill. The problem is 50 yards downhill and slightly east from TR#1. You will know you found the line when you are standing in front of an overhanging, heavily chalked west-facing flake. Just to the left of the chalked line is a thin seam awaiting some sicko hardman.

Phillip Benningfield on The Scoop V1

Trixie Tartasky on Corner V3

AIR BOULDER

All boulders, whether granite or sandstone or limestone, should have the qualities of Air Boulder! The boulder is just the right height at 15-odd feet, square for the most part, solid but for the intermittent chip or flake, with one line for downclimbing, and great landings (although extra pads help out on one or two problems). It is hard to think of anything which would improve the Air Boulder experience; possibly one more tree for shade—but the tree would be detrimental to worthy photos. The boulder shows its undying popularity by the number of nubbins, all over the rock, caked in chalk, even on desperate topropes, or possible new problems (that were probably done by some tennis-shoe clad guy in painter pants back when I was a wee lad). And lastly the boulder has a sumptuous view of Pikes Peak to add flavor to the already tasty scenery.

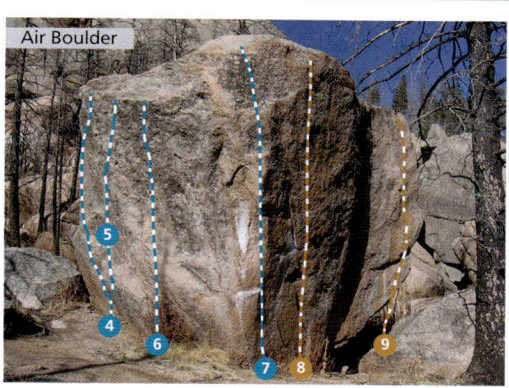

Air Boulder

Directions: From the Dinosaur Boulder you will pass numerous blocks. Continue past these boulders staying on the trails that head northwest around the talus slopes. Walk past the obvious chalked boulders staying below most of the blocks to the northwest. After passing a firepit (if you happen to run into it) continue to the northwest for 90 yards to a big west-facing boulder that looks better than any of the others on the hillside. The boulder lies on the western edge of the huge boulderfield leading down from Sheep's Nose.

☐ **1. V0**
The left side of the north face, up diagonal jugs. Also the downclimb. There are a couple of desperate looking lines to the left through the steep east face: done, undone?

☐ **2. V2** ★★
The sloping face before the right arête of the north face.

☐ **3. Little Air V3** ★
Climb the northwest arête from a low start.

☐ **4. The Waffler V3** ★
This might be a new one—but it might not! Climb the northwest face starting from #5 then moving directly left to a hidden edge and the top.

☐ **5. Air Boulder V4** ★★★★
This problem is on the cusp of classic. It received three stars in the first guide, so what the hell—it gets four here! Climb the left side of the west face off good sidepulls to a big reach up high and right.

☐ **6. V5** ★★★
Can't quite muster the vote for four stars. The rock is bing-bing but the moves are a tad unrelenting. Climb straight up the edges and undercling to the flat jugs in the middle of the west face.

☐ **7. Big Air V3** ★★★★
This one gets all the stars! It looks like a great granite line and climbs like one as well. The problem ventures up the right arête of the west face with an interesting top-out crux.

☐ **8. Into Thin Air V8** ★★★
As classic as any other problem on Air Boulder and far more sustained. Starts the same as Big Air and moves up the south face on good edges and sidepulls to committing moves to reach the lip.

☐ **9. Scary V6** ★ 🌀🌀
This one has a hazard factor. One just can't tell if a bad fall will send you into the adjacent block. There are definitely big reaches up high after pinner micro-edges begin the festivities. I think I once heard—this may be the definition of sandbag—that the problem was 5.12+. The first moves feel that hard and left my flesh in disarray. A bolt is on top.

Chul Lee on V8

Air Satellites

V0s Slab and Surrounding Blocks

A long slab with numerous dirty V0s through the horizontal breaks. The block is a mere 15 yards southeast from Air.

Golden Dihedral

❒ 1. Golden Overhang V2 ★
A golden overhang 20 yards due east from Air. Walk under a giant fallen tree and past V0s Slab to get there.

❒ 2. V4 ★
A double arête problem that is a tad dirty, due north of Air Boulder. Bring pads.

❒ 3. Golden Dihedral V4 ★★
Uphill from Air Boulder to the northeast approximately 80 yards on a very faint trail. The boulder is actually visible from Air Boulder, if you have a keen eye for chalk and bolts; a large tree sits in front of the dihedral. The problem begins low on well-chalked edges and leads out right in a seam to a right-facing dihedral. Bolts on top.

Additional Blocks

These are found uphill from Air Boulder and below Ten Years After (the huge right-facing dihedral on Sheep's Nose)

Pete Zoller on Golden Overhang V2

❒ 1. Fin V4 ★★
Uphill from Air Boulder to the northwest approximately 125 yards. This block is due west of Golden Dihedral. The boulder is fin-shaped and it has an east-facing overhang with a couple of variations.

❒ 2. Bolt Flake V2
A great, immaculate little line located 140 yards northwest from Air Boulder. Stay at roughly the same height on the hillside and contour to a thin flake with bolts above the southwest face/arête. A V1 traverse can be done along the entire lip from right to left.

❒ 3. V0s
A nice short boulder with three or four casual lines is located uphill to the north from Bolt Flake approximately 50 yards.

Ten Years Before

TYB is a massive boulder resting below the ultra-classic dihedral Ten Years After on Sheep's Nose west face. From Air Boulder head straight uphill 200 yards towards the giant right-facing dihedral (easily visible from Air Boulder).

South Face

Extremely steep problems venture up the south face. The lefthand corner has a toprope bolt, which ain't a bad idea, as the upper move requires full commitment in a fairly precarious position.

Chris D on Vegetarian's Delight V6

❒ 1. TR #3 (Vegetarian's Delight) V6 ★★★
You're gonna think sandbag on this one. Starts low under the roof and moves through two gigantic jugs to a difficult dyno or very insecure set of moves to gain the right-hand jug. This problem is the epitome of a tall person's problem. If you are taller or burly you have a 100% better chance of sticking the dyno.

❒ 2. ASAP V4 ★★
Found right of the V6. Start on the far left side of the sloping ledge in the white stripe and move ASAP to the right, then up. An undone nasty line moves up and left from the start utilizing excruciatingly minute crimps.

❒ 3. V1 ★★
Climb the far right side of the sloping ledge system. A low start boosts the grade a whole bunch.

❒ 4. The Pillar V2 ★★
Hidden away on the uphill side of the boulder is an alcove with a straight-up vertical wall to a detached pillar for the ending moves. A significantly harder problem is directly left. A few miniscule sit-down starts could be done on the thin face to the left.

Chris D on Black Mariah V3

5. The Shadow V4 ★★★

The slightly overhanging, lichen-striped and brilliant block resting against TYB and facing The Pillar. Start left of the mini right-facing corner on a solid edge and move into the corner with the right hand. Continue up, up and into the danger zone on good edges and sidepulls. Make sure to bring at least five pads for the landing zone. A direct start in the corner, off the obvious underclings will make the climb harder.

6. Black Mariah V3 ★★★

On the north face resides a seemingly blank slab with an awful landing. Climb the face on itty-bitty edges and pebbles. Bring your footwork and a bunch of pads with you or forgetaboutit.

7. V3

The short arête directly next to the slab. Start on two good edges and throw to the top.

Wash Boulders

These granite boulders are littered along the hillside below the west face of Sheep's Nose. The boulders here are not as cute as the Air Boulder but a line or two show some cloning to be occurring. Feel free to keep an open mind and explore the area more thoroughly: boulders line the hillside like hippies at a Dead concert. To reach them walk along the hillside from Air Boulder staying at the same level, give or take a few feet, for 200 to 250 yards. The boulders appear as the woods open up into small meadows above the sandy wash.

Washout Boulder

The first real block that appears to have some bouldering opportunities. The boulder, with problems on the west face, sits 40 yards from the wash.

1. V0

The far left side of the southwest face.

2. Adventure Bouldering Part One V5

The hard south bulge problem on very questionable rock. Be careful, laddy.

Second Boulder

Couldn't come up with a better name at 11:50 p.m. This block is 45 yards north from The Washout.

1. V0

Climb the easy right-trending ledge on the north face.

2. V2 ★

Up the northwest face, near the aspen, from a low start.

3. V0

Climb the south face's right-trending ledge.

4. V0

Climb the southeast bulge.

Mouth Boulder

This boulder with a horizontal seam along its lower expanse is located to the north 20 yards from Second Boulder.

1. V3

Climb the vertical seam on the west face. Much harder from a sds.

Tonsils Boulder

This block is directly behind Mouth to the northeast.

1. V1

Climb the left arête on the southwest face and left of the good flake.

2. V0 ★

Go from the flake to the horizontal and top out on the southwest face.

3. V0

Climb the short arête to the right of #2.

Fifth Boulder

I'm getting quite creative with the names. This mean boulder is 30 yards north of Mouth.

1. Wash Your Mouth Out V4

This one doesn't get a star due to the pain factor. Start high and muckle through the sharp crystal and seam. A low start would be even more fun.

Smashing Boulder

This block has two very fun—one might even say smashing—problems on the northeast face, and a jump for a downclimb. The boulder has a number of other lines to be completed.

1. It's a Wash V1 ★

Climb the beautiful vertical northeast face in the middle utilizing the sloping left arête.

2. V2 ★★

Climb the right side of the northeast face on very good holds.

Second Boulder

Tonsils and Mouth

Smashing Boulder

WESTERN HILLSIDE

The giant talus field on the west-facing hillside houses some of the most bad-ass looking lines in Colorado. Years and years pass with little development of these fine house-size and smaller boulders. And thankfully so for the motivated boulderer who hates crowds.

All problems are easiest to locate from Air Boulder. As well, all the problems are within the massive boulderfield above and between Boulder G and Air Boulder.

THE CORRIDOR

A tight slot located southeast approximately 100 yards uphill from Air Boulder. Weave through and under a gigantic block (no problems) headed slightly uphill (southeast) to a gorgeous southwest-facing white slab (South Block) with a splitter crack leading right.

SOUTH BLOCK

The southern boulder making up The Corridor. Problems exist on every side!

Southeast Face

The massive slab face with a beautiful crack leading up and right. Problems have only been done on the shorter 18-foot right side. The face tops out at over 30 feet on the left.

☐ 1. **Safety First V3** ★★★ 🌐🌀

The rightmost slab on the southeast face.

North Face

Within The Corridor the South Block offers spectacular problems along the just-past-vertical north face and northwest arête.

☐ 1. **Will's Left Line V5** ★★

Climb the left set of thin edges for a second, then it's pretty much over.

☐ 2. **Badmouth V8** ★★★

Start right of Left Line on perfect built-in edges and exit left past the top squeeze.

☐ 3. **New Freedom V7** ★★★ 🌀

Climb the northwest arête via balancy and powerful moves.

☐ 4. **Something for Nothing V4** ★★★ 🌐🌀

Two lines can be done on the west face, which require some gumption as the wall tops out at over 20 feet.

NORTH BLOCK

The north boulder making up The Corridor.

☐ 1. The Blade V4

North face slabular problem heads up directly across from the South Block's V5.

☐ 2. Above the Corridor Arête V3

Northwest Face

A couple of V0–V1 lines head up the northwest face.

The author on New Freedom V7

Above the Corridor Arête V3

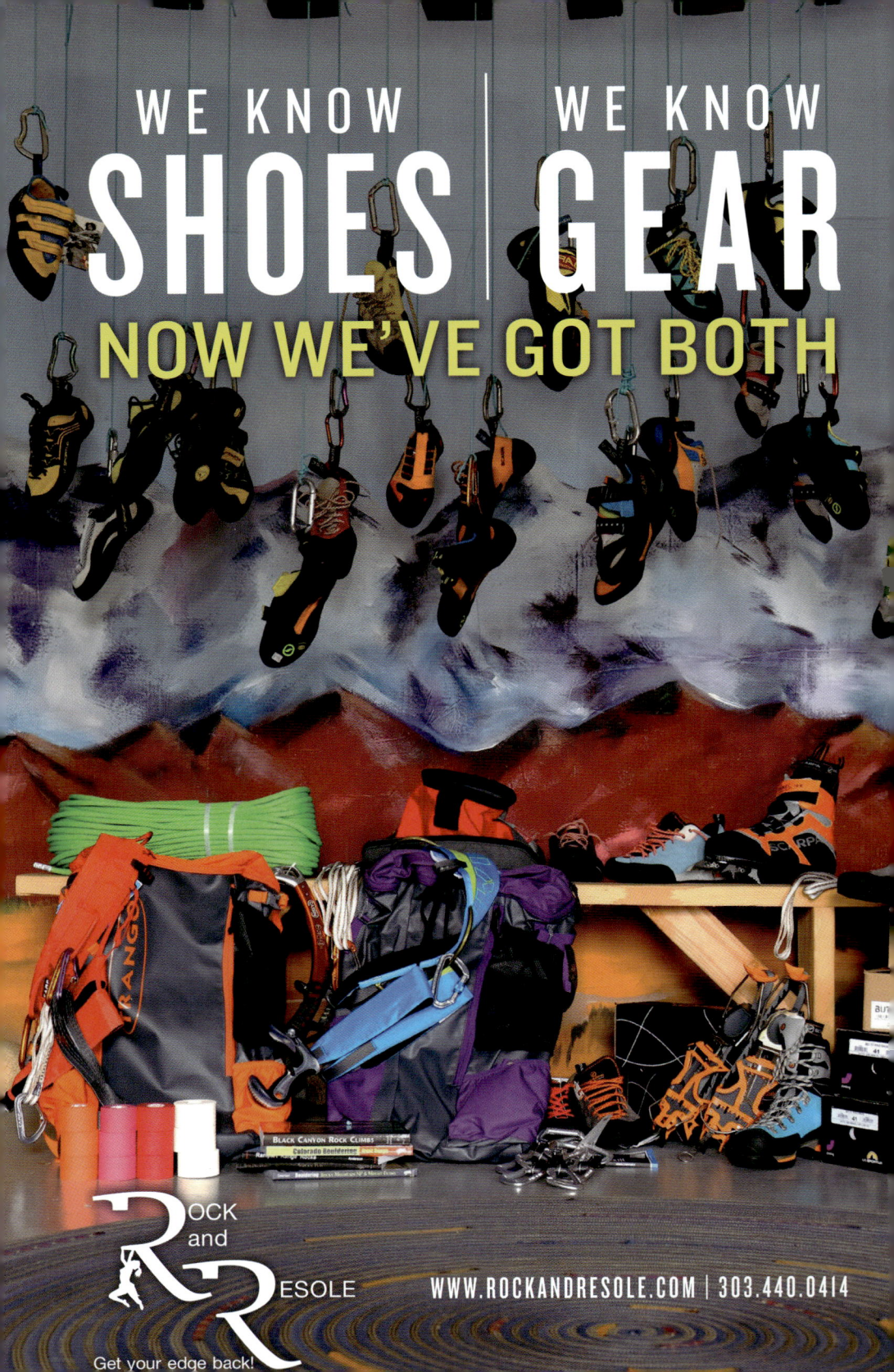

Tony Hosek on East Twin's Triangle Face V2

ELEVENMILE CANYON

If you desire a fine granite bouldering area away from the mayhem of all the "coolest places" like the Poudre, Chaos Canyon, and Mount Evans, you can find it here. What Elevenmile offers is off-the-radar (thank the lord) killer camping, superb fishing, and even better—excellent classics . There are hundreds of blocks of all shapes and sizes that for some crazy reason remain undeveloped. There are plenty of established lines, but the potential is staggering as the canyon stretches over eight miles along the South Platte River with mostly casual approaches. The areas listed only scratch the surface…

Directions: From Woodland Park drive west on US Route 24 to Lake George turn left on Park County 96 (brown sign for Elevenmile Canyon State Park) and drive one mile to a right turn for Elevenmile Canyon (big brown recreation sign at turn). Go 0.1 mile to the kiosk and pay. All mileages are from the kiosk!

The park charges a daily fee of $7.00.

Mileages to boulders:

Spray Boulder: 2.1 miles across river.

Undeveloped: 3.7 miles across river. Reach these blocks by parking up the road 0.1 mile at the bridge, cross over troubled water and head back downstream.

Lone Boulders: 4.2 miles across river.

Undeveloped: 4.7 miles across river.

River Boulders: 6.5 miles across river.

Undeveloped: 8.0 miles across river.

Spillway Boulders (Overlook Boulders): 8.5 miles, in Spillway Campground.

SPRAY WALL

The first set of boulders with developed problems. Located across the river below a severely overhanging wall with bolted routes. The largest block lies below the wall with a couple of smaller ones downstream.

SPRAY BOULDER

The overhanging boulder below the bolted routes. The dark, northwest overhang has excellent problems on novel holds for the canyon.

☐ **1. V6** ★★★
The left problem on huge flakes that ends high and right.

☐ **2. V8** ★★★
A more demanding problem that begins in the low V-slot then traverses right staying below the lower roof.

☐ **3. Anger Management V11**
Start at a low slot and move left on sidepulls to reach the left arête.

SATELLITE BOULDERS

The boulders to the east of Spray Wall. One sits a couple of feet away; the other is close to the river approximately 25 yards away.

☐ **1. V0** ★
The short sds problem on the left side of the north face.

☐ **2. V1** ★★
A two move problem on the northwest arête.

☐ **3. V3** ★ 🌓
On the boulder closest to the river is a short overhang on the east face. The landing has a couple of ankle twisters to keep things interesting.

LONE BOULDERS

This set of blocks rest in a meadow on the opposite side of the South Platte River. A wade is necessary to reach them. A few lines are waiting to be done.

LONE BOULDER

The obvious block sitting alone. It has a blocky roof on its south face (faces the river).

☐ **1. V0** ★★
The left side of the west face. Also a good downclimb.

☐ **2. V1** ★★
The right side of the west face up zigzagging cracks.

☐ **3. V4** ★★
The sds problem on the south face overhang. Be ever mindful of the loose block.

☐ **4. V3** ★
The north face has a dingy problem above the low slab. Fight through the tree to finish.

☐ **5. V2** 🌓
The northwest arête.

☐ **6. V1** ★
The southwest arête. Fun laybacks (fragile) and good feet. Look for a sinker pocket.

☐ **7. V0** ★★
On the boulder to the east approximately 50 yards from Lone Boulder. The dihedral on the east face.

Spray Boulder

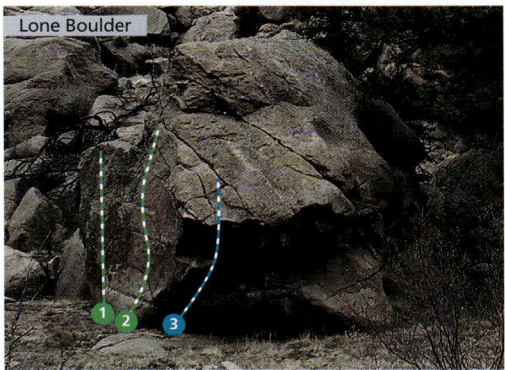
Lone Boulder

RIVER BOULDERS AKA THE MURRAY BOULDERS

These two boulders are the crème de la crème of boulders in the canyon (also the state). Perched next to the river, and having flat landings, they're hard to beat. A pull-out is directly across the river from the boulders. A short wade will get one to the blocks, easily identified by the East Twin's triangle-shaped face. Many harder sds boost the grade on most of the lines.

WEST TWIN

The western block of the two. A down-jump is necessary off the west face.

☐ **1. V2** ★★ ⚫
The right-facing dihedral on the south face. Pine needles cover the top-out.

☐ **2. V2** ⚫⚫
The east face seam that starts vertical then turns slabby and moves left.

☐ **3. V3** ★★
The left arête on the north face. It is just left of the passage between the Twins.

☐ **4. V3**
The middle of the north face has a filthy, lichen-covered problem.

☐ **5. V2** ★★★
Climb the right-angling corner on the right of the northwest face.

☐ **6. V3** ★★
The northwest arête up a layback.

☐ **7. V6** ★★
The thin edge face on the left of the west face.

☐ **8. Murray Right V5** ★★
The faint layback seam on the west face.

West Twin

West Twin

Andrew Null on West Twin's Route #6 V3

EAST TWIN

The eastern block with a triangle-shaped wall facing the river.
Downclimb the east face.
The first three problems are not pictured:

☐ **1. V5** ★★★ 🔵⚫
A sds problem that begins left on the north face then moves
up and right to finish on the tall slab left of the pine tree.

☐ **2. V1** ★★★
Just left of the huge pine tree is an awesome vertical face.

☐ **3. V4** ★★
The arête just right of the huge pine tree.

☐ **4. Bob's Wall V5** ★★★ 🔵
Climb the small edges surrounding the left-angling seam in
the middle of the west face.

☐ **5. V3** ★★★ 🔵
The small, right-facing corner on the right side of the west
face. Begin low and right using the arête.

☐ **6. Triangle Face V2** ★★ 🔵
Begin on the left jug of the south face and traverse the lip to a
left-facing corner on the slab then up.

THE AMPHITHEATRE

A somewhat hidden wall that is approximately 150 yards
upstream from the River Boulders . A short, long block with a
small overhang lies between The Amphitheatre and the river.
The best access is to cross at the River Boulders, then walk
west along the river for 150 yards.

☐ **1. Black Corner V2** ★ 🔵
The black groove that is often wet.

☐ **2. Crack Traverse V2** ★ 🔵
Climb out right on the horizontal crack. A variation pulls out
the overhanging crack in the roof but the top-out is very dirty.

☐ **3. V2** ★
The short problem on the boulder facing the river. Start in an
undercling on the right.

The author on Bob's Wall V5

The Amphitheatre

The Pyramid

SPILLWAY BOULDERS AKA OVERLOOK BOULDERS

An awesome collection of boulders situated to the north and west of Campsite 1 in the Spillway Campground.

THE PYRAMID

The second large boulder on the right of the Overlook Trail which begins at the Pay Station sign for the Spillway Campground. The Pyramid is 25 yards up the trail.

☐ **1. Triplet V1** ★★
The problem on the west face that climbs through the diagonal seam/cracks.

☐ **2. Sit Down V2**
The overhanging crack on the south face. Grovelly pulling on to the slab.

The Fire Boulder

THE FIRE BOULDER

The large blackened boulder on the east side of Campsite 1.

☐ **1. V1**
The far left problem that climbs the crack on the west face.

☐ **2. Firepit Direct V4** ★★
Climb the black rock above the firepit through laybacks and cracks.

☐ **3. V2**
Dynamic! Start under the east face's small roof.

CAMPSITE 1 BOULDER

The slabby boulder next to the picnic table.

☐ **1. V1** ★★
The left seam on the south face.

☐ **2. V2** ★★
The middle seam on the south face.

☐ **3. V0** ★
The right problem on the south face.

☐ **4. V2** ★★
The seam on the east face.

☐ **5. V0**
Just right of #4.

☐ **6. V1** ★
The west face problem that climbs over a bulge. A sds makes this V4.

Campsite 1

Derek Young on the sds of #6 on the Campsite 1 Boulder

DRAGON'S HEAD

The largest boulder in the campground. It is located to the right of the Campsite 2 picnic table.

❑ 1. **V3** ★★

The left problem on the north face. Starts off big holds to a long throw reaching the lip. A sds is V4.

❑ 2. **V5** ★★★

The left-diagonaling seam starting low in the overhang. Tough top-out.

❑ **V1**

The northeast arête on the small boulder to the east of Dragon's Head.

CAMPSITE 2 BOULDER

Not the crystal choss boulder! The small block left of the crystal boulder.

❑ 1. **V1**

A dynamic problem off the jug on the east arête.

❑ 2. **V0**

The short dihedral.

TURD BOULDER

Uphill approximately 20 yards from Dragon's Head. A tall vertical wall faces south.

❑ 1. **V3** ★★

Climbs the left side of the east face through a short bulge.

Dragon's Head

Turd Boulder

Jordan Chamberlain ponying her way up Singular Affair V3

NEWLIN CREEK

Newlin Creek in the Wet Mountains is a sub-alpine canyon seemingly in the middle of nowhere. The granite blocks differ in quality from the ubiquitous moss-covered piles to sparkling clean overhangs and slabs. For those boulderers who desire convenience and sunshine, the Creek will not suffice. The highball, ankle-breaking bouldering requires multiple pads and attentive spotters for the best problems. There are many more completed lines than described here.

***More important than any problem here, the fragile riparian ecosystem needs to be trod on very carefully (some areas that have extensive damage have not been included so they can recover).

Directions: From Colorado Springs head south on Colorado Highway 115 (towards Shelf Road) but continue over US Highway 50 just after Penrose and go to Florence. In Florence take a left (south) on CO 67 towards Wetmore/Westcliff and drive 4.3 miles to a right on 15 Road (a brown National Forest sign points the way to Newlin Creek). Drive 6.8 miles to the trailhead parking area for trail #1335 (the final mile may require a 4x4 if the road is wet). Park and walk up the trail 20 minutes (past a wooden bridge over the creek) to the Behemoth Block on the trail's left side. Singular Affair is just past the Behemoth (two minutes) on the trail's left side. The Conglomeration is approximately 10 minutes up the trail from Behemoth (the boulders are trailside after crossing the creek for the second time). Meander through the boulders towards the big cliff to reach the problems.

Kristen Kirkland working the tall and classic Walk Softly V9

THE NICKNESS BOULDER
AKA THE BEHEMOTH BLOCK

A lone monstrosity sitting just off the trail's left side with a massive north face. The remainder of the north face is terrifyingly high (exceeds 25 feet with a jumbled talus landing) and looks super-duper burly. The south face sports luscious slabs and a long downclimb with a steep overhang on the east side.

☐ 1. Brilliant Wings V11 ★
Start sitting, matched on a good jug. Climb left on amazing rock and huge moves. An Austin Geiman classic.

☐ 2. The Nickness V10 ★★
A classic Newlin Creek testpiece. Start standing with a left hand on a flat sidepull and a right hand on the lower of two underclings. Make a very powerful move to the lip, then continue up the arête to an easier but tall finish. Climbers occasionally finish early by rocking onto the slab. The stand start V8, which is a classic problem in its own right, does the Nickness from one move in.

☐ 3. The Nickness Right V11 ★★
Start the same as for The Nickness, but head right first, topping out on the tall but easy slab.

☐ 4. B3PO V10 ★
Start standing, matched on a flat jug and head left, reversing The Nickness Right, and then finishing on The Nickness.

☐ 5. Project
Around the corner on the tall and imposing face is a beautiful highball project that has been cleaned and tried, but never completed.

☐ 6. William Shatner V12 ★★★
On the far right side of the face closest the main trail is a unique scoop with great rock. Start sitting, left hand on a sidepull and right hand on a pinch. Move up through terrible pinches and crimps and finish up the tall face. A Chuck Fryberger testpiece.

Southeast Face:
An immaculately clean slab littered with crisp edges and slopers. You will want numerous pads to climb the problems safely, as all problems are way highball. Just around to the left side of the boulder when facing The Nickness.

☐ 7. V0 🪨
The uneventful, although terribly high, downclimb on the far left side. Be extra careful, as the traffic on this downclimb has not cleaned off every last flake.

☐ 8. V2 ★★ 🪨
Climb the tall slab just right of the open dihedral/ramp. To finish straight up, instead of bailing out right or left, is slightly harrowing.

☐ 9. V2 ★★ 🪨
Start on a big, flat sloping edge and venture up the face on crimps to a committing sloper move up high.

☐ 10. Fun with Fatty V5 ★★
Climb up the open corner then into the right hand slopers directly below the grassy break.

☐ 11. V7 🪨
An undercut problem on the east face that appears more like a jump problem than power problem.

THE TRAIL BOULDER

☐ 1. Singular Affair V3 ★★ 🪨
Up the trail a short distance from The Nickness. A distinct vertical face sitting directly beside the trail. A fun line follows the left arête with a perfectly flat landing. Easier lines are found to the right, but aren't as cool.

The Nickness Bould

The author having Fun with Fatty V5

Phillip Benningfield on Singular Affair V3

The Wall of Destiny

THE WALL OF DESTINY

Facing The Nickness, head left and up the hill (away from the creek) for 250 yards on a well-worn social trail. The Wall of Destiny is an imposing cliffband with several hard established problems.

❒ 1. Sing the Sorrow V7 ★

Stand start on a small left-hand crimp and a right-hand sidepull in the crack. Move up to a sharp gaston. Sing the Sorrow V9 sit starts down and right, matched on a right-facing sidepull and climbs into the stand.

❒ 2. Walk Softly V9 ★

Start matched on a low, rounded jug and climb straight up the face. A superb and tall testpiece from Justin Jaeger. This has been climbed from down and left, at V11.

❒ 3. Walk Softly Sit Start V11

Start on Sing the Sorrow Sit Start and climb up and right, finishing on Walk Softly.

THE WALL OF DESPAIR

Facing Walk Softly, walk around the right side of a huge but blank roof to the right. The Wall of Despair will appear on your left.

❒ 1. Livin' on a Prayer V8

Stand start with a left hand on a small crimp and right hand on a flat right-facing sidepull. The first move is the crux.

❒ 2. Finger on the Steel V7

Stand start with a right-hand undercling and left-hand sidepull. Good edges in a seam lead straight up to some miserable crimps and a crux move. The sit start is V9 and begins low, matched on a good rail.

❒ 3. Amitabha V6

Sds to powerful sidepulls and a big bump to a perfect edge.

PINEAPPLE EXPRESS

Continue on the Newlin Creek Trail for 160 yds, past a small talus pile on the left just before Bear Trap. Just beyond the talus pile is a social trail that heads left up into a drainage. Follow this winding trail for 150 yds to a large boulder in the drainage, on your left.

❒ 1. V3

On the left side of the north face follow slopers to a left-to-right diagonal crack.

❒ 2. V2

The right-facing corner above the bulge. The landing on this baby is very, very bad and will require actually paying attention.

❒ 3. Pinapple Express V5 ★★★

Start sitting, left hand on a flat slot-like hold and right hand on a flat triangular hold. Climb straight up worsening holds on great rock.

❒ 4. Magister's Terrace V10

Walk up the gulley another 100 yds to a big, imposing arête.

The Wall of Despair

Pineapple Express

BEAR TRAP

☐ 1. Bear Trap V7 ⬤

A beautiful overhanging power problem below the trail, next to the creek, 90 yards past Singular Affair. A V3 slab can be done to the right.

Chris Lesher on Bear Trap V7

ATARI AREA

This killer cluster of boulders is passed on the way to Newlin Boulder. A distinct, open V-corner in the boulders west face helps you know where the hell ya are.

ALARM CLOCK AWAKENING

☐ 1. **Alarm Clock Awakening V6**
Faces the trail on the large boulder to the left. Start matched on a low jug and climb fun moves out the low roof to a difficult finish on the bulge.

NEWLIN BOULDER

☐ 1. **V0** 🌙
The steep jug haul on the left side of the west face. A tad slabular breaching the overhang.

☐ 2. **Spooookie V6** ★★ 🌀🌙
In the middle of the west face is a V-corner problem. Figuring out this gem is a mother! Exit to the left past the bulge.

☐ 3. **Friday the 13th V7** ★★★ 🌀🌙
Start the same as Spooookie and fight up the right side of the V-corner. Finishing off the festivities might make you think twice.

☐ 4. **Atari aka Double Dike Spider Arêtes V4** ★★★
An obscure little affair marked by a gorgeous double arête and sits below and left of MMM Block with a good flat landing.

Newlin Boulder

Sam Sommers on Atari V4

Phillip Benningfield on Spooookie V6

MMM Block (Green Iguana)

The highest boulder in the field with three good problems on the west face. A comfortable hang is near the cliff and next to the block.

❑ 1. V1

The face on the left side above the drop. Climb on the big holds at the bottom up to the left-angling arête. A low start makes it a bit harder.

❑ 2. M7 aka Green Iguana V7 ⚫⚫

A magnificent outing starting down in the pit and moving through the distinct undercling. Bad feet make the crux moves a tad slippery! Green Iguana traverses right to the arête!

❑ 3. V3 ⚫⚫

Climb the left-angling arête on the west face right side.

❑ 4. South Slabbers V0-V1

On the south face are cruiser slabs with the right side offering a bit more delicacy.

Dark Hole Boulder

Immediately west of MMM and down in a dark hole (north face) are a few steep affairs with lay-down-start potential. Problems listed left to right:

❑ 1. V3 ⚫

The first problem encountered as one comes around to the north face. If you're looking at a bunch of flatish, sloping jugs to an easy top-out, you got it, but you don't! One long move defines the crux.

❑ 2. V3 ⚫

Just right of the first V3, and over the detached boulder, is a jug-haul-like line.

❑ 3. Geiman in a Blender V6

In the middle of the overhang, follow a seam with good right-hand sidepulls. Not a gem but a decent power problem. First move is the crux, to a good left-hand edge.

Passion Boulder

❑ 1. The Passion V9 ★★

A Newlin classic. Start sitting, very low, matched on a sloping rail. Move up through an amazing pinch and delicate balance moves to a tricky top.

❑ 2. NBA Pro Jams V11

Start matched on a big shelf and dyno up and left to an impossibly bad sloper. Top-out.

Megalodon Boulder

Continue on the Newlin Creek Trail for 160 yds, past a small talus pile on the left, and a short V1 with nice edges. Cross the small creek and head up hill for 25 yds. Cut back left on a social trail. Megalodon is the large boulder on your left.

❑ 1. Megalodon V7 ★★★

Stand start, matched in a high jug and climb up the tall and gorgeous face. Highball, committing and classic.

❑ 2. Three Barrel High V7 ★

Start on Megalodon and head left.

MMM Block

Passion Boulder

Passion Boulder

Megalodon

WATERFALL BOULDER

Continue up the side stream beyond Megalodon for 50 yards until the path is closed off by a small but scenic waterfall.

☐ **1. The Waterfall Project V10**
Start matched on a sloping crimp rail and head straight up on bad hands and feet.

TOJO RISEN

☐ **1. Riders on the Storm V3** ★★ 🌀 🔵
Start sitting matched on a good hold, head straight up.

☐ **2. Tojo Risen V6** ★
Start the same as Riders on the Storm but head left, then up, through an incredible tufa-pinch and a difficult encounter at the lip.

☐ **3. Mojo Risen V7**
Start left of Tojo Risen on two triangular-shaped underclings and head up and left.

SLAB

☐ **1. Slab V3** ★★ 🌀 🔵
Start standing on edges and climb the slab behind Tojo Risen.

THE NEW SECTOR

Located 575 yards and across two small drainages (problems exist on the left of the trail through this area) up the trail past Atari Area.Cross the creek on the left to arrive at Meat Wallet. To continue to the rest of The New Sector walk up a contouring trail to the south and east for approximately 150 yards to a "pass" between two rock outcrops. A large dead tree marks the spot. From here the trail descends for 75 yds. Look for a clearing and several large boulders on your left, below in the drainage. Head straight down the loose hillside.

MEAT WALLET

☐ **1. Meat Wallet V10**
Just beyond on the river crossing is a large overhang that faces upstream. Start standing, matched on a jug, and head right then up through a crazy flat undercling feature.

RIGHT GUARD BOULDER

The first boulder reached after heading downhill from the approach trail.

☐ **1. Burned at the Stake V11**
Start sitting, matched on a jug. Head immediately left to left-hand gaston and climb poor holds up the arête. A Megan Mascarenas FA.

☐ **2. Uncivilized V8** ★★
Just right of Burned at the Stake. A magnificent outing. Start sitting down matched on a jug. Climb the prominent arête.

☐ **3. Old Guard V8** ★★★
Classic Newlin Creek. Stand start on a good edge at head-height. Climb straight up the wall finishing slightly left. The sit start is V9.

☐ **4. Right Guard V7**
Start sitting make a big move up, then head right on good holds and top out up the arête on easier climbing.

Waterfall Project

Tojo Risen

Meat Wallet

Right Guard

❏ 5. Project

Around on the opposite side from Right Guard is a huge overhang. Climb out on terrible sloping holds and pinches.

❏ 6. Pretentious Vendor of Invention V10

Start low and matched on a good left facing edge. Climb up the tricky arête.

GREAT GUMBY BOULDER

Follow the approach trail down hill to the next boulder on your right.

❏ 1. The Great Gumby V8 ★★

Start standing, matched on a large left-facing sidepull. Make a big dynamic move up, right hand, to a small edge, and finish up the left arête.

JACQUES COUSTEAU

Walk left from the Great Gumby and around to the backside of the boulder.

❏ 1. Jacques Cousteau V11 ★

A Colorado gem. Stand start matched on a jug in the back of the roof. Move out to a good hold and dyno to the lip.

Pretentious Vendor of Invention

Jacques Cousteau

Pete Zoller on The Great Gumby V8

The V4 just past the Sixth Block

GUANELLA PASS

This alpine pass is inundated with hikers and four-wheelers during the summer and early fall but allows the lowland dweller a quick escape from the blistering Front Range summers. Guanella offers scads of moderate boulder problems and mean, steep, and committing testpieces on well-featured rock with extremely easy access and nearby camping. New problems are unearthed every year.

Directions: From Interstate 70 take the Georgetown exit #228. At the first stop sign (where mileages start) after passing under the highway go right following the blue signs for Guanella Pass. At the second stop sign go left into the historic downtown area, then take a right at the third stop sign and continue straight through the fourth stop sign. The road will begin to gain altitude through a few switchbacks.

FLIM Boulder
Located 5.4 miles up the pass. Many more boulders are located to the north and east of the powerlines. These boulders can be reached by parking at Clear Lake and walking along the west side of the lake to two boulders lakeside (Bob's Boulders which are often inundated with water) then straight uphill to FLIM.

Dark Horse Boulder/MM19 Boulders
Park just after mile marker 19 against the chain fence. Cross the road and walk back down the pass 60 yards to a distinct trail leading uphill (120 yards) to an incredible large block with impressive lines. Bring at least four big pads.

Clear Lake Campground Boulders
Located at 6.9 miles on the right. For the Campsite One Boulder enter the campground and walk uphill (SW) between campsites #1 and #2 onto a faint trail past an innocuous block to the upper boulder. Total walk is 50 yards. For Campsite Two Boulder go to campsite #2 and the boulder sits directly above an old restroom.

Of note, the tiny boulders in Clear Lake Campground are superb for kids to scramble on.

Mike Frieschlag on FLIM Traverse V4

FLIM Boulder

North Face

☐ 1. **V?**
Straight up the north face following edges to a small overlap at the top.

☐ 2. **V2**
An extremely long problem starting at the bottom of the ramp and moving progressively up and right on good edges.

☐ 3. **V2**
On the northwest corner, start in a hole between two blocks and move up and left to finish above the top of the ramp.

☐ 4. **V4**
Start on an atrocious left-hand crimp and pinch/slopers on the right. Move up a shield below the upper overlap. A painful V7 can be done from a sds.

☐ 5. **V?**
A beautiful pinch problem utilizing the pinches between the two V4's.

☐ 6. **V4**
A magnificent traverse problem on the west face starting on the lowest edge/slopers and cruising up and right.

☐ 7. **V1**
The far west arête moving up and left on great holds.

Dark Horse Boulder/ MM19 Boulders

☐ 1. **V?**
The southeast steep overhang.

☐ 2. **Dark Horse V10**
The gorgeous long, steep line up the middle of the east face starting from an obvious matched large edge. Move up and left on sloping holds and edges. A sds that finishes straight up has been done.

☐ 3. **Crazy Horse V5**
Slightly right of Dark Horse start low to slopers then fine edges up to a left-facing small corner. V8 with sds.

☐ 4. **V4**
Again right a little is another problem moving up to a crack/corner.

Campsite One V3

CLEAR LAKE CAMPGROUND BOULDERS

CAMPSITE ONE BOULDER

A relatively short boulder littered with holds. If you and your kids desire shorter problems on good rock this boulder will suffice.

❒ **1. East Face V3** 🌀
A well-defined overhanging problem on big flat holds. Use a spotter, as the landing is uncomfortable on the spine.

❒ **2. West Face V2** 🌀
In the gray rock start on a left-hand sidepull to a sloping edge then juggy arête.

❒ **3. South Face V2** 🌀
Climb the white face starting on extremely thin sidepulls to a small white edge.

❒ **4. South Face V1** 🌀
On the short side of the south face a couple of problems can be done off a low flat jug.

Campsite One Boulder

Campsite One Boulder

CAMPSITE TWO BOULDER

A tall east face defines this boulder. Be aware that the problems are not well traveled but are easy slabs on good rock.

☐ 1. V0/V1 ☻

The main east-facing slab has three cruiser slabs with the problems getting progressively more interesting from left to right.

☐ 2. V5 ☻ ☻

On the right side of the east face start on a good edge in the burnt orange lichen then make a big throw up to tenuous slopers. A good sidepull is up and right once the feet are situated on the left-angling foot ramp.

Campsite Two Boulder

Phillip Benningfield on Campsite 2 Boulder

Dawn Heigele on Campsite 1 Boulder #4

GUANELLA PASS MAIN AREA

Located at 8.0 miles. Park just after the culvert on the right. From the eastern (downhill) side of the culvert follow a trail headed south past a fire ring approximately 220 yards. You can't miss the boulders as the trail is well defined and goes right by them.

FIRST BLOCK

This nice boulder is smack dab in the middle of the trail and has a distinct vertical north face with a pine tree directly in front of it.

North Face

☐ 1. **V2**
Climb the left arête to a big move up high.

☐ 2. **V5**
The best problem on the boulder! Climb the middle of the north face with left-hand sidepulls and right-hand slopers to a hard move to reach a flat, sharp edge.

West Face

☐ 3. **V2**
Climbs the left arête to a horizontal sloping edge, then up to an obvious horn.

☐ 4. **V2**
Directly right. Start on sloping edges to a big right hand side-pull then you're on your own.

East Face

☐ 5. **V0** 🌐
The low-angle slab facing east. A superb easy problem that requires a little patience figuring out the best sequence.

South Face

☐ 6. **V0–V3**
Numerous slabs can be done for boulderers afraid of heights.

SECOND BLOCK

Follow the trail 35 yards south past the First Boulder. Problems are not listed as the lines are definitely not classic in nature, but the boulder has good warm-ups.

THIRD BLOCK

Directly uphill 25 yards from the Second Block.

West Face

☐ 1. **V3** 🌐
An excellent problem behind the spruce tree utilizing right hand laybacks and an undercling then dyno using terrible footholds to a big-ass jug.

North Face

☐ 2. **V1**
Climb the obvious discontinuous crack.

First Block

First Block South Face

Second Block

Third Block

Fourth Block

Walk 50 yards south from the Second Block then straight uphill (east) 15 yards.

Northwest Face

☐ 1. **V2**

From the righthand pocket reach up to an in-obvious edge then sloper.

Southwest Arête

☐ 2. **Bessie V10** ★★

A very hard sloper creation! Start on the good flat edge then bear hug the viciously sloping arête.

South Face

☐ 3. **V5** ⬤

Start on the good incut and head straight up on miniscule sloping edges. An easier, yet miserable variation, follows the seam to the right.

Sixth and Seventh Blocks

Walk 75 yards south past the Second Block on the trail and come around to the south-facing problems.

Sixth Block

☐ 1. **V3**

There is one main problem on the south face. Start from the right side on big flat holds and move up and left on incut edges and a gaston to reach the right-angling top. A pumpy V5 traverse can be done from the far left finishing on the V3.

☐ 2. **V4**

Nice edges most of the way!

Seventh Block

South Face

☐ 1. **V4**

Climb the middle of the south face starting on thin edges to a high right-hand sloper. One-move wonder!

☐ 2. **V1**

Climb the right blunt arête.

☐ 3. **V3** ★★

Just past the 6th Block the trail goes by a short problem.

Fourth Block

Sixth Block

Sixth Block

Seventh Block

8TH BLOCK/MIND MATTERS BOULDER

This is certainly the most committing boulder with some horrific landings and hard problems. Walk farther south a couple of minutes from the 6th Block on a trail that winds slightly uphill to a hidden boulder.

☐ **1. Sloping Matters V8** ★★

From the southwest arête's slopers move up into the undercling crack. A sds catapults the grade.

North Face

☐ **2. Stemming Matters V6** ★★★

The superb left line! Start low in the hole and move up the open corner.

☐ **3. Compression Matters V7** ★★★

The right line that involves, you guessed it, compression moves to an excellent left-jug then dyno to a sloping pinch. Another variation has been done to the right that appears to require far more compression.

East Face

☐ **4. Crimping Matters V10** ★★★

The left line beginning down in the pit like Mind Matters. This vicious problem looks on par to the neighboring V12.

☐ **5. Mind Matters V12** ★★★

Steep east face that climbs above jumbled talus to the high right-facing corner in the middle of the wall. Bring every single pad you can find and plenty of spotters.

☐ **6. V?**

The right side of the east face has another line.

9TH BLOCK/LOVE MATTERS

Located from the 8th Block by walking south and east from the east face of Mind Matters for a couple of minutes. You will know you found this one as it looks like a small mining claim below the beautiful block.

☐ **1. V?**

The south face has a horrendously steep problem created by strong arms digging and crimping.

☐ **2. Love Matters V8** ★★

This climb has broken a number of times. The right-to-left traverse beginning off the low jug on the west face moves through slopers to the apex of the south and west faces.

☐ **3. Beyond Matters V8** ★★

Straight up west face, from the low start with a heel hook, on mean slopers. Climbing Love Matters into Beyond Matters is Life Matters V8.

ROAD BOULDERS

Located 0.1 mile past the Main Area parking are two small blocks on the west side of the road. Problems range from V0–V4.

8th Block

8th Block East Face

9th Block

Sheyna Button on Boulder E V0

RED CLIFF—THE KLETTERGARDEN

These well-hidden granite boulders lie above 9000 feet and have good conditions in the summer and are magnificent in the fall when the aspens turn. As the hordes congregate on the Front Range, the flawless pristine granite near Red Cliff is quieter and welcoming. The boulders allow a multitude of fun problems on featured stone.

Red Cliff used to be a quiet dump for local trash, but the advent of hungrier and hungrier traveling boulderers has turned this area into quite a destination spot. New development occurs on a regular basis, so go out and find some! You would be wise to come during the week or off-season months.

Directions: From Interstate 70, west of Vail, take US Route 24 (exit #171) towards Minturn/Red Cliff. Follow the road out of Minturn and up the switchbacks then past the suspension bridge, which comes just after the north entrance to Red Cliff. Stop at the south entrance to Red Cliff. Park on the dirt pullout between the entrance and Hwy 24. Directly across Hwy 24 is a dirt road that leads to the boulders. The short hike takes a minute or two. Social trails lead to all the blocks.

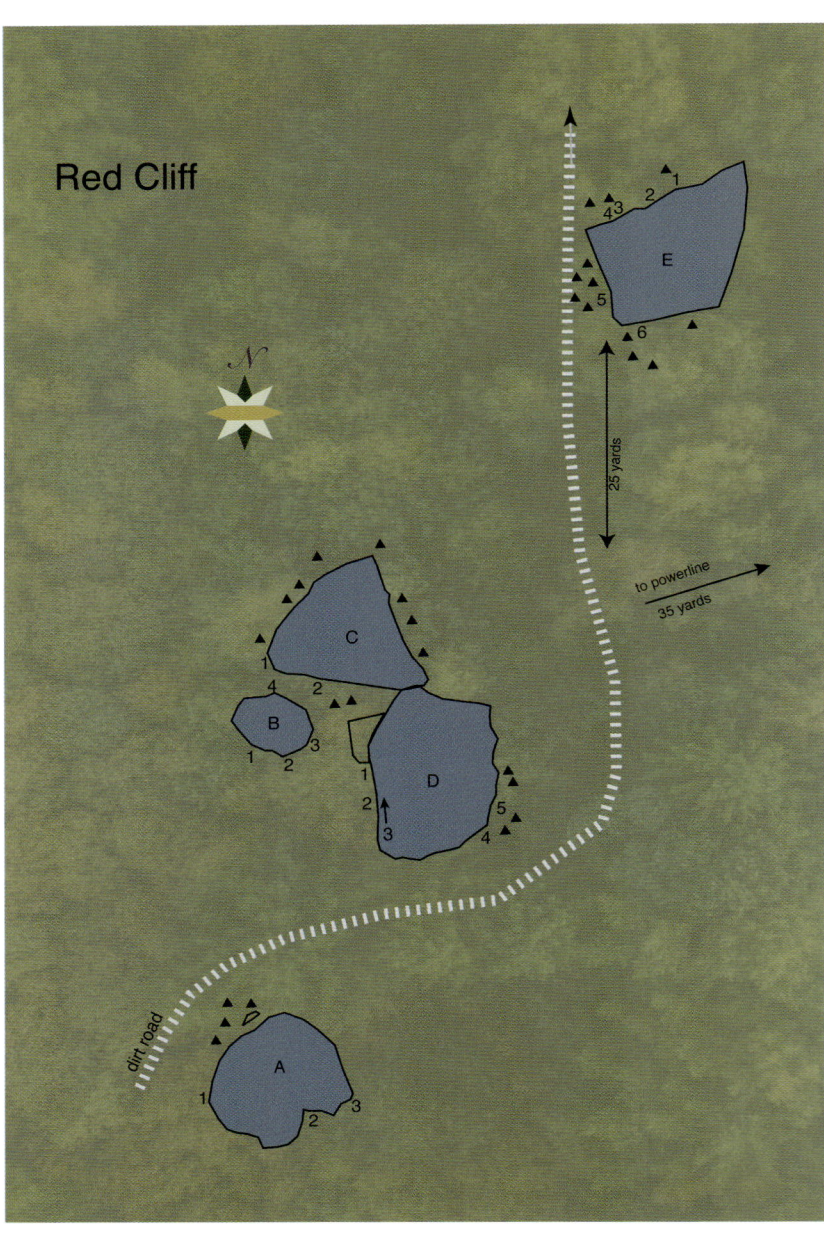

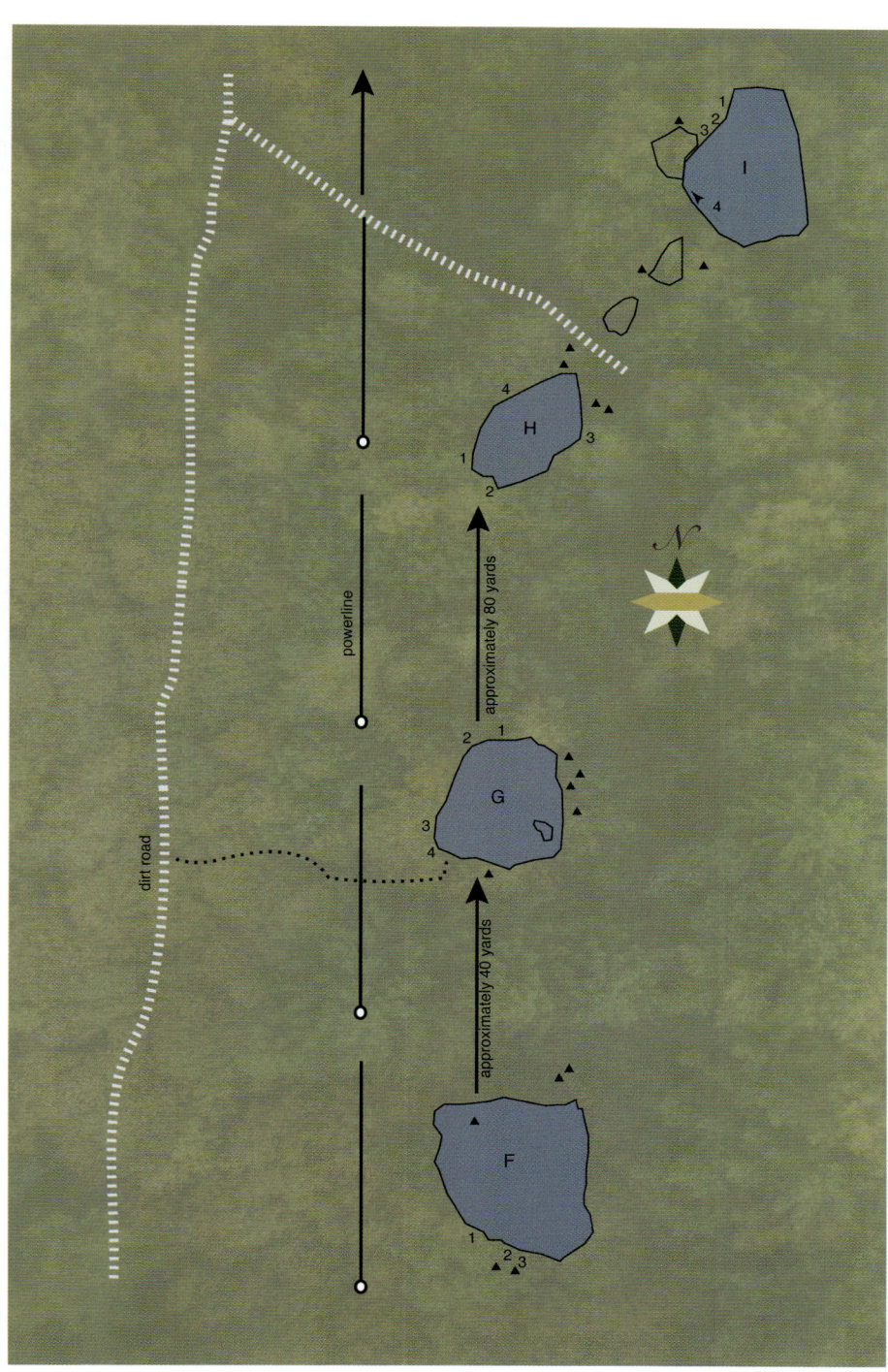

A.
The first boulder encountered up the road on the right. A severely overhanging dihedral is on the southeast face.

❏ **1. V5** ★★
The west face has a distinct problem that starts below an undercling and sidepull and makes a big reach up and right to a bomber flat edge. A short V1 sloper problem is a couple of feet to the left.

❏ **2. V6** ★
The overhanging dihedral on the southeast face with sharp holds and mandatory stemming.

❏ **3. V6**
A grungy sit down start that moves slightly left on painful bulbous holds and finishes right of #2. A few variations exist to this problem.

B.
Directly across the dirt road is a cluster of three boulders. The smallest left one has a number of sit down start problems.

❏ **1. V1**
Starts on two sidepulls on the left of the south face and make one move to a huge jug.

❏ **2. V1** ★
A couple of feet right of #1 is a sit down start on the south face. Also the downclimb for the boulder.

❏ **3. V1** ★
Again to the right is another sit down start on the blunt southeast arête. A V3 traverse moves left and finishes on the west face.

❏ **4. V2** ★
On the north face is a problem with thin edges and terrible feet. A sit down that starts on two opposing pinch/sidepulls is substantially harder.

Melissa Love on #1 on Boulder A

Boulder A

Boulder A

C.

The boulder just north with a beautiful 20-foot slab on the south face.

❏ 1. **V0** ★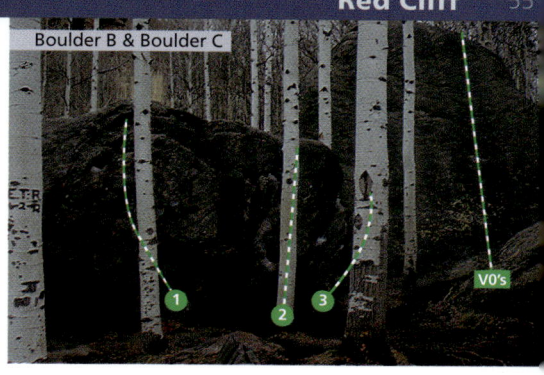

Climb the blunt southwest arête.

❏ 2. **V0** ★★

A high slab on the south face with progressively better holds as one gets higher. A V0 variant starts to the right and shares the finish.

D.

The large boulder attached to the right side of the south face of Boulder C.

❏ 1. **V2** ★

Four feet right of the end of #3's ending holds is a sit down start that uses slopers to jugs.

❏ 2. **V3** ★

Seven feet right of #3's end is another low start off an incut edge then straight up the blank slab.

❏ 3. **V5** ★★

A traverse on the west face that begins in the scooped overhang and moves left on slopers. It ends straight up before the attached small block. Pulling straight out the scooped overhang at the beginning is V3.

❏ 4. **V1**

A low start on the southeast arête that climbs straight up. A short traverse right to the crack is V3. Continuing past the crack and across the entire face is V6.

❏ 5. **V0**

Climb straight up from below the crack.

Boulder B & Boulder C

Boulder D

E.

A lone boulder found on the right after walking north on the dirt road for approximately 25 yards. This distinguished boulder has many demanding problems on the overhanging north face.

Boulder E

☐ 1. V8 ★★★
A sds on the north face that climbs up the obvious line in the middle of the overhang then takes a sharp left onto the slopers to a mean finish.

☐ 2. V6 ★★
Straight up from the middle sds then surmount the vicious slab crux.

☐ 3. V6 ★★
Start three feet right of #2 on sds slopers and climb up to the same finish as #2. A short V5 starts on the tiny lip crimps above and right of the start to #3 and tackles the slab.

☐ 4. V4 ★
To the right and five feet off the dirt are opposing sidepulls. Climb straight up to bad slopers and a small edge.

☐ 5. V0
The juggy right side of the west face.

☐ 6. V1
A sds on the left of the south face. Climb through the green lichen at the top.

F.

Due east 30 yards from Boulder E is a massive boulder sitting on the opposite side of the powerline. The problems on the boulder are tall and difficult with lichen-covered top-outs. It is the largest block by the powerlines, with a tall southwest face undercut on the left side. Walk through the first set of boulders along the dirt road then look right across the meadow and Boulder F sits out in the open facing the road.

Boulder G

☐ 1. V3
On the far left side of the roof start standing and muckle over the lip. A direct start boosts the grade substantially.

☐ 2. Tragedy Resides in You V6 ★ 🌀
A terrifying escapade—rather like dealing with pissy locals. Start on the right side of the undercut roof and dyno from crappy holds to gain the small right-facing corner. Be ever-so careful climbing the problem unless some fine person went to the trouble of cleaning the corner.

☐ 3. Immortality V7 ★★★ 🌀
Climbs the 24-foot-tall part of the boulder via secure edges at the bottom and a difficult crux to gain the upper right-facing corner.

☐ 4. Sticky Fingers V5 ★★ 🌀
A low start problem that climbs up and left then makes a terribly long reach back right to finish.

☐ 5. Anaphylactic Shock V6 ★ 🌀
This problem begins in the low slot and moves up and left through indistinct holds. The problem begins the same as Sticky Fingers.

☐ 6. V6 ★★
Start this dynamic problem the same as #4, but bust right and finish up the slab with pockets.

G.

Forty yards north from Boulder F, along the powerline, is a boulder littered with many tiny edges.

☐ 1. V3 ★★
A one-move dyno that starts on two decent crimpers to the left of the massive jug.

☐ 2. V4
A short traverse that starts below #1 and moves right to the massive jug on a diagonal seam.

Phillip Benningfield on the FA of Tragedy Resides in You V6

Boulder H

Scott Leonard on Boulder E V8

☐ 3. **V1**
The slab with positive edges and bomber feet, left of the crack on the west face.

☐ 4. **V0**
The jug haul that follows the crack on the west face.

H.
Follow the powerline another 75 to 80 yards to this boulder outside the pine trees.

☐ 1. **V1**
An easy problem on the west face that uses one sloper side-pull up to good edges.

Boulder I

☐ 2. **V1**
Just right on the southwest face is a problem starting on sloper/sidepulls then up to a huge, flat jug.

☐ 3. **V0**
An easy problem on the east face with secure jugs and edges.

☐ 4. **V0**
The slab on the northwest face.

I.
Continue north along the powerlines past two large blocks to a boulder in the woods. A steep west face has a small adjacent boulder lying under it with a plethora of sloping and micro holds that have been beaten into submission to create problems verging on V10—and maybe, just maybe V11. The problems are far too contrived to describe. Rest assured plenty of leathery flesh is necessary to pull on the horrifically minute crimps.

☐ 1. **V1**
The low start on the left of the northwest face.

☐ 2. **V0**
Climbs the scoop just right of #1.

☐ 3. **V2**
Start right of the scoop in front of the adjacent block and climb over the small overhang.

☐ 4. **V5** ★★
The traverse from right to left on the southwest face. Many variations can be done in and around this traverse.

The author on Boulder F Immortality V7

Melissa Love one of Boulder F's V6

THE KLETTERGARDEN, ETC.

This area has numerous tiny blocks with a handful of climbable boulders; the area is mostly devoid of the old machines formerly found at The Klettergarden. To reach The Klettergarden Etc. boulders walk down the dirt road to the main Klettergarden (you walk right through the middle of the boulderfield) then go approximately 175 yards farther. The dirt road goes under the power-line, and the boulders are roadside to the northeast, before heading downhill. Please tread ever-so-lightly when climbing at Red Cliff's dump.

V0 BLOCK

This lone boulder sits 25 yards off the road, past an old fire pit. It has an overhanging arête on the south side (V3). All other problems on the boulder are V0 and make for uneventful warm-ups.

RED BOULDER

Uphill from the V0 Block to the east about 45 yards. This boulder and its neighbor are easily seen through the trees.

❏ 1. **V0** ★★
A boulder problem requiring a mixture of stupidity and curiosity to climb. The landing defines Bad Landing but the climb is fun and worthwhile. The problem heads up the middle of the west face on good crimps to progressively better holds.

❏ 2. **V3** ★
Climb the southwest arête on good sidepulls to a throw for the lip or hard crimping over an unsuitable landing.

❏ 3. **V1**
Climb the horribly sharp right side of the south face.

WHITE RIGHT BOULDER

The huge block adjacent to Red Boulder, with an undercut roof at seven feet, on the west face.

❏ 1. **V0**
Climb up the dirty left side of the north face.

❏ 2. **V0** ★
Climb the open north face dihedral. A V3 starts on the sloping ramp left of the dihedral and finishes in the dihedral.

❏ 3. **V1**
Climb out the left side of the roof on the west face, starting from a big jug.

❏ 4. **V3**
Climb out the filthy right side of the west face roof. A difficult problem is immediately right, through the miniature overlaps.

❏ 5. **V1**
Climb—or don't if you are smart—the loose southwest arête.

Red Boulder

V0 Block

White Right Boulder

Additional Blocks (pictured right)

This assortment of squatty boulders is located along the road before heading northeast to the better and bigger blocks. Problems range from V0 to V5 sit down starts.

Squatty Boulder

Sign Boulder

A singular boulder graced with solid rock and distinctive problems. The boulder is visible from the parking area on Highway 24 to the east, above the sign for Leadville and Buena Vista. Approach up the hillside on a trail, which starts from the dirt road.

❏ **1. V2** ★★
Climb the vertical line on the left side of the west face. Easy up to the midway jug, then you encounter a sloping edge to reach the top.

❏ **2. V2** ★
Just right of #1 up the right-diagonaling seam.

❏ **3. V1**
Climb the far right side of the south face in a broken ramp to a long reach at the top.

❏ **4. V6** ★★
Climb the southeast arête staying on the south face.

❏ **5. V5** ★
Climb the blunt south face arête right of the black stripes, starting with a jump to reach the left-hand sidepull.

❏ **6. V3**
Climb the thin edges on the southeast face (left of the broken rock).

Sign Boulder V5

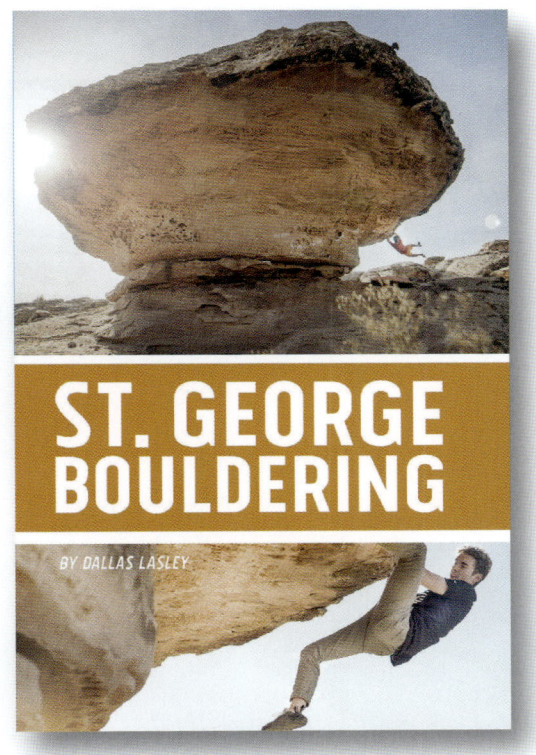

HORNSILVER

The granite boulders in this area are mostly undeveloped. The two areas with known problems are the Day Use Area and Hornsilver Campground. The boulders are scattered throughout the woods from the Red Cliff Boulders all the way to the Hornsilver Campground and beyond.

Directions: From the south entrance to Red Cliff continue on Highway 24 going south. The Day Use Area is located on the right 0.5 mile up Highway 24. The Hornsilver Campground is another 0.5 mile up on the left.

HORNSILVER DAY USE AREA

The lone boulder sitting in the meadow offers a few problems in the V0 to V2 range.

HORNSILVER CAMPGROUND

This area has potential for problems in the campground and below the Hornsilver cliff. The boulders northeast of the campground have a couple of problems. Some fun problems can be done along the small granite slabs south of the campground.

Trixie Tartasky on Star Crossed Lovers V5

HORNSILVER CAMPSITE 6

For convenience to the cooler stuffed with libations, this slabby area can not be beat. Be sure and bring loads of beer, I mean pads, as the majority of problems have sloping landings and top out around 30 feet. Rest assured, these slabs are high quality (minus the pine needle covered top outs) and committing.

LOWER WALL

Problems listed from left to right. The distinct gray slab with a wide left-leaning crack in the middle and directly above the voyeuristic picnic table at Campsite 6.

☐ **1. Affinity V2** 🪨⭕
Climbs the far left blunt arête above a detached stone. Scary as a couple of the high edges are not fully attached.

☐ **2. V3** 🪨⭕
Right of the dirty corner up the clean gray slab. The problem moves slightly right after the initial moves.

☐ **3. V3** 🪨⭕
A few feet left of the wide crack is another tall slab with itty-bitty crimps to start.

☐ **4. V3** 🪨⭕
The wide left-leaning crack with ultra-polished footholds.

☐ **5. Ichi Ban V6** 🪨⭕
The overhanging face/arête right of the crack. Depending on where you flop onto the slab, the difficulty and landing become sicker.

☐ **6. V0** 🪨⭕
The low-angle slab on the face right of the arête. A silly, yet entertaining thin affair (V3) is on the holdless face just before the dirty, left-facing corner.

☐ **7. Abyss V2** 🪨⭕
Right again is a fun steeper affair through sidepulls to yet another highball slab finish.

QUIMBY BOULDER

☐ **1. Quimby V2** 🪨⭕
A monstrous slab that gets the juices flowing. The distinct line is found above the lower tier's left side and up the steep slope. Climbs the left side of the tallest face on secure, albeit sloping edges, to a long reach to gain a right-facing sidepull.

☐ **2. V2** ⭕
On the right side of the face is a little safer companion to the Quimby.

☐ **3. Top-out or Tapout V4** 🪨⭕
The hidden line left of Quimby on thin edges.

Scott Neel on Lower Wall V3

HOMESTAKE CREEK BOULDERS

This secluded and perfect summertime and fall retreat has scads of boulders but only the Aircraft Carrier Boulder and the Cool Arête seem to attract enough takers to hold chalk. Although the neighboring boulders see less traffic, there are plenty of fun highball lines. Killer boulders are constantly developed up and down the creek.

The Homestake Creek Boulders and the Aircraft Carrier Boulder are located 1.1 miles past Hornsilver Campground (headed towards Tennessee Pass and Leadville). From Leadville it is 17.8 miles from Highway 24/91 intersection. Go right on Homestake Road (FR703) and down the hill and over the creek to the first righthand parking area just after the creek crossing (0.6 mile). Walk north down the creek on a distinct trail system for approximately 420 yards. Take the left hand trail for 50 yards, which goes uphill slightly and past a large, lone boulder (V5). Continue on the trail another 50 yards until you hit a chalk-choked block with a big overhang on the north face and undercut roof on the west face. Other fun, undocumented problems reside on the neighboring blocks.

V5 on the way to Aircraft Carrier
V5

Quimby Boulder
3
1

Aircraft Carrier
aka Romeo and Juliet Boulder

This is a beautiful big boulder hidden down the west side of Homestake Creek and littered with a couple of classics, numerous contrived lines, and short (safe) warm-ups on the east face.

North Face

❑ 1. Romeo V6 ★★
This line gets a higher grade from some (maybe burrowing into the dirt) but really isn't that hard from a sit start left of the chalk-caked V5 (Star Crossed Lovers) that climbs to a reasonable top-out.

❑ 2. Star Crossed Lovers V5 ★★★
An absolutely classic boulder problem that climbs straight out the north overhang on the obvious chalked jugs.

❑ 3 V? ★
Just right of SCL is a tough problem that may have been climbed. Word had it the problem was V11 but a V9 does move into this line of horrendous edges from SCL.

West Face

❑ 1. Rhythm of the Saints V8 ★
The leftmost roof problem from a stand start or breach the low-to-the-ground overhang/roof at a harder grade (V10?).

❑ 2. V7
Right of ROTS is a fairly contrived problem. A butt start under the overhang is V?.

❑ 3. V0
The far right side has an easy line.

East Face

❑ 1. The Cool Arête V7 ★★★ 🌲🌀
On the massive (now covered in bolts) boulder just west of Aircraft Carrier is an eye-catching line up the south arête from a butt start. A V10 can be done traversing in from the right.

Aircraft Carrier North Face

Aircraft Carrier West Face

The Cool Arête

Lisa Raleigh on the Pyramid Boulder Photo by Duane Raleigh

REDSTONE

The Redstone boulders are situated just north of the historic coal-mining town turned tourist trap. The boulderfields consist of two areas separated by the Crystal River. However, their close proximity does not mean similar bouldering. The boulders offer various styles from vertical faces with sloping pebble pinching and incut rails to vicious slopers. Look to the Stein Boulder for the former. The Weider Boulder and Corkscrew provide the latter. If the waterside Corkscrew doesn't satisfy your appetite, venture among the aspens and enjoy a plethora of phenomenal face problems. Conditions are generally good, except during the dead of winter and early spring.

Directions: From State Route 82, at the Carbondale exit, take State Route 133 south from Carbondale until reaching Redstone's north entrance. The Corkscrew is located just south of the north entrance on the west side of the Crystal River. Park in the first pull-out (still on State Route 133) after the north entrance. For the other boulders turn left at the north entrance onto the frontage road and drive one mile and park on the left before the town sign for Redstone. Walk up the dirt road from the parking area until a trail appears (50 yards) on the left. Follow the trail approximately 80 yards until a fence ends on the left. Continue another 60 yards looking for an extremely faint trail on the right. Go up this trail and the boulders appear after 20 yards.

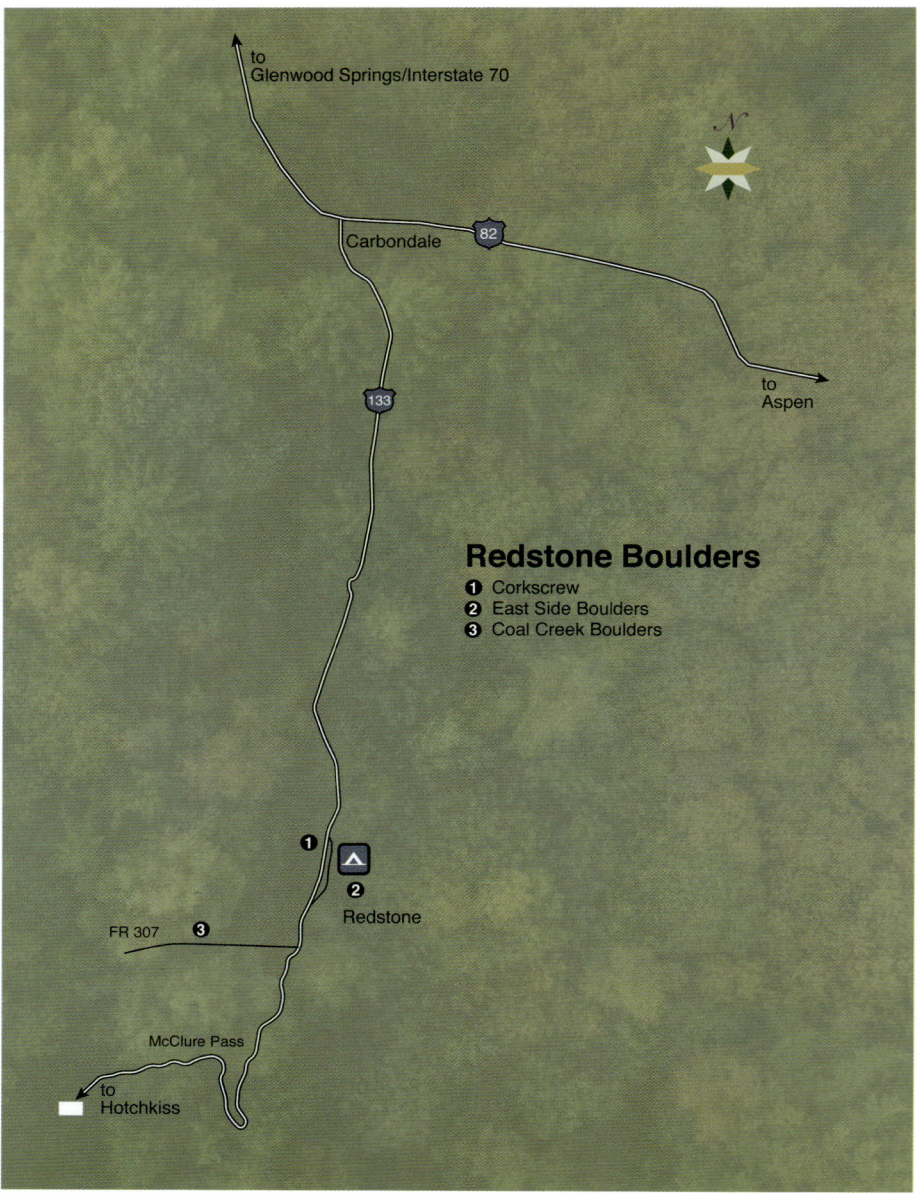

to
Glenwood Springs/Interstate 70

Carbondale   82

133

to
Aspen

Redstone Boulders

❶ Corkscrew
❷ East Side Boulders
❸ Coal Creek Boulders

❶

❷
Redstone

FR 307   ❸

McClure Pass

to
Hotchkiss

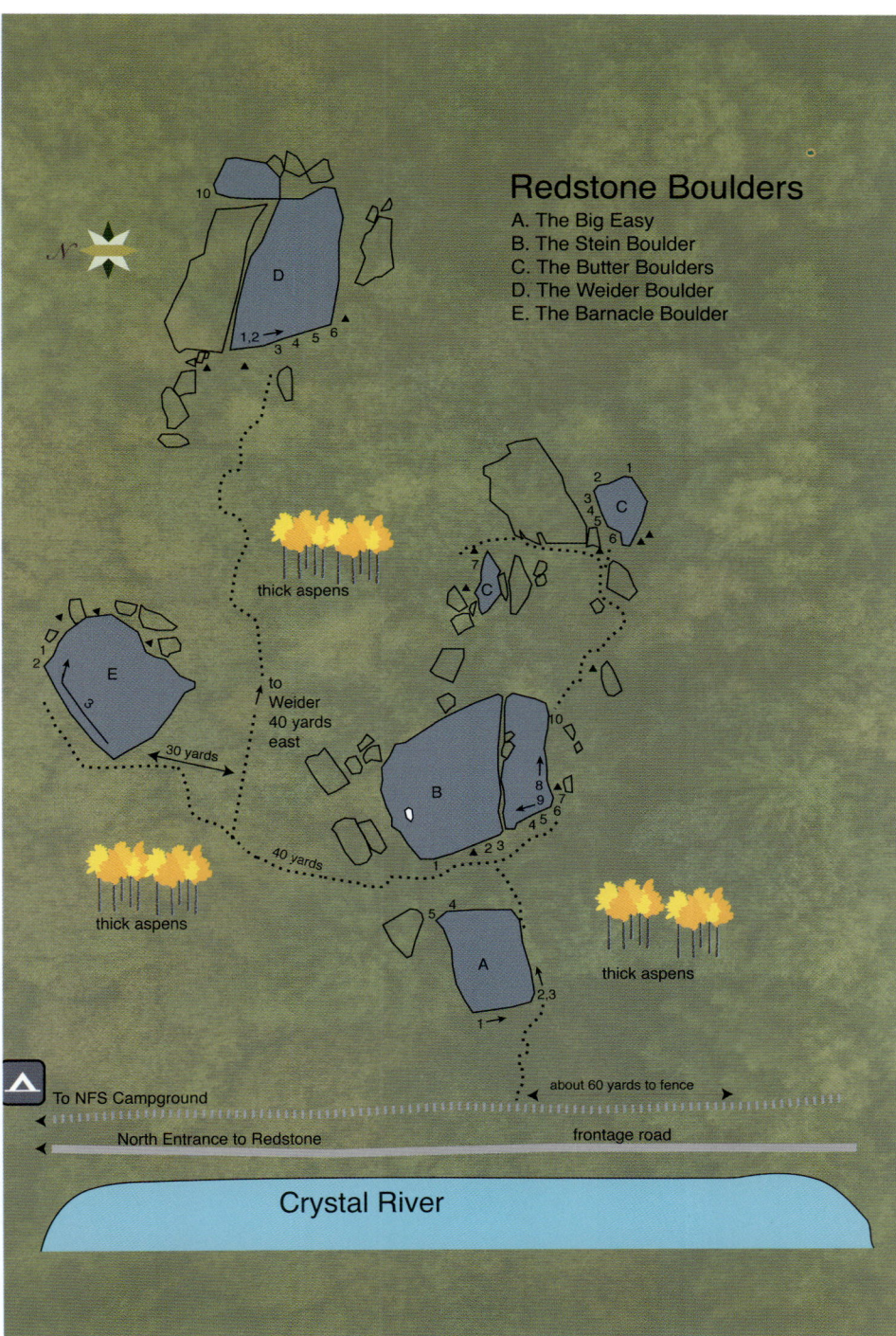

Redstone Boulders

A. The Big Easy
B. The Stein Boulder
C. The Butter Boulders
D. The Weider Boulder
E. The Barnacle Boulder

N

10

D

1,2
3 4 5 6

thick aspens

2 1
3
4
5
6

C

7

C

1
2

E

3

to
Weider
40 yards
east

30 yards

10

B

8
9

7
6
5
4

1 2 3

40 yards

thick aspens

5 4

A

1

2,3

thick aspens

To NFS Campground

about 60 yards to fence

North Entrance to Redstone

frontage road

Crystal River

CORKSCREW BOULDER

A beautiful boulder in an awesome setting—located on the west bank of the Crystal River. The varied bouldering on this one block is hard to beat. From highball slabs, sloping dynamic problems, and bizarre corkscrew moves, almost all the techniques are given a chance to be thwarted.

❏ 1. Left of Corkscrew V5 ★★

Start on a sidepull pod and reach to a matched sloper then a throw out right. A V5 variation climbs straight up on a small crimp followed by a hard throw to the sloping top. A V2 climbs off a left-hand undercling from the matched sloper then the top.

❏ 2. Corkscrew V5-V6 ★★★

Probably the most novel boulder problem in the state. Start facing the river (V6) and work like a corkscrew until facing the final moves over the top to the left. The problem can be done straight on at V5 unless one's flexibility is akin to an I-beam.

❏ 3. The Main Squeeze V6 ★★

A sds that climbs the severely overhanging arête right of Corkscrew. Finish straight up from the arête or move around the corner onto the sloping shelf. A V8 continues traversing left through Corkscrew, ending with the dyno on #1.

❏ 4. Guns and Roses V6 ★★

A low traverse of the northwest face on good edges and ending on the south slab.

❏ 5. Northwest Slabs V0-V2 ★★

A number of high, outstanding routes on the northwest face.

❏ 6. Worm Drive V4 ★★

Climb the tallest section of the northwest face not using the good edges left of the west arête. Begins directly above the crux of Guns and Roses.

❏ 7. South Slabs V1-V3 ★★

The slabs on the left are more committing than the northwest face slabs, but shorter on the right. The Mental Problem (V1) climbs the middle of the south face from good edges that are manteld to gain more good edges then a dyno to the lip.

Corkscrew Boulder

THE PYRAMID

The second boulder a few yards downriver from the Corkscrew. Most of the year the water surrounds the block but if you're lucky a number of fine, short problems, dynamic throws, and traverses can be done. Problems range from V0 to V6. (Don't be fooled by the earlier photo; the Pyramid has shifted since that picture was taken).

IMMERSION BOULDER

Downstream and across the river from Corkscrew approximately 200 feet. This block also sits in water most of the year. Luck may be on your side in late summer or early fall.

❏ 1. V2 ★★

Traverse the upstream side of the boulder to Total Immersion.

❏ 2. Total Immersion V2 ★★

Climbs the prow over the deep water.

Mike Benge on the Immersion Boulder Photo by John Sherman

The Big Easy

Crystal River East Side Boulders

A. THE BIG EASY

The first boulder encountered from the trail in the woods. The trail skirts the right side of the boulder (the beginning of the Big Easy Traverse) and opens into a small clearing where the Stein Boulder can be seen.

1. Front Traverse V6
The traverse of the boulder's west side from left to right.

2. The Big Easy Traverse V1 ★★
From the left side of the south face, traverse around to the east side and end on a white cobble on the far right side of the east face.

3. Low Traverse V10
The same traverse as #2 except use the low set of pebbles across the south and east face. Finishes by climbing up #5.

4. Straight Up Pocket Problem V2 ★★
Begin from a deep sharp pocket on the right side of the east face. Pull pebbles up to the sloping shelf. A sds from the big hueco makes it V5.

5. The Arête V6 ★★★
A sds problem that climbs the northeast arête. One of the classics in the area. A V8 starts on #4 and moves right to finish The Arête.

B. THE STEIN BOULDER

The second huge boulder found in the woods. Just to the east 15 yards from The Big Easy.

1. Slopenstein V6 ★★★
Start at the far left of the west face and traverse the sloping holds before moving up to a bucket. A longer traverse exits on small pebbles (just left of the aspen) and is V7.

2. Gertrudestein V9
A gross problem just right of the tree on the west face that starts on a low sloper.

3. Arêtestein V7 ★★
The problem just left of the nasty offwidth crack.

4. Frankenstein V8 ★★
Just right of the offwidth crack is a right-facing dihedral. Start with an underclinged crystal with the right hand and make long slaps up and left to slopers then the top. A sds that uses the left arête to the slopers is V7.

5. Grisseltwist V10 ★
Climbs the right-facing dihedral with bizarre moves.

6. Pinchenstein V4 ★★
A sds to the right of #5 that uses underclings to reach the high slopers and a reasonable top-out.

7. Melonstein V6 ★★★
A classic that starts on the blunt southwest arête's low sloping jugs and moves through pebble underclings and pinches to good holds.

8. Linkenstein V5 ★★★
From the sloping shelf on the southwest arête traverse right across the entire south face on the high set of bomber rails. A few big moves between rails and a down-move near the end get the juices flowing.

8a. Simplestein V0-V2
Starts the same as Linkenstein but tops out early where the sloping shelf ends.

8b. Low Linkenstein V10
Starts as #8 but traverses low on sloping pebbles.

9. Lichenstein V6 ★★
From the right end of the sloping shelf traverse back left on the high holds below the lip. Round the southwest corner and exit up the high slopers on the west face before reaching the Frankenstein dihedral.

10. Assorted Stein V2-V7 ★★★
Tons of contrived problems can be done on the south face. The best ones are on the far right climbing either right or left off the obvious line of pebbles (V5).

Stein Boulder

Lisa Raleigh on Linkenstein V5 Photo by Duane Raleigh

C. THE BUTTER BOULDERS

A set of three boulders (two have problems) found southeast from the Stein Boulder approximately 20 yards. The boulders are defined by low-angle slab and arête problems, with one overhanging problem that climbs opposing arêtes.

☐ **1. Left Arête V6** ★★
On the left arête of the east face of the south boulder is a technical problem with a mono and bad feet to start. Finish on the blunt arête.

☐ **2. Middle Arête V2** ★★
The right arête on the east face that ascends the left-angling arête.

☐ **3. The Prow V7** ★
On the left side of the north face (just around the corner from #2) is a difficult slab to a tough mantel.

☐ **4. The Scoop V2** ★★
Climb the scooped-out section just right of The Prow.

☐ **5. Pocket Route V1** ★★
Climbs the face directly above the down-facing pocket.

☐ **6. Right Arête V1** ★
The easiest problem on the boulder that cruises up the west arête.

☐ **7. V6** ★★★
On the north face of the easternmost Butter Boulder is a classic overhang that utilizes terrible opposing arêtes. A sds makes it V8.

Butter - Left Arête

Butter- East

The Weider Boulder

Lisa Raleigh on Barnacle Boulder Traverse V8 Photo by Duane Raleigh

D. THE WEIDER BOULDER

This is another massive block that is hidden in the woods northeast of the Stein Boulder. Walk the trail that heads north from the Stein Boulder for approximately 40 yards until a faint trail heads due east. Walk up this trail (marked by parallel logs on the ground) for 40 yards until a huge block appears. The problems face west and tend to be gritty.

❒ 1. **High Traverse V2** ★
The hardest V2 in the state. If one can get to the high holds traverse right.

❒ 2. **Low Traverse V8** ★★
Bad, sloping handholds and nonexistent feet epitomize this problem. Climbs left to right.

❒ 3. **V5** ★★
Starts on the sloper at arms reach and makes one atrociously hard move to the upper shelf.

❒ 4. **V7** ★
A harder variation to #3. Starts directly left of the crack.

❒ 5. **The Crack V10** ★
How can three moves equal ten? Give it a try and see if it adds up.

❒ 6. **Right of the Crack V6**
Try and hold the flaring fist jam to reach the higher holds. Finishes on the good rail. A V5 climbs the right side of the arête and is the only problem to top-out the boulder.

❒ 7. **V5** 🏃
Climb the southeast arête all the way to the top if you dare.

❒ 8. **South Face V3s** 🏃
Highball doesn't really do this justice. You will surely be free-soloing for your life up the numerous choices across this wall.

❒ 9. **Project V?** 🏃🏊
The line just left of the aspen tree on the left side of the south face may be done by the time this guide hits the news stands. A one in many try move is the biz down low.

❒ 10. **Sex After 50/51 V8** ★★ 🏃🏊
Easily the best new addition to the already plentiful classics at Redstone. A distinct, lone, tall arête with a relatively safe landing depending on your top-out sequence. Start low (51) and slap and pinch your way up the arête. Exit with an insecure mantel off the high sloper on the left face, or continue up the high groove above the bad landing. Found at the north end of the Weider Boulder.

❒ 11. **V0-V3** 🏊
Left of SA50 is a tall slab with a couple of choices to get the juices flowing.

E. THE BARNACLE BOULDER

Located past the trail to the Weider Boulder. Follow a faint trail approximately 40 yards north veering uphill and slightly right (a couple of trails venture through the woods—head northeast). Take your time, as the boulder can be difficult to ascertain until you see the pebbles and chalk on the northwest face.

❒ 1. **V4** ★★
On the northeast face is a problem that climbs the center line of holds to large pebbles. Scary top-out.

❒ 2. **V7** ★
Just right of #1 is a difficult pebble-pulling affair.

❒ 3. **Traverse V8** ★
Starts on the far right side of the northwest face and traverses left around the northeast arête. Exit past #1 on a difficult slab.

Krong on the Sunshine Boulder   photo: Chris Goplerud

CHAPMAN RESERVOIR

Chapman Reservoir area has a concentration of boulders near the water and sporadic blocks spread up the western side of Hagerman Pass. The granite boulders are very diverse. The boulderfields around Chapman Reservoir tend towards thin and lower quality; the Hagerman Pass boulders tend to be smooth as butter and crisp.

Directions: From Basalt drive east up Fryingpan Road (FR 105) towards Ruedi Reservoir (a couple of decent boulders are passed before reaching Ruedi). Pass the reservoir and continue past Meredith (an occasional granite block is roadside) for six miles. Turn right for Chapman Reservoir (dirt) and drive to the group site gate (may be closed) and park. Walk up the dirt road (east) to reach the boulders.

CANINE BOULDER

Two huge blocks, once one, have been split down the middle forming a wide chimney. The uphill block has a couple of extremely tall problems on the southeast face.

Directions: From the gate take the obvious trail on the right for 175 yards (southeast) up the hillside.

☐ **1. V3**
Climb the tall middle section of the southeast face.

☐ **2. V0/V1**
Climb the shorter right side of the boulder. Exit the boulder to the right.

Canine Boulder

BOULDER A NUMBER ONE

This block sits just off the right side of the dirt road after a short walk from the gate.

☐ **1. V3 ★**
Traverse the north face; many options to head upwards before reaching the west face.

☐ **2. V3 ★**
Climb the open scoop on the left side of the west face.

☐ **3. V5 ★**
Climb the southwest arête starting from the west face.

☐ **4. V0**
Climb the south face slab.

UNKNOWN ASCENTS

A set of boulders sits on the left side of the road a minute past Boulder A Number One. It is unknown whether any problems have been done on the block.

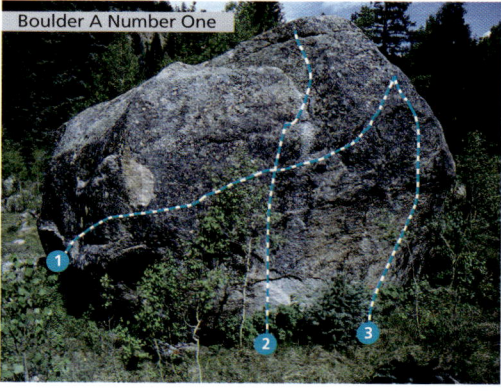
Boulder A Number One

CAMPSITE 22 BOULDERS

A pair of boulders located up the road a short distance from Unknown Ascents. Look for a trail sign on the left and follow the trail leading to the right off the road for 80 yards to the boulders. The described boulders are only a taste of the boulders in the area as many more sit on the hillside to the west.

ROOF BOULDER

The first boulder encountered on the left side of the trail. A distinct head-height roof is on the east face. Not pictured.

☐ **1. V1**
The overhang on the far left side of the east face in the chasm.

☐ **2. V5**
Climb the left side of the roof on sharp holds. The problem starts off underclings to painful crimpers over the roof. Not a clean problem.

Back Boulder

This block rests on the southeast side of Roof Boulder and has a number of vertical problems on the south and east faces.

Back Boulder

❏ 1. **V1** ★
Climb the east-face traverse from left to right.

❏ 2. **V1** ★
Climb directly up the vertical south face on positive edges.

❏ 3. **V0**
A one-move-wonder slab on the low-angle east face. Not visible on photo.

❏ 4. **Trite Bologna V2** ★★
Probably the best problem in the Campsite 22 Boulders. Climb the north face, starting in a left-facing corner, to slopers at the top. The problem is V4 from a sds.

Due West Boulder

This lone boulder sits directly across the trail and up the hill a short distance (easily seen from the trail) from the Campsite 22 Boulders. No photo.

❏ 1. **V0**
Climb the black south face. Not clean.

❏ 2. **V3**
Climb the southeast arête.

❏ 3. **V0**
Climb the low-angle east face.

Giant Steps Boulder

From the east face of the Back Boulder head east through a drainage for approximately 100 yards. The boulder sits on the edge of the Group Campsites.

Giant Steps Boulder

❏ 1. **Giant Steps V4** ★★
A difficult slab that climbs up the thin west face.

Note: More unrecorded problems have been done on the boulders located past the Group Campsites. To reach these boulders continue on the dirt road past the trail sign and enter the Group Campsite then continue east on the road to the boulders.

Hagerman Pass Boulders

Boulders located on the lower slopes of Hagerman Pass vary substantially from exfoliating granite piles of lichen and spider webs to splitter cracks and solid edges. The two blocks described here are as good as granite boulders get with independent lines and spectacular settings. Rest assured, these boulders are obscure and best visited in the fall. For the intrepid soul the east side offers a wealth of spectacular granite both lining the road as well as in the wilderness. Go see and show respect for the wilderness!

From Basalt drive east up Fryingpan Road (FR 105) towards Ruedi Reservoir. Pass the reservoir and continue past Meredith (an occasional low quality granite block is roadside). Continue east past Chapman Reservoir and past the right hand turn for Fryingpan Lakes. For The Best Boulder Problem in Colorado go right on FR 105.3 for 1.4 miles. Park and head uphill 35 yards on the right side of the talus field (the boulder is visible from the road). More undocumented boulders are further up FR105.3.

Sunshine Boulder

A spectacularly clean granite boulder with a magnificent view of the upper Fryingpan Valley and the Hunter Fryingpan Wilderness to the south. The boulder looks insignificant from the road (the short side faces the road).

Directions: From the hairpin turn (after driving east past Chapman Reservoir) drive one mile up FR 105 (headed northwest) to boulders on the left side of the road.

☐ **1. V5** ★★
A sds problem on the far left side of the boulder with a hard move to start.

☐ **2. V6** ★★
Just right of #1, start on good edges and move left and utilize the left-facing corner to better holds up high.

☐ **3. V8** ★★
Right of #2, climb the right-angling seam.

☐ **4. V?**
A difficult traverse along the bottom of the boulder from right to left ending on #2 or continue to #1.

☐ **5. V6** ★★
Climb the blunt corner on the right side of the boulder before heading around the corner. A few variations exist to this problem.

☐ **6. V2** ★★
Climb up the only part of the boulder's south face with obvious good holds.

☐ **7. V4** ★
Climb the thin southeast face. There a multitude of small edges so find the V4 sequence or tweak out on the thinner edges for a harder variation.

Sunshine Boulder

Green Boulder

Green Boulder

The slabby boulder east of the Sunshine Boulder. A couple of tall dirty slabs (V0) can be done on the southwest face. Not pictured.

☐ **1. The Best Boulder Problem in Colorado V8** ★★★
A lone block with a right to left traverse along a seam. A slightly easier variation exists by pulling to the top halfway across the traverse.

☐ **2. East Seam V?**
A distinct vertical seam on the bottom western edge of the talus field (a mere 10 yards from the road). The 15-foot problem faces due east and is found on the far left of the huge granite block sitting in an aspen grove. No photo.

Greg Loomis on Ineditable V6   Photo by Cody Blair

INDEPENDENCE PASS

The Pass is undoubtedly one of the state's premiere alpine bouldering areas. Boulders included here are both newly developed and old-time classics. Bouldering on the Pass is a wonderful alpine treat. The granite boulders are hidden throughout dense aspen groves as well as roadside talus slopes. With reasonable temperatures throughout the summer months, as well as superb spring and fall temps, the friction is hard to beat. For the diehard granite boulderer the low lying Patrol Boulder can be reached before the Pass opens in late spring. One can bike to the upper boulders prior to the Pass opening. In addition to the quality bouldering, the solitude and evening alpenglow heighten the experience. Views of New York Peak and Independence Mountain further the scene. Be sure to try the ultra-classics like Jaws, The Ineditable, ICBJ, the left dihedral of Dihedral Rock, Whirlpool Arête, Lightning Bolt Crack, and the Goal Post. Of the newly developed boulders included here the must-do's are Root Down, Black Beard, Ace of Spades, White Face, Funky President, and a whole lot more.

Directions: Areas are listed from Aspen towards the summit of Independence Pass. The mileage begins at the east intersection of State Route 82 (Original Street) and Cooper Avenue before leaving Aspen and beginning up the pass.

Patrol Boulder is located 2.8 miles up the pass on the left (visible in the dense bushes). A three-car dirt pullout is just past the boulder on the right. Cross the highway and a distinct trail leads to the boulder.

Jaws Boulder is located on the downhill (east) side near the creek. Park at a large cement pullout on the right 7.7 miles up the pass.

Morning Wood is located 0.1 mile past Jaws (7.8 total). Park on the right or left just past the Weller Campground entrance. A distinct path heads north and west for approximately 425 yards past sub-par cliffbands (cairns may be in place occasionally). The first boulder encountered is Beastie Boulder.

Hernando's Hideaway is located 8.0 miles up the pass. Park in a small two-car pullout on the right. From the pullout walk up the road approximately 100 yards (where the small cliff band ends) and go up a white slab. Walk north across the granite slab into the aspen grove. A faint trial leads through the aspens heading northeast and skirts the right side of a black cliff. Walk north above the cliff (approximately 125 yards) crossing small tiers of slabby granite. The Hideaway is up and right on a small black cliff with a pine and aspen standing in front of it. Chalk abounds on the barely visible problems.

ICBJ is located 8.4 miles up the pass. A small two car pullout is on the left under the Pass Walls. Walk directly across the road (the creek side) and a dark overhang can be seen just down the hillside.

Whirlpool Area is located 8.6 miles up the pass on the left. Park in a large righthand pullout and cross the road to a trail. Hike up the trail 65 yards towards the cliff and go left at the telephone pole into the talus field for 45 yards.

Treeline Area/Mirror Pond
Park at the Grotto Day Use parking at 8.8 miles. Walk across the highway and past the swamp for 135 yards (north). Go right (50 yards) to two large boulders with distinct west arêtes and a large crack separating the two. Problems range from V0-V7.

Goal Post Area is located 8.9 miles up the pass on the right below the road. Park at the Grotto Day Use parking at 8.8 miles. Walk east from the parking area along the river keeping in mind the boulders are located approximately 120 yards up stream then approximately 85 yards back into the woods and below the highway.

Ice Caves are located on the opposite side of the creek from Goal Post Area.

Grotto Wall Boulders AKA The World of Hurt are located up the pass 9.0 miles. There are cement parking areas on the left or right after the hairpin turn. The boulders are west in the massive boulderfield west from the Lower Grotto Wall. The Husky and White Boulder are located past the guard rail. See directions after Grotto Wall Boulders.

Black Caesar boulder is located on the left side of the road (basically in the roadway) at 9.1 miles (just after passing the roadside expanse of the Lower Grotto Wall and before Lincoln Creek Road). Park at the Grotto Wall parking area and walk up the road.

The Cube and Sunset Boulders are 9.8 miles on the right at Lincoln Creek Road. Park immediately before the bridge. Cross the bridge then head left (southeast) along the creek. Walk 150 yards to a cairn (oftentimes destroyed by meatheads) then go right and head straight uphill following distinct cairns on a well-traveled trail for approximately 275 yards. The Sunset Boulder is 30 yards back downhill to the north and can be seen through the trees if you squint. Just past Sunset (60 yards) is an obvious clearing in a talus field with a superb, tall white block on the right (The Cube).

Lincoln Creek is located 9.8 miles up the pass. Turn right into the Lincoln Creek Road and head down the rough road and turn into the Lincoln Creek Campground. The boulders begin on this dirt road and continue into the campground.

The Treasure Chest is located down Lincoln Creek Road (4x4 or beater old car) past the right hand turn for Lincoln Gulch Campground. Drive a couple of minutes to the right-hand pullout with camping information for Lincoln Creek Road and park (if you are lucky enough to get Campsite 2, take it). From the information board, walk upstream along the creek for two minutes and the small, hidden wall is creek side and adjacent a magnificent swimming hole.

For the Camp 5 Boulders follow the same directions as The Treasure Chest but drive farther and park at or near Campsite 5 (on the left side of Lincoln Creek Road at 1.1 miles). The Main Camp 5 Wall (V0-V2) is directly above the campsite. To reach The Boulder, Aspen and Right Boulder walk through Campsite 5 to the east on a trail headed to the hidden crags a few minutes uphill and past Beetle Juice (150 yards uphill on the right of the trail) then continue another 125 yards to The Boulder. Dihedral Boulder and Right Boulder are located 90 yards right (south) from The Boulder in a conglomeration of big boulders.

Storm Boulder (Ptarmigan Creek Area) is located at 10.4 miles up the Pass. Park on the left just before mile marker 52 in a small parking area (four cars tops). A distinct trail with cairns begins at the parking and heads straight uphill (northwest) past Greg's Cliff to below Storm Jumper and Kaos Cliffs. Total distance is approximately 350 yards. Continue uphill past Greg's Cliff on the left side. Once past Greg's Cliff head east (right) through some talus (cairns may be present) and skirt the top of Greg's Cliff for 50 odd yards. The boulder sits on top of Greg's Cliff and faces southeast with a small cave on the right side.

Bliss Boulder is just past the Storm Boulder parking at the next hard right turn between MM 52 & 53. Park on the left (space for six cars). Walk back down the road 60 yards to a faint trail (by an old, small cement foundation). Cross a seasonal stream and walk north uphill for 160 yards past many tiny cairns to a large talus field. The Bliss Boulder is the lowest climbable block in the talus field.

James Brown Boulders are located at 10.8 miles. Park in a righthand pullout and cross the highway. Follow a number of paths towards Wild Rock staying to the left side of the massive talus/boulderfield (approximately 100 yards northwest of the highway). The boulders are located on the flat terrain below the talus slope.

Wild Rock and Project Wall: Park at James Brown Boulders parking. Just past James Brown Boulders is the Wild Rock boulders. For The Project Wall hike up steep hill for five minutes to a huge rope-length, bolted boulder (Wild Rock). Facing this impressive sport crag is an overhung 50-ft wide face with a multitude of projects.

Upper Boulderfield aka The Bulldog Boulders are located 11.1 miles up the pass on the left side of the road. A huge dirt pullout is located next to the boulders.

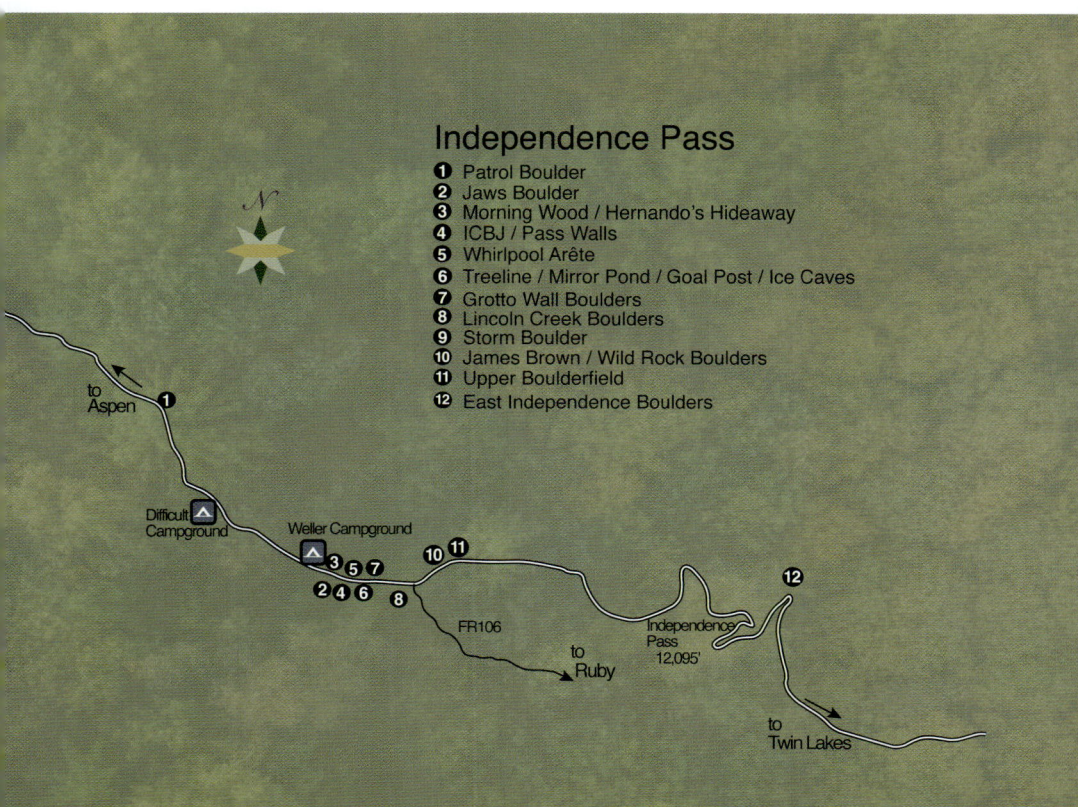

Independence Pass

1. Patrol Boulder
2. Jaws Boulder
3. Morning Wood / Hernando's Hideaway
4. ICBJ / Pass Walls
5. Whirlpool Arête
6. Treeline / Mirror Pond / Goal Post / Ice Caves
7. Grotto Wall Boulders
8. Lincoln Creek Boulders
9. Storm Boulder
10. James Brown / Wild Rock Boulders
11. Upper Boulderfield
12. East Independence Boulders

PATROL BOULDER

Closest to Aspen, this boulder makes for a great quick fix. The majority of problems are in the V0 to V2 range.

Patrol Boulder

❒ 1. **V0** ★
A right to left traverse on the south face.

❒ 2. **V1** ★★
A left to right traverse through a diagonal seam on the east face. Starts on a jug at the base of the seam.

❒ 3. **V2** ★★
A straight-up problem into the seam, off a flat jug.

❒ 4. **V2** ★
The thin edge problem on the right side of the east face. Start on a crimp/seam up to progressively better edges.

❒ 5. **V2** ★
The arête just right of the V2. Ends on a lichen-covered slab.

❒ 6. **V0** ★
The low-angle north slab. Also the downclimb.

❒ 7. **V0** ★
Climb the left-facing dihedral/ramp to the top of the west face.

❒ 8. **V1** ★
Climb the white crystals on the west face to a small right-facing corner just right of the dihedral.

❒ 9. **V0** ★★
Just right of the crystal problem is a jug haul that starts with bad feet. The problem to the right on the southwest arête is also V0.

JAWS BOULDER

This beautiful riverside block has a couple of highball problems on its north face. It is located downhill (east) in the parking area. The nearby Piranha Boulder is just north of Jaws.

Jaws Boulder

❒ 1. **V3** ★★★
The obvious roof problem starting up the east face then moving onto the arête. Bomber edges and exposure are the rule.

❒ 2. **V1**
The slab just left of the crack.

❒ 3. **V0** ★
The crack on the north face slab.

PIRANHA BOULDER

A small block 10 yards north of Jaws. There are a number of sit down start problems that face the creek.

❒ 1. **V2** ★★
The left sds problem on the east face.

❒ 2. **V4** ★★
Climb the middle of the east face with a difficult deadpoint to get things going.

❒ 3. **V5** ★★
The sds on the right side with arête pinches and small crimps for the left hand.

Piranha Boulder

MORNING WOOD

A superfine collection of blocks at the base of a talus field with more than a few two-scoop lines. Five or six main boulders make up this aspen-shaded boulderfield, which is defined by the word pleasant. Having seen the array of new zones and killer finds, the Morning Wood (for obvious reasons for all concerned), is the best newfound zone on the Pass alongside Husky, White Rock, Sunset Boulders new development, and Wild Rocks Project Wall. That's just how good the Pass bouldering is!

❒ 1. **Morning Wood Mantel V2** ★
The namesake problem of dubious belly-scraping notoriety located 40 yards west from Beastie Boulder. Starts on the south face matched on a big sloper above the head and muckle over the lip without losing belly flesh.

BEASTIE BOULDER

The first block with a highly chalked classic on the east face.

❑ **1. Root Down V5** ★★★ 🌸
A damn good line on the southeast face starting on two low slopers then right to a hand-size sloper then sharp matched crimps and the distant sloper top-out.

❑ **2. V7**
Start on the far right low sloper and traverse left across a mini corner/roof to jugs at finish. A few variations can be made by pawing the numerous grips.

P BOULDER

Directly uphill from Beastie a few yards is a tall boulder with vertical problems on the east face.

❑ **1. Left V?** 🌀 🌸
Undone highball arête/face on the southeast arête and east face.

❑ **2. Paw Me V0** 🌸
The open crack with nice sloping laybacks.

❑ **3. Blunt Pinch V1** 🌸
The right arête on good edges.

The next two problems are west from P Boulder on a companion block.

❑ **4. F Stop V5** ★★ 🌸
The left arête from low sidepulls to a left-hand undercling, then up above the brain-crushing boulders. Shares a couple holds with the right V5.

❑ **5. V5** ★★★ 🌸
Starts matched on a nice incut to a neck-straining reach and mantelesque finish. Superb problem!

ROLLER GIRL BOULDER

Faces the previous V5s with problems on the south and east faces.

❑ **1. Creamtime V4** ★★
Climbs the sloping hand-shuffling arête from low left to the right. Bad feet.

❑ **2. Seam V?** ★★
A two-move strain out the left-diagonal to the middle of Creamtime's arête.

❑ **3. Roller Girl V2** ★★ 🌸
Up the slightly overhanging east face. Exit up the slab.

❑ **4. V?** ★★ 🌀 🌸
A steep project just right of Roller Girl…to a disconcerting top-out over nasty bone-crushing blocks.

❑ **5. V3** ★★ 🌸
On the dark backside of the block is a sweet little face from a sds. Very nice edges over uneven talus.

❑ **6. Ice V1** ★★★ 🌀 🌸
The tall vertical face with an undercut start. Fun jump start to great holds. A very, very bad landing zone. Harder without the jump.

❑ **7. Amber Waves V3** ★★ 🌀 🌸
The southeast arête above an atrocious landing. Start left of the low open corner.

Beastie Boulder

P Boulder

Roller Girl Boulder

F Stop

Ice

Amber Waves

HERNANDO'S HIDEAWAY

A rare occurrence for the Pass bouldering. This small area is a wonderland of variations and contrived problems. A few distinct traverses and straight-up problems can be done.

❒ 1. **V0**
The right-to-left low traverse. Stay off the obvious big sloping mid-height hold.

❒ 2. **V6** ★★
This circular traverse begins left to right and finishes by traversing back left on the high traverse.

❒ 3. **The Crescent V4** ★★
The left side of the cliff has a distinct crescent-shaped hold just below the high traverse's holds. This problem climbs from below and left to the crescent and ends on the high traverse slots.

❒ 4. **V6** ★★
The high traverse starting on the far right side then moving left. Finishes where the stone becomes loose and dirty.

❒ 5. **V2** ★★
A straight-up problem on the far right side. Begins on the low traverse and ends on a high flat hold. Drop off.

ICBJ AKA PASS WALLS BOULDERS

Below the Pass Walls is a severely overhanging boulder with a terrible landing. Not pictured.

❒ 1. **V3**
Just left of ICBJ is a shorter part of the wall. The problem climbs good holds up a seam to a filthy top-out.

❒ 2. **Ice Cream Blow Job V6** ★★★
Pulls out the overhang above back-breaking talus.

WHIRLPOOL AREA

At the base of Whirlpool Rock is a small talus field. A couple of problems from V0 to V7 grace the blocks.

❒ 1. **Whirlpool Arête aka The Battle Royale**

V7/V10 ★★★
Sds. A severely overhung arête with a perfect landing and moves.

❒ 2. **V0-V1** ★
Just right of the Whirlpool Arête are a couple of problems on vertical faces. A steep overhang is farther right approximately 25 yards away. Not pictured.

TREELINE AREA

A newer area with scads of fun problems (V0-V9) that are still in need of cleaning, but are well-worth a session. The boulders included here are a good sample, with many more available.

MAIN TREELINE BOULDER

East Face

❒ 1. **Into the Woods V3** ★★★
An excellent problem involving sloper tension on the left side of the east-face pillar.

❒ 2. **Walden V5**
Really bad landing without a proper spot. This is a very thin, sloping edge line next to the adjacent boulder that utilizes the right-hand arête.

❒ 3. **V0**
Fun little line of jugs on the far left side of the south face.

❒ 4. **West Arêtes V3-V7**
Numerous arête problems can be done above the bad rocky landings.

Hernando's Hideaway

Whirlpool Arête

Greg Loomis on Walden V5

Greg Loomis on Assault of a Minor photo: Zac Reynolds

Minor Boulder

Uphill a few minutes to the northeast from Main Treeline Boulder is a distinct cave holding a classic problem. Tall slabs can be climbed as well!

☐ **1. Assault of a Minor V9** ★★
Starts in the back of the cave and finishes up the left crack!

Orange Face Boulder

Continue east towards the World of Hurt approximately 90 yards to a gorgeous burnt orange east-facing problem. Located before the hillside en route to the World of Hurt!

☐ **1. Setting Sun V4** 🌀 🌀
Climb the attractive face from a matched low pinch to opposing sidepulls and small overhang.

Big Nose Boulder

Located approximately 100 yards west of Orange Face and down from Main Treeline Boulder. The boulder has problems ranging from V4-V7.

Mirror Pond Area

Finding these gorgeous rocks requires patience for the length of the approach. Waiting till later in the season is best as the boulders have running water and the air can be filled with voracious bugs. Go north past the Treeline Area and climb steeply uphill. The trail goes through a talus field and then enters another grove of trees. When the trail enters the trees look for an alternative trail traversing left. The traversing trail goes below the talus field and up to the main area which has a large flat terrace below the Mirror Pond Face. Problems range from V3-V8.

Orange Face Boulder

John Georger on Big Nose V6

Goal Post Area

A collection of boulders on the hillside below the highway before reaching the Grotto Wall parking area. The mosquitos in this area are unbearable during the summer.

❑ **1. V4** ★★
The left slab on the west face. Not pictured.

❑ **2. V0**
Obvious sloping edges left of the right-facing crack/dihedral. Not pictured.

❑ **3. V0**
Right of the crack. Not pictured.

❑ **4. V0**
On the southwest arête is an easy problem. Finish right.

❑ **5. V3** ★
Just left of the crack on the south face.

❑ **6. The Goal Post V4** ★★
The clean black face right of the crack. Don't use the right-facing dihedral's jugs.

❑ **7. V0** ★
The problem using the right-facing dihedral's jugs.

❑ **8. V2** ★
The far right arête to a dirty top-out.

❑ **9. V4** ★
On the block to the east is an overhanging problem starting on sloping holds from a sit down. Not pictured.

❑ **10. Merotica V2** ★
Just right of Goal Post and above #9 is a problem that starts in a low slot and climbs straight up on the high slab. Not pictured.

Downhill to the southeast approximately 35 yards are more problems on a lone boulder.

❑ **1. V1**
Climbs the left side of the block from a high flat edge.

❑ **2. Lesoterica V5** ★★
Begin from a low start below the blunt arête and finish on the arête with a dyno from a bad left-hand edge.

❑ **3. V2** ★★
Climbs the right side of the prow using sloping edges in a seam on the slab.

❑ **4. V1**
On the right of the boulder is a low start that uses a right-leaning flake.

Mirror Pond V4 Photo by Cody Blair

Goal Post

Lesoterica

GROTTO WALL BOULDERS

AKA THE WORLD OF HURT

This huge mass of talus blocks are just west from the Lower Grotto Wall. Many of the problems have atrocious landings.

❏ 1. **Parking Lot Block V4**

An undercut block sitting in the parking area below the Lower Grotto Wall. A tough problem muckles across the lip then plops onto the slab. A direct start to this problem waits to be done. Not pictured.

❏ 2. **Felix V6** ★★

The first boulder on the west-heading trail from the west parking area (left side of the road). A sds problem starts on the north face and traverses left up the entire arête. A V3 begins midway off a good edge.

SOUTH FACE ROCK

This boulder is located approximately 20 yards west of Felix. No photo.

❏ 1. **V2** ★

Starts off a bomber jug then moves up and left. A low start makes it V4.

INEDITABLE BOULDER

Located above the hairpin turn before reaching the Grotto Wall parking. To reach the boulder walk west down the trail leading away from the parking area (on the side of the highway with the Grotto Walls). Trend left after passing South Face Rock across granite slabs for approximately 50 yards. The problems face south.

❏ 1. **V5** ★

A traverse starting on the left of the south face and ending around the right corner.

❏ 2. **The Ineditable V6** ★★★

Climb the 30+ foot right side of the south face. One of the best highballs in the state. Begins down and left on small edges then moves right and up past a right-facing crescent-shaped layback. A V7 direct start, Green Drake, begins low and right and finishes through the crescent crux. A sds adds a couple grades.

❏ 3. **V3** ★★

The small overhang right of The Ineditable. Either ascend the arête or move right to the crack/layback. Escape right.

❏ 4. **V2** ★

On the gray slab on the block just north of Ineditable. Found on the north face. Not pictured.

❏ 5. **V4**

The blunt arête just left of the gray slab. Starts low and grovels up the arête and sidepull seam. Not pictured.

❏ 6. **Orange Face V3**

A short block located 45 yards to the west of the Ineditable Boulder. The problem faces south.

The next problems are located in the bowels of The World of Hurt. Each problem is on its own boulder. Patience is necessary to locate these problems, as a distinct trail is nowhere to be seen.

Felix

Orange Face V3

Child of Darkness V9

❏ 1. **Child of Darkness V9**

A sds problem on ultra-thin and sloping edges. This south-facing problem is located up (north) in the talus slope, from the Ineditable Boulder (about 50 yards).

❏ 2. **V2** ★★

Ten yards west of Child of Darkness is an excellent east-facing problem. Begins low and right on slopers and moves left.

❏ 3. **V3**

On a separate block that faces the V2 is a gray right-leaning flake on the northwest face. Not pictured.

Deep Six Holiday

Husky Boulder

V0 V2 V2 V5 V6

WHITE BOULDER AREA

Walk past the Husky Boulder for a couple of minutes upriver on a faint trail to a large talus field. Walk to the far end of the talus to a lone free-standing boulder. The White Face faces the river. A number of ultra-committing lines, as well as safer outings, can be done throughout the talus field.

❐ 1. White Face V11

An absolutely stellar line just right of middle. Starts on little bitty edges to higher, more and more committing slopers.

❐ 2. Reanimator V8

Just right is a shorter outing.

❐ 3. V3

Opposite the WF is a thin slab above a bad landing.

Paul Robinson on White Face V11

❐ 3. Deep Six Holiday V6

This is probably the boldest problem in Colorado. A fall from the mantel crux would invariably break half the bones in the body. It is located north of Child of Darkness about 20 yards. A V3 named Meathook Junior starts on the left of the same block and climbs straight up.

❐ 4. V2

Walk east across the talus approximately 25 yards from Child to an overhanging block with a black southwest face. Another problem deserving of World of Hurt status.

HUSKY BOULDER

A fine addition with stiff grades and immaculately landscaped landings. Park at the Grotto Wall then go across the road over the railing. Follow a trail through the trees approximately 100 yards to a big wall facing the creek. Problems range from V1-V7.

Greg Loomis on Husky V5

Sunset Cruise V8 Photo by Cody Blair

BLACK CAESAR BOULDER

This cliffband is located at the thinnest double-lane section of pavement in the entire state. Three distinct problems can be done in the V3 to V6 range.

SUNSET BOULDER

A near endless expanse of granite bouldering, but not for the faint of heart. Most of the lines are highball and hard but the setting is quiet and conducive to wearing the flesh off fingers. There are more than a few projects on this excellent block.

❒ **1. Project V?** 🔵
The sloper arête left of Target Practice.

❒ **2. Target Practice V4** 🔵 ⚫
The overhanging problem on the far left side of the south face. A V8 sds can be done.

❒ **3. Sunset Cruise V8** 🔵 ⚫
Starts right of TP on a sloping rail to a jug. Move right then back left.

❒ **4. Projects V?** 🔵 ⚫
A couple of projects are right of Sunset Cruise.

❒ **5. V1**
The east arête.

❒ **6. V2**
The dihedral to the right of the east arête. Sds is V5. Move right to finish.

❒ **7. Motze V7**
A dyno problem on the next arête. How many arêtes does this block have?

❒ **8. Spades V6**
On the north face is a fun line that starts on a sloper and finishes moving to the left.

❒ **9. Ace of Spades V4** 🔵 ⚫
In the middle of the kick-ass north face, make a jump start to get situated, then move left up weakness to a very high, I said high, finish.

❒ **10. Projects V?** 🔵
Once again you are enticed to come and see the fine projects Sunset Boulder offers.

Sunset Boulder

Sunset East Face

CUBISM AREA

Starting at The Cube are a number of developed blocks with problems from V0-V4 and of course a few projects. Get your butt up here and find out.

THE CUBE

☐ 1. **5.12a/V?** 🪨 ⏱ ★★★
The lone 20-plus foot boulder on the right edge of the clearing. A toprope bolt is above the southeast arête. A boulderer with enough pads and gumption could do the problem and scare the crap out of herself.

☐ 2. **V3** 🪨 ⏱ ★★★
Climb straight up the northeast face.

Numerous boulders are to the south and west and feature rarely ascended lines from V0-V6.

EGG BOULDER

Yet another monstrous granite block in the woods with as many projects as completed lines. The beauty of Independence Pass bouldering is all too evident when you discover this fine block. No photo.

Park at the first switchback on the Lincoln Creek Road before the entrance to the Lincoln Gulch Campground. Hike up trail (on left of road) towards cliffs. The trail is not always obvious and the boulder is not as easy to find as indicated in other resources. Ten minutes will bring you to the enormous Egg Boulder. If the directions were easy everyone would find this boulder (it took the author a number of tries before succeeding). Good luck. More problems, up to V9, have been done.

☐ 1. **V1**
Start on jugs at start of V5 then up and over as soon as possible.

☐ 2. **V5**
The left line following the diagonal seam/crack.

☐ 3. **Voltaire V8**
A difficult problem to the right of the V5 that starts on high crimps, moves to a V-shaped hold then up to an easy top-out.

Sunset North Face

The Cube

LINCOLN CREEK BOULDERS

These boulders are found on the road to Lincoln Creek Campground or in the campground behind the outhouse.

Intruders

❑ 1. **Intruders V4** ★★★
A classic boulder problem that's name is befitting. Located on the right side of the road 40 yards after the entrance to the campground. The problem faces south and comes out into the road.

❑ 2. **V4s**
Fifty yards down the road from Intruders is a roof band with a couple of problems starting low and finishing on the right slab. Not pictured.

URINARY TRACT WALL

Located just down the road from Intruders on the right side of the road approximately 110 yards. This obvious crag has an overhanging sport climb on its southeast face and a finger crack right of the main scooped wall.

❑ 1. **V0** ★★
The crack left of the water streak.

❑ 2. **V2** ★★
Climbs up the black water streak.

❑ 3. **V6** ★★
The right-to-left slanting crack. Starts on either a stem between the aspen and the cliff or left on the crack. Ends up the black water streak.

Urinary Tract Wall

OUTHOUSE WALL

The long wall directly behind the outhouse in the campground. Numerous easy slabs are on the left side of the wall.

❑ 1. **V3** ★
Traverse the wall from left to right ending at the roof.

❑ 2. **V1** ★
The Z-shaped crack on the wall's left.

❑ 3. **The Lump V1** ★★
A tall problem that climbs through a distinguishable hold (lump) just left of the roof section of the wall. A V0 highball is just left of The Lump.

❑ 4. **V2** ★
Climbs the left side of the roof.

❑ 5. **High Wire V4** ★★
Climbs up the double diagonaling seam under the electrical wires.

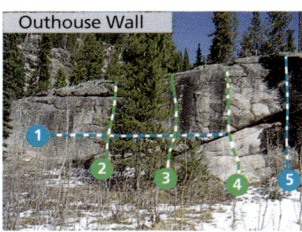
Outhouse Wall

GLACIAL ERRATICS

Uphill from the Outhouse Wall. Go 80 yards northeast up old road/drainage right of Outhouse Wall then 35 yards northwest to two smallish boulders above the creek.

Slope Boulder

SLOPE BOULDER

A fun little block with a couple of reasonable V1 lines on the southwest face.

MAIN BOULDER

A few yards to the northeast is a bigger block with thin slabs on the south face.

❑ 1. **Left Slab V1**
Climb up the left side of the south face.

❑ 2. **Center Slab V2**
Might be harder depending on where you start. Up the thin slab in the middle of the south face.

❑ 3. **Erratic Arête V2** 🌀
Follow arête that faces river. An entertaining problem on good holds.

THE TREASURE CHEST

A hidden gem that sees very little traffic and offers a couple of superb lines, shaded in the summer and near an idyllic swimming hole. Found below and next to the creek from Campsite #2.

❏ **1. Captain Kid V6** ★
Climbs the far left blunt arête and deals with a one-move wonder.

❏ **2. Black Beard V3** ★★★
Bouldering lines are seldom this distinct. Climb the perfect dihedral in the middle of the wall.

❏ **3. Queen Ann's Revenge V5** ★★
Climb the right arête of Black Beard on a difficult high step move to an inobvious edge.

❏ **4. The Pyramid V0** ★★★ 🌐 ⭕
Right of the main wall is a tall jug-haul facing the swimming hole. A more congenial setting might be the forest of Font.

CAMP 5 BOULDERS

There are a number of walls and boulders in this area, but only the best boulders are documented here. All the boulders and walls in this area are worth a visit, especially The Boulder (if you like to climb superb problems with committing top-outs).

Problems listed left to right:

THE BOULDER (CAMPSITE 5)

A monstrous boulder located below the crag. The east face is steep with a perfectly flat landing zone. A great hang in the afternoon.

❏ **1. Sliver V7** ★ 🌐
On the far left side of the overhang is steep line starting on the biggest low jug and moving through underclings and surmounting the 30-plus foot slab.

❏ **2. V5** ★★ 🌐
Same start on a low jug and finish by moving right to gain the lip. Pulling over is cruxy. For a V6 start low and left from the V5 and finish the same.

❏ **3. Faded V9** ★ 🌐
Start low in middle of face on jugs, traverse left on crimps into the V5 finish.

Treasure Chest

The author failing on the V5

Greg Loomis on Faded V9

❏ **4. Robinson's Rail V9** 🌐
Begin on a high pinch rail and move right to finish before the dihedral.

❏ **5. V4** ★★ 🌐
Directly right is a distinct line of right-leaning holds that leads to the upper slab. Try to figure out where the problem busts onto the slab and you might do a V4. Otherwise getting situated on the slab is harder than V4 by a long shot.

❏ **6. V2** ★★★
In the corner on the face's right side is a low or sit-start line on excellent incuts to the lowest exit. A V3 supposedly has the same start but finishes higher in the corner. A V7 exits left onto face holds before the action eases.

ASPEN BOULDER

A beautiful block with a couple of enticing arêtes on the south face.

❑ **1. Barracks V2**
Climb the west face.

❑ **2. Aspen Arête V7** ★★★
The stellar arête with an aspen at your back.

❑ **3. Sloper Arête project V?**
The south protruding arêtes that say no way. I said protruding.

❑ **4. Sprung V5**
Up crimpers on backside of boulder.

DIHEDRAL BOULDER AKA STOMPIN

The boulder directly uphill from Aspen Boulder. A beautiful highball northwest arête and impossible-looking southwest arête could be done with tons of pads and gumption. This boulder is a perfect example of names gone awry. These fine problems were done years ago, but the simple fact they saw little traffic allowed them to get silly new names.

❑ **1. V3**
The northwest arête.

❑ **2. Stompin V7**
Start on an undercling, jump to a sloper and move into an excellent slopey top-out.

❑ **3. V0** ★★
Climbs the open dihedral to mid height then moves around to the right and finishes on the committing slab. A straight up variation would be terrifying and very, very high on insecure moves.

❑ **4. Mike's Arête V2** ★★
Just uphill to the right of the Aspen Boulder is a distinct lowball left-leaning arête above an adjacent block. Starts low and follows the arête.

Greg Loomis on Aspen Arête V7 Photo Cody Blair

Mike Frieschlag on Mike's Arête V2

CAMPSITE 10 GROTTO

A gorgeous grotto with superlative deep water soloing lines above the ice-cold creek. Continue up Lincoln Creek to Campsite 10. Head down to the creek and an obvious grotto. Use a rope to get to the grotto without getting wet. (Photo this page of Ryan Olson on WWOE by Andy Mann.

☐ 1. **Wonderful World of Entertainment 5.11**
30-plus feet on the right side of the grotto up the low corner then exiting up the black face.

☐ 2. **5.11+**
Same start as WWOE but continue across the face to the blunt prow and exit up the seam.

Ryan Olson on Wonderful World of Entertainment

Storm Boulder

Boulders do not have a more aesthetic setting than this one. The landing is flat as a pancake, the southern exposure is warming, and the view is unsurpassed. What the boulder lacks in travel by climbers, the setting makes up for it as soon as you arrive. An unclimbed vertical wall is approximately 30 yards east of Storm Boulder and would offer up a couple of sweet harder problems. Problems are listed from left to right.

❑ 1. **V0**
On the far left side is a low-angle endeavor.

❑ 2. **V2**
Follow the black stripe starting in the horizontal crack.

❑ 3. **V3**
Follow the golden stripe utilizing small crimps and avoiding the big right hand holds.

❑ 4. **V0**
The right side of the block has a couple of easy problems on big holds.

❑ 5. **V3** ★
The small separate block immediately right of the Storm Boulder. Start on a flat edge and move to a sloping right-hand hold then incut edge and top. The finishing flop is really stupendous.

Bliss Boulder

Bliss is an appropriate name for this 30-foot tall monstrosity. Rarely are blocks loaded with enjoyable problems in a beautifully shaded alpine setting.

❑ 1. **Traverse V2** ★★★
A juggy traverse from the south face into the open dihedral. Keep some focus for the committing, slabby finish. An undone highball could be completed on the super-tall face to the left.

❑ 2. **Directs V3** ★★
Directly below the high dihedral are two variations to get situated in the dihedral.

❑ 3. **V5** ★
Just right of Directs is a large, low jug and a left-hand sidepull. Get situated on the face and make a big reach to a crumbly edge. Exit to the left past the obvious jug/horn. A straight-up variation would be substantially more committing.

❑ 4. **Prow V6**
On the far right end of the Bliss Boulder is a steep bulge. Slap up the sidepulls to a disconcerting mantel.

❑ 5. **Separate Wall V3**
On the boulder just right of Bliss is a straight-up problem starting from two small crystal edges.

James Brown Boulders

A superlative zone of four or so blocks that revolve around the neighborly James Brown Boulder (three massive blocks next to one another). There are plenty of high problems with questionable landings, but a few lines are plenty safe with a couple of pads.

First Boulder

A lone block 15 yards east before running smack dab into the James Brown Boulder.

❑ 1. **V3** ★
Climb the northeast overhanging arête starting on the left and moving to the right.

❑ 2. **V2**
The short low start variation to #1.

Mike Benge on the Bliss Boulder's V2

Mike Benge on Prow V6

JAMES BROWN BOULDER

The boulder (15 yards west of First Boulder) sits closest to the talus slope headed up to Wild Rock and still on flat ground. A distinct boulder on the north side of the massive three-block collection. (Problems listed left to right).

❏ 1. **It's a Man's World V5** ★★
The super tall gray east face. The epitome of a bad landing as the tall problem rests gingerly on a shelf. A fall up high could be rather catastrophic without many a pad and spotter.

❏ 2. **Funky President V4** ★★
Climb the right side of the northeast arête. A problem of the same grade, maybe a tad harder, climbs the left side of the arête over a bad landing.

❏ 3. **Hot Pants V3** ★★
Start on good edges on the north face. Gain the triangular hold then move right to finish.

❏ 4. **Sex Machine V4** ★
Start on the small crimps directly below the triangular hold and climb straight up.

❏ 5. **V3** ★
A lone problem uphill 20 yards to the north that faces southwest and climbs left of the arête. The backside of this huge boulder has a V4 on the far right side, left of the arête. Big-time projects await left of the V4.

JB MIDDLE

The middle of the three blocks that constitute the James Brown Boulders.

❏ 1. **V3**
Climb the tall face up the black rock left of the tree.

❏ 2. **Get on Up V7** 🔄
To the right, start with a right-hand undercling to a sloping shelf and terrible crimper. Keep utilizing atrocious crimps to a committing final move. Classic slab climbing.

❏ 3. **Get on the Good Foot V5** 🔄 🔄
Get a damn good spot. Start just left of the pine and pop to the big, flat shelf directly behind the tree. Go straight up to a terrible left-hand hold and right-hand layback. Finish the same as Get on Up.

❏ 4. **Body Count V2** ★★
Climb straight up the gray face to the right of the pine tree.

James Brown Boulder

JB Middle

Chris Goplerud on It's a Man's World V5

Chris Goplerud on Get on the Good Foot V5

JB Left

The left boulder of the three, with a short overhanging tier capped by a sloping ramp and a vertical wall.

❏ **1. Moon Tide V1**
Climb the left seam of the V-seam to a glorious mantel top-out.

❏ **2. Chick Climb V2** ★
Climb the V-seam on the low tier from a sds and finish up the right seam. A V2 climbs the up the arête right of #2.

❏ **3. American Hero V4** ★★
Climb the golden white corner via a little contortionism. Be aware of a loose block up high

Wild Rocks Boulders

At the bottom of the large talus field below Wild Rock is a vast area of undeveloped stone. A few good problems have been done on separate blocks.

❏ **1. Slam Dunk V3**
On the right side of the long black face is a steep problem that climbs just left of the arête.

❏ **2. V5**
Just left of Slam Dunk V3.

❏ **3. The Yardstick V9** ★★★ ●
The most striking line up the black streak was finally climbed after many years of effort. Rest assured it ain't a walk in the park. Start on bomber edges off the block and make either a massive dyno to the lip or crimp a tiny left-hand edge and throw to the lip.

❏ **4. V6** ★★ ●
The thin, almost too thin, and painful crimpfest between the V1 and The Yardstick.

❏ **5. V1** ★★ ●
On the far left side of the east face, directly right of a large pine, is a right-facing set of laybacks to good jugs. A sds makes it V7 if you don't use the separate block underneath for the feet.

JB Left

Wild Rocks

The author on The Yardstick V9

Josh Wharton on the sds of #5 (V7) on Wild Rocks

□ 6. **Tree Hugger V2**

On the opposite side of the boulder from The Yardstick is a low-start problem just right of the twin trees. Three other problems have been done to the right from low starts (V0, V4, V3) and have new names (not mentioned here) attached to ancient ascents.

□ 7. **V1** ★

On the boulder opposite Slam Dunk is a steep roof. Climb up and left. A V2 climbs up and right.

□ 8. **V4** ★

On the right side of the long black face is a steep problem that climbs just left of the arête.

□ 9. **V7** ★★

Approximately 45 yards down the hillside to the west is a tall toprope boulder. A traverse from left to right, starting under the roof, climbs across the face. Not pictured.

WILD ROCK PROJECT WALL

Located directly underneath Wild Rock. Walk, I mean trudge, up the steep hillside to the north for 200 yards from Wild Rock Boulder. The boulder underneath Wild Rock has steep powerful lines facing the bolted cliff (some contrived and sds). All the problems have a terrible landing requiring no less than two big pads. All tall, all bad landings, but absolutely the coolest, hardest, neato to-be-completed lines on the Pass.

□ 1. **Count Clovis V8** ●

On far left side of overhang starts on a jug under a roof. Go left on underclings and edges to a flat finish.

□ 2. **Jamrock Part 1 V7** ●

A little right of Count Clovis, start low on a finger lock and undercling then left to finish on CC.

□ 3. **V?** ●

Starts under the overlap down in the dark recesses and pulls through continuous power moves to higher edges. Steep and good.

□ 4. **V?** ● ●

The left-facing mini-corner at mid-height from a low start. Moves through the corner somehow.

UPPER BOULDERFIELD AKA BULLDOG BOULDERS

This is the largest developed boulderfield on the Pass with numerous problems bordering on classic. The boulderfield stretches over 200 yards and has leg-breaking problems, short power problems, and a multitude of fun slabs. Problems are listed from the western boulders going east.

THE OTHER WARM UP BOULDER

The last developed boulder on the west end of the boulder-field. It is located approximately 45 yards west of the parking area and has a large pine standing in front of the north face.

❒ 1. **V0** ★★
The left arête on the north face. A good sds can be done to gain the arête.

❒ 2. **V4** ★
Just right of the arête are two small underclings. Climb straight up on atrocious sloping crimps to a lunge for the top.

❒ 3. **V1** ★
Starts off the huge jug in the middle of the face to sloping left-hand edges.

❒ 4. **V0** ★
Climb the bomber edges in the right-angling dihedral.

❒ 5. **V1** ★
On the far right of the north face is a problem beginning low and moving up and left to good edges. Not pictured.

❒ 6. **V5** ★
A traverse across the north face from right to left. Stay low and the grade is stiff. Start not pictured.

DYNAMIC PLAN BLOCKS

These two blocks rest right next to one another approximately 20 yards northwest from the parking lot.

❒ 1. **Bleed V6** ★
A sds on the southwest arête of the left block. This is truly a one-move wonder.

❒ 2. **V2** ★★
The slab on the south face.

❒ 3. **V1** ★
From the middle jug on the right block throw to the top. A V7 sds begins off terrible opposing pinches then throws to the middle jug and up.

❒ 4. **V2** ★★
On the boulder 10 yards to the east is an excellent slab prob-lem up the south face.

A couple of V0s are on the short north face of the boulder.

THE WARM UP BOULDER

The obvious block sitting in the parking area. A long chalked traverse skirts the west face. Many variations exist on the west face.

❒ 1. **V3** ★★
The high traverse on the west face.

❒ 2. **V4** ★
A short problem up the middle crimpers of the west face.

❒ 3. **V2** ★
The sds problem on the right that follows the low, right-angling jugs.

❒ 4. **V6** ★★
A sds in the left scoop of the north face. A three star problem called No Camping Here (V7) begins right behind the huge tree and traverses into the V6 on terrible slopers.

Other Warm Up Boulder

Dynamic Plan Blocks

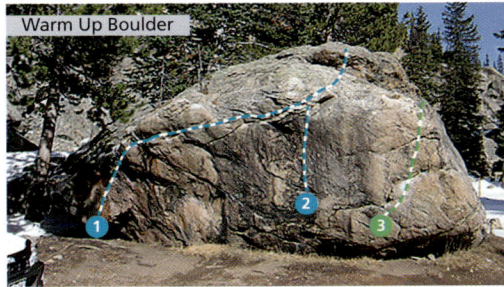
Warm Up Boulder

Warm Up Boulder

LIGHTNING BOLT BOULDER

The big overhanging boulder 25 yards north of the parking area. It is defined by a flat, white roof left of a crack.

☐ 1. **V3** ★
Start low on the south face and move to a slot. Left of the roof.

☐ 2. **V2**
Just right is a problem that climbs out the white roof to a horrendous mantel.

☐ 3. **V3** ★★ ⬤
Starts on a low, separate block and climbs up to sloping rails heading left. The finishing moves are scary and dangerous.

☐ 4. **Lightning Bolt Crack V0** ★ ⬤
The crack/jug haul right of the dangerous V3. Many variations exist to this problem.

☐ 5. **V3** ★
A dynamic problem, approximately 15 yards west of the Lightning Bolt Boulder, in a hidden cave.

LIGHTNING BOLT NEIGHBORS

☐ 1. **V3** ★
A sds on a block just east of LB Boulder. The problem faces south and starts on a low overhang to a slab finish. Not pictured.

☐ 2. **V4** ★
A sds located directly behind (north) the Lightning Bolt Boulder. The problem is on a short overhang that faces downvalley. Muckle over onto the slab. Not pictured.

DIHEDRAL ROCK

Forty feet east from the Lighting Bolt Boulder is a west-facing duel dihedral system with jumbled blocks for the landing zone.

☐ 1. **V2** ★★★ ⬤ ⬤
The super-classic left dihedral. Good jams and laybacks with decent feet.

☐ 2. **V3** ★★ ⬤ ⬤
The right dihedral with one hell of a terrible landing—definite broken bones without a lot of spotters and pads.

☐ 3. **Mike's Prow V2** ★★
A sds on the block just south from Dihedral Rock. Climbs the southwest prow on sloping sidepulls to an easy top-out.

DEPENDENT BOULDERS

These two blocks are located 10 yards to the east of Mike's Prow. Both blocks have problems and remnant chalked holds. Not pictured.

☐ 1. **The Thing V3** ★★ ⬤
A low start on the north face of the left Dependent Boulder that climbs small crimps to an easy top-out. Best reached by scrambling behind Mike's Prow.

☐ 2. **Figure it Out V4** ★
Faces The Thing. On a short bulge with a low start.

☐ 3. **V3** ★
Climbs the left arête of the left boulder just behind the tree. Start low on a good left-hand crimp and right flat edge.

☐ 4. **V2** ★★
The slab just right of the arête. A sds from the low scoop makes it V3.

☐ 5. **V2** ★★
A sds on the right block's left-leaning arête. A V3 traverse can be done into it from the right.

☐ 6. **V4** ★★
Traverse the southwest face from right to left past #5 and end on the slabby, lichen and pine needle covered leftmost face.

Lightning Bolt Boulder

Dihedral Rock

LONER STONE

☐ 1. **V4** ★
A sds on the north face starting on a hollow flake. Approximately 35 yards east of the Dependant Boulders. Not pictured.

PAPPY BOULDER

This east-facing overhanging block is located uphill from the Loner (approximately 50-plus yards east of Lightning Bolt Boulder—a lone block trailside with a sds V4 on the north face) in the talus.

❏ 1. El Vere V6 ★

Climb the far left side of the overhang.

❏ 2. Che it Loud V8 ★

A low start up the middle of the overhang through a good undercling. Only V3 from the undercling to the top.

❏ 3. Pappy V1 ★

The casual problem from the right side of the overhang climbing left along the lip.

Pappy Boulder

THE PASS BOULDER

Located 45 yards east of the Loner Stone (a singular short block with a V4 sds on the north face) is a set of large blocks uphill (north) 20 yards with a highball south-facing problem (The Pass) hidden in an alcove.

❏ 1. The Pass V?

The biggest, smoothest, steepest, burnt orange south face on The Pass, that'll make you think about passing on this one. It also has the most back-scraping potential of any highball if one falls onto the adjacent slab. You'll need four or five substantial pads to safely ascend this beauty. The doable line starts from two arms-reach holds in a horizontal break and moves up, up, and away into the no fall zone. A low start will make this problem one of the hardest lines on The Pass.

OVERLOOKED BOULDER

This boulder is directly uphill (north) from The Pass. You can not see the problems from the trail as they face either north or west.

❏ 1. V2

Starts on secure edges on the right of the north face and makes delicate moves up the face. A low start from the jug makes it V4.

❏ 2. Collage V4

A gorgeous line up the northwest face. Start on the left-hand crimp in the middle of the face and right-hand gaston to the obvious set of holds straight up. The exit is on slopers at the lip. Make sure to bring along at least three big pads, as the landing is atrocious. A low start from the left arête's low jug is hard V6.

The Pass

Overlooked Boulder

UNBEATEN PATH BOULDERS

Located 20 yards east of The Pass Boulders and slightly uphill (north). These boulders see nary a speck of chalk as everyone goes to the Warm Up Boulders to start sessions. The V0 problems on the super juggy east face are not super clean, due to non-existent traffic (but the holds can each hold an ape-sized hand). The crimpy V0s on the north face make for a good start to a session. More fun lines can be found in the talus slope above.

HAND JIVE BOULDER

Further east, approximately 80 yards, is a massive boulder (30+ feet tall) with a small pine on top.

☐ **1. Triple Decker V4** ★★
The problem on the east arête starting on a detached block under the huge boulder.

☐ **2. V2** ★★
On the north arête (white stone at the bottom) are sloping edges that lead out left. Going straight up is V5.

SLAB ROCK

Just downhill from Hand Jive is a slabby wall facing south (towards Hwy. 82).

☐ **1. V0**
Climb the groove on the left.

☐ **2. V1** ★
Climb the angling crack just right of the groove to a left-leaning crack.

☐ **3. V4** ★
A traverse from left to right across the face, starting right of the groove.

☐ **4. V1**
The entire left-leaning crack from the low start.

FAR EAST BOULDERS

A small set of blocks approximately 90 yards east of Hand Jive. A trail leads through the woods to the blocks. Additional parking is next to these blocks.

☐ **1. V3** ★★
On the upper block is an east-facing tiered roof with a funky problem coming out the roof.

☐ **2. V1**
On the closest block to the road (just east of the V3 is a dirty east face that has a problem on good edges following a faint seam.

☐ **3. V2** ★
The overhang on the west face that faces #1.

Unbeaten Path

Hand Jive Boulder

Slab Rock

Far East

EAST INDEPENDENCE

Hidden on the east side of Independence Pass is a small boulderfield exposed to the alpine elements. The boulders are granite, like their western neighbors, but are more featured. The problems, which tend to hover in the V0 to V3 range, have little to offer for the tough guy yet their quality warrants a stop. All techniques are required on these slabs, traverses, and quality overhangs.

Directions: Head east on State Route 82 and go over Independence Pass summit. At the third hairpin turn down the pass turn left on a dirt road and park by a green fence. Walk a couple hundred yards down the dirt road to the boulders. From the east the hairpin turn is 12.7 miles from the Twin Lakes Store.

SOUTH BOULDERS

The first set of boulders seen on the left from the dirt road. The west face of the largest block has fun problems.

❒ **1. V3** ★★ ⬤
Traverse the west face left to right ending on the jugs on the far right side of the south face.

❒ **2. V1-V2** ★
The straight-up problems on the west face with many variations on the sloping edges. The top-outs are covered in gravel.

NORTH BOULDERS

A set of two boulders, one on each side of the road, approximately 60 yards past the South Boulders. Only problems on the largest boulder are listed.

❒ **1. V3** ★★ ⬤
Ascends the left side of the south overhang on laybacks and heelhooks.

❒ **2. V2** ★★
The seam just right of the overhang. Move right to the lichen-covered top-out.

❒ **3. V3** ★
Traverse left to right across the southeast face. Dirty at the far right end.

❒ **4. V1** ★
At the start of the high ledge, climb straight up to excellent edges over the top.

❒ **5. V0** ★
Straight up the middle of the southeast face ending in a left-facing corner.

❒ **6. V2** ★
The left-angling layback just after the low shelf ends.

❒ **7. V0-V1** ⬤
A number of slabs on the northwest face. Very licheny and a little fragile. No photo.

Phillip Benningfield on Tempt Fate V7

BUENA VISTA

There is more rock around Buena Vista than a boulderer can shake an extendo-brush at. Decades of fine ascents range from fully obscure lines at the Davis Face, rarely used and oftentimes bad blocks along Chaffee County 304 Road (1.8 miles east from US 24/285 junction-Collegiate Peaks Overlook), Turtle Rock, the many new problems between tunnels 2 and 3, etc...The trouble is that much of the granite is low-grade and friable. The best newfound bouldering is included here. Many problems have been renamed!

***The heat of summer, with so many boulders facing south, makes visiting in the cooler months or dead of winter the wise choice. Besides, the massive influx of tourists (boaters, vacationers, and fishermen) make the area overrun and noisy.

Directions: From US Route 24 turn east onto Main Street in BV and head east across the railroad tracks and turn left on Colorado Avenue. Drive 3.2 miles over the river and through the tunnels (chalk-less boulders exist between all the tunnels) to a right turn on a dirt road (just after Almost a Tunnel). Turn immediately right and park at the end of a small turnaround under the Tunnel Boulders. All the blocks are near the parking and up the hillside.

Tunnel Boulders

TUNNEL BOULDERS

(ALMOST A TUNNEL BOULDERS)

A massive boulderfield just past Almost a Tunnel (a tunnel without a roof) with varying quality of rock, lines too dangerous to send without a dozen pads, and a number of undocumented easier (V0-V2) lines. The climbable problems number merely three-dozen, but make for a superb session. Rest assured there are a few undone lines strewn across the boulderfield.

A. PARK BOULDER

The lone burgundy block with one hard problem facing the road.

☐ 1. **V3**

This short affair starts on a sloping sidepull and small bulb with bad feet to a powerful move to the right-facing corner then the top. A low start is much more tenuous and difficult (V7).

Park Boulder

Phillip Benningfield on Nuthin' Beats Cope V7

B. THE MONSTER

Directly above the lower quality, ground level blocks and above the Park Boulder is a nice block with three V1 warm-ups on a slightly overhanging face. The problems face west, start low above a sloping landing and pit, and require a few pads for safe outings.

❏ Orange Crush V1 ★★

The spectacularly thin, clean, orange flake to the east and above The Monster. This boulder is distinguished by its atrocious landing and aesthetic position.

❏ Flyer V6

Along the big talus, as one heads south towards the Solar Collector, is a steep overhanging blunt arête problem moving from a low start on very small crimps and utilizing small feet, sloping handholds, and a big throw to reach the jug. A shorter V1 traverse lies a couple of feet left and finishes the same.

❏ V2

A very steep juggy arête moves in from the right of the V6 and finishes roughly the same.

C. THE SOLAR COLLECTOR

This miniature amphitheater basks in the wintertime sun and offers a near panoramic view of the Sawatch Range. Two blocks make up the Solar Collector and require plenty of pads and highball hunger.

LEFT BLOCK

The flat gray south face making up the left side of the SC.

❏ 1. V2

On the far left side of the south face before the rock turns to crap is an outing with a terrifying top-out on detached blocks.

❏ 2. Tempt Fate V7 ★★

Start on good incuts in the fluorescent lichen, on the wall's left side, and head straight up on progressively smaller edges and longer reaches in the horizontal seams. End right by traversing below the detached block resting above the face or tempt fate by pulling over on the detached block. See opener photo.

❏ 3. V?

On the far right from Tempt Fate is a thin, less than ideal face possibly lacking, enough holds to reach the juggy top-out.

RIGHT BLOCK

The bulbous boulder making up the amphitheater's right side and facing west. Numerous fun problems are strewn across the front and back sides.

Frontside Problems

Problems listed left to right across the west face.

❏ 1. Nuthin' Beats Cope V7 ★★★

The superb steep left arête! Looks like a classic problem and it is! Start with a high right-hand crimp and lower left hand incut edge. Fire up the arête. You can start by matching on the incut edge to make a hard V8.

Caption: Mike Freischlag on Orange Crush V1

❏ 2. Husky V3 ★★★★

Directly right of NBC. Start this awesome problem on a killer jug for the right hand and move up the diagonal seam on sloping holds to a committing throw or lock off. Very bad landing so bring lotsa pads.

❏ 3. Bandits V1

The next problem right, which starts on a great jug with a long reach to the first good incut seam and cruiser finishing moves. Start low on Big League's low start for a good V3.

❏ 4. Big League V8 or V9/Growler V10 ★

The steep, classic, right-trending, rounded arête. From a matched slot directly right of Bandits' start, begin the 18-move traverse by heading right through bad crimps to the matched sloper where the line moves up and around the blunt arête. More slopers and pinches lead to a good crack. A full lowball start from a sloping rail and edge makes it V9. Wrong sequences make it V10.

Backside Problems

Listed left to right across the south face.

❏ 5. Manginalogues V4

The left seam on the shorter backside (south face) of the Right Block. Starts low on a big right-hand layback and left-hand edge.

Brad Durbin on Husky V3

❏ 6. **V2**
The right seam from a low start. Start with the right hand on a good edge in the low seam and the corner/edge for the left hand.

❏ 7. **V2**
The right arête with one substantial move.

❏ 8. **North Back Breaker V4**
On the dark north face of the Left Boulder making up the Solar Collector is a far left problem starting on a giant jug then traversing right above the impaling talus then up. Finish left.

❏ 9. **Tribulation V7** ★★★
Fantastic problem above the landscaped fall zone!

D. Squat
The small boulder on the north side of The Solar Collector's left boulder and before reaching the Back Breaker. Problems are south facing but dark due to the Solar Collector's size. Expect good, short lines graded V1 (left arête), V2 (straight up middle), V3 (traverse from right to left onto thin pebbled low angle slab finish). A fun V0 is on the north side.

E. Great White Boulder
Directly above The Solar Collector is an obvious, stellar, triangular white boulder with a ankle-breaking landing. Best reached from the top of the backside problems.

❏ 1. **Blunt Arête V2**
The far left arête above a horrible landing.

❏ 2. **White Power V1** ★★★
Straight up the middle of the southwest face to the high right arête.

❏ 3. **V0**
The hand traverse up the right arête from a low start on a massive jug.

White Power V1

F. Panorama Boulder
Forty feet directly above Great White to the northeast (left as one looks at Great White's white face) is a southwest-facing block with a couple of problems on the far left side of the southwest face. An excellent hang on cold, windy days.

❏ 1. **V3**
The far left short arête moving slightly right to pull over. Start on a matched thin edge.

❏ 2. **Belly V5**
The short problem just right of the arête that starts off a good right-hand sidepull and tiny left-hand edge then jumps to the sloping lip and insecure top-out.

❏ 3. **Never End V6**
On the left side of the north face is a crimpy as s*#t, sloping blunt arête from a sit start. Bust left after the initial moves to the right-angling arête. Bring flesh. Bad landing.

Panorama Boulder

G. FITB Boulder
The block touching Panorama's left (northwest side). A small slot gains entrance to the east face. Pads are necessary!

❏ 1. **Cauliflower Traverse V7**
A tasty 18-foot long left to right traverse along the sloping lip of the east face. Exit before ATF for a good V6 or make it all the way to the exit of ATF. Bring pads for the terrible landing.

❏ 2. **A Transient Filament V5**
On the right side of the southeast face is a short problem starting off a good right hand sidepull and low gaston then dynoing to the lip.

FITB Boulder

❏ 3. **V4**
On the small block facing ATF on the north face is a superb sloping traverse down in a pit. The nicest, tightest hunk of smooth rock at the Tunnel Boulders.

B BOULDER

A mere 30 feet to the south from Manginalogues. The problems are south-facing on a fairly short block. A good warm up wall. Problems are listed left to right .

❏ **1. Lowball V1** ⬤
On the far left side of the face is a good problem.

❏ **2. Right to Your Left V2** ⬤
In the corner to the right of Lowball. A sit start makes it V5.

❏ **3. Centerline V2** ⬤
Starts with a left-hand undercling and the biggest flat edge right of the corner. Climb straight up.

❏ **4. Right V4** ⬤
Start on the fragile incut edge and flat hold on Centerline then crimp the hell out of a right-facing edge then straight up. Kinda fingery for the grade.

❏ **5. Shortie V0**
On the backside of B Boulder facing Manginalogues is a quality little warm-up starting low on incuts and utilizing edges or pinches to a jug top.

BONE BOULDER

This singular block is located farther north up Colorado Avenue (371 Road) past the Tunnel Boulders. Continue driving north until reaching Railroad Bridge then go 0.3 mile farther north to a small pullout on the right (6.5 miles from Main Street). The boulder is above the pullout, barely visible through the trees, and less than 40 yards from the road.

❏ **1. West Bulge V2**
Start low on good flat holds then over the lip to decent coarse slopers.

❏ **2. Press Test V3**
In the open scoop is a horrendous high step and press problem. Multiple pads or actual flexibility make it more doable.

❏ **3. The Bone V5** ⬤
The south-face problem starting off terrible slopers to a good left-hand layback then up…Don't even think about it in the sun. V8 starting with the right hand under the roof.

❏ **4. Make no Mistake V6** ⬤
Just right of TB is a sit start off the adjacent boulder, a perfect place to sit and definitely spot, then up to pinches and good edges…one hell of a bad landing.

❏ **5. V0-V1** ⬤
On the north and east side of the boulder are a couple of decent short problems.

ONE MILE BOULDER

This excellent boulder is located on County Road 305 as one heads east on US 285 from Johnson Village (5.6 miles from the Arkansas River). Turn left on CR 305 and drive just under one mile to a pullout on the right (the parking has a fairly deep rut getting off the road). From the parking area walk up the road or parallel the road on the east side heading north squirting below a small cliff. Walk 175 yards slightly uphill (northeast) to a nice boulder behind a large ponderosa pine (the boulder is visible from the road). A short distance up the road past One Mile is a wall just off the road's right (east) side with a couple of cracks and slabs (unknown grades).

West Face

❏ **1. V2** ⬤
On the northwest arête is a nice jug haul up a wide trough.

❏ **2. Cigarette Pack V4** ⬤
To the right following a left-angling dike is a superb little outing with a couple of hard moves. Start as low as possible to make a V5.

❏ **3. Dead Soldier V6** ⬤
Starts on two atrocious underclings to terrible crimps just right of Cigarette Pack.

South Face

❏ **4. V1**
Climb the left-angling seam for a terrific warm up.

❏ **5. Smoker's Delight V3** ★★
The best problem on the boulder (i.e. classic) that climbs up the steep slot/seam directly right of the V1.

❏ **6. V5**
Climb the right wide overhung crack to a fairly nasty exit on sharp crystals.

East Face

❏ **7. V0-V1**
A downclimb V0 ventures down the insecure, loose middle of the east face. A V1 is left of the downclimb as well as to the right.

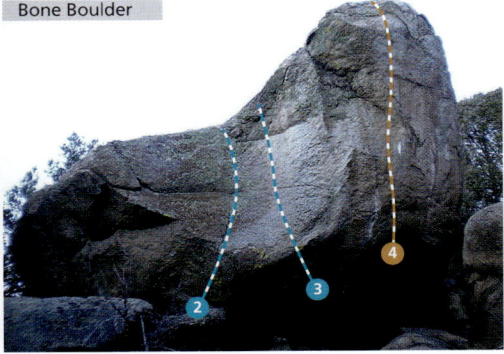
Bone Boulder

One Mile Boulder

COLLEGIATE PEAKS OVERLOOK AND THE CRACKED BOULDER AREA

This easily-accessed zone has plenty of potential and one developed, exceptional boulder.

Directions: From the turn for Collegiate Peaks Overlook off Highway 285, go 1.3 miles past the overlook to a left on 304 Road. Drive another 1.7 miles (the Cracked Boulder is visible to the east approximately 200 yards from the road on the hillside) to a righthand pullout on the right. Walk up the drainage past a couple of big blocks on the left at 150 yards. At 165 yards exit on the right side of the drainage to the south for 70 yards to the Cracked Boulder.

CRACKED BOULDER

A pretty fine block with a couple of exceptional crack problems. The boulder gets plenty of winter sunshine and is probably best during the colder months.

❒ 1. **East Side V0-V1**
A couple of decent cracks exist on the darker east face. This side is certainly the safest as the top-out comes around 10 feet.

❒ 2. **V5** ★★★
An all-time classic crack reminiscent of a thin offset flake from the better granite crack areas. The arête to the right is V4.

❒ 3. **V3**
The super tall arête directly left of the V5.

❒ 4. **Southwest Face V?**
The right line near the southwest arête.

❒ 5. **V?**
Directly up the middle of the southwest face through thin and unfortunately sub-par stone to an easy top-out.

Mike Freischlag on the Cracked Boulder's V5

Chris Jones on Chained Heat V6   Photo by John Sherman

NATHROP

Nathrop bouldering is a maze of private property boundaries and undeveloped stone. The known bouldering is the Buena Vista Boulder. The BV Boulder is tiger-striped ryholite, littered with pockets, in an arid environment. Gorgeous views of Mt. Princeton and Mt. Antero fill the western skyline.

Directions: Take US Route 24 south past the intersection with US Route 285. Continue south from Hwy. 24/285 intersection for 3.4 miles to Chaffe County Road 301. Take a left and cross the Arkansas River. Go 0.5 mile down 301 then turn right on Chaffe County Road 300. Drive down this dirt road for 2.1 miles (do not take the side roads on the left). The Buena Vista Boulder sits next to the road on the left next to a huge, dead tree.

BUENA VISTA BOULDER
The largest block in the boulderfield lying at the base of a talus slope.

❏ **1. V2** ★
The 20-foot tall arête problem using the diagonaling crack.

❏ **2. Light Sentence V3** ★★
On top of the flat block is a short one-move power problem that reaches sinker pockets.

❏ **3. Chained Heat V6** ★★
Begins just right of the flat block. The 13-foot overhang follows a faint seam on pockets and laybacks. Dyno all the way to the lip for a jug or use the sharp pocket below the lip (harder).

❏ **4. V4**
One foot right of Chained Heat is a short ultra-thin problem that climbs out right.

❏ **5. Northwest Face V2**
A one-move problem from a sharp layback and sloping pocket. Punch left to a sinker flake then over the bulge.

❏ **6. West Face V0**
Climb the face just left of the bush.

❏ **7. Southwest Face V0**
The downclimb off the boulder. The slabs are a little loose.

❏ **8. South Face V1** ★
Just left of the northeast arête's V2 (#1). Climb straight up, staying left of the seam.

NORTH BOULDER
A few yards north of the BV Boulder is a short block with a few easy problems.

❏ **1. V1** ★
Traverse right from the northeast face, across the north face, and up at the far right end.

❏ **2. V0**
The pocket-pulling affair on the north face.

❏ **3. V0**
On the south face is an undercling problem.

SOUTH BOULDERS
Approximately 40 yards south from the BV Boulder is a conglomeration of boulders with excellent face problems.

SOUTH ONE
The first boulder encountered on the right when walking south from the BV Boulder. Problems are on the northeast face.

❏ **1. V2** ★
A difficult problem utilizing a throw from an undercling or crimping terrible edges. V6 sds.

❏ **2. V0**
Directly right is a short, pocketed face.

SOUTH TWO
The next climbable boulder to the southeast.

❏ **1. V3** ★
On the east face is a problem with pinches for both hands.

❏ **2. V0** ★
On the arête to the right is a fun face ending on a lichen-covered slab.

SOUTH THREE
The tall boulder with problems facing the BV Boulder just past South Two.

❏ **1. V1** ★★
A 13-foot problem on the left block that is hard to read. The jug of all jugs is on top.

SOUTH FOUR
The small block touching the taller South Three.

❏ **2. V1**
A sds problem climbs the west face.

Mike Freischlag on South Three

HECLA JUNCTION

Hidden away between Buena Vista and Salida is a quiet and beautiful granite bouldering area nestled next to the Arkansas River. With easy access and a relatively short and definitely flat approach hike, the seldom-visited boulders offer solitude during autumn and early spring months. Problems range from easy V0 slabs to awkward higher V8 lines…and of course much harder lines.

***This area is hot and loaded with rattlesnakes, tourists, and boaters during the summer.
***A State Parks Pass or daily fee is required.

Directions: South of Buena Vista (the intersection of US Route 24/US Route 285) head south on highway 285 for 13.3 miles to a left turn for Hecla Junction (brown state recreation sign). From Salida head north on State Route 291 (Main Street) to the intersection with US Route 285. Go north (right) and drive 1.3 miles to the right turn for Hecla Junction. Follow this dirt road 2.1 miles and park in the Day Use Area. Follow the casual trail (changes between trail and old roadbed) down river (east/south/then west) to reach all the boulders.

RIVERSIDE

The first quality boulder encountered on the trail's left side (approximately 420 yards from the Day Use parking) with quality lines. The boulder rests on the bank of the Arkansas River.

❏ 1. V0s
The west and north faces have a couple of uneventful slabs to warm up on.

South Face
Two arêtes make up the short south face.

❏ 2. Don't Stop Believing V5 ★
The left sloping arête starting on a distinct right-hand edge and the arête. Muckle onto the sloping arête to an easy finish. You can lowball this sucker to get a sicker problem.

❏ 3. Hold on to that Feeling V4
Climbs the right arête from a hurtful edge or pinch and a low sidepull to a big ol' reach.

❏ 4. The Up Side of Down V7 ★
On the east face is a beautiful corner that is surmounted by figuring out a bizarre sequence. The top out is scary and requires good padding and spotters. V8 sit start.

GOOD TIMES BAD TIMES

As you walk down river on the trail a few minutes (approximately 900 yards) from Riverside an impressive 20-plus foot block rests on the trail's right side. The completed lines are on the uphill (west) side and have a superb flat landing.

West Face

❏ 1. V?
On the northwest arête is a series of layback edges up the arête. Make sure to bring plenty of pads and spotters.

❏ 2. Too Good to be True V2 ★★★
The most distinct line leading out the left side of the west face. Start low on the big rail and move left and over the small overhang.

❏ 3. V5
The thin line immediately right of TGTBT. Starts on the lowest jug on the rail and pulls through the bulge to small edges and nipples. I said nipples.

❏ 4. Tasty V2
Right of the V5 on the vertical face, climb through the small overhang to a sloping right-hand edge and little left-hand crimps. Feels more like a V3.

❏ 5. Downclimb V0
On the far right edge of the west face follow the decent edges and layback flake.

Riverside

THE GROUP

Continue along the trail a couple minutes (approximately 250 yards) headed down river. After 150 yards a small block (Waves) is trailside on the left with a couple of vertical faces and thin slabs (V0-V3). Continue and a group of larger boulders will be run smack dab into. Many lower quality problems are undocumented or too short to warrant description.

TWO-FACED BOULDER

On the right approximately 25 yards past Waves is a block 15 yards off the trail with an undercut south roof and tight line on the back next to a back-shredding mini block.

❏ 1. The Roof V?
Trying to even think about getting on under the roof makes ones head hurt. Start at arms reach and fight over the roof.

❏ 2. Back Stab V8
When we mention bad landings, this one problem is the definitive example. Starts low on matched underclings then ascend the fairly sharp edges and slopers on the left arête to a big dyno above a Ginsu knife landing.

TRAIL BOULDER

The big block next to the trail on the right. The west face has a couple of kinda hard lines that improve every time a foot or fingernail knocks off an exfoliating chip. Not the best rock but fine enough for government standards.

❏ 1. Left Line V?
The harder painful route in the middle of the west face starting from a matched edge to either the undercling or edge above. Not good stone.

❏ 2. Monkey Boy V4 ★
It's a damn good line with a real bad landing so bring a couple of pads. Big edges and sidepulls with a simple sequence even a monkey could figure out.

White Stripe Boulder

After passing the biggest block on the trail's right side (you can touch it from the trail, hence the name Trail Boulder), and a few yards uphill, is a slabby face with a white crystal band on the upper third of the south face.

☐ 1. **V2**

White Dike V0

Climbs the middle of the south face from a right-hand layback to decent edges.

☐ 2. **White Dike V0** ★★

Climb the right side of the south face to a jug at mid-height. An excellent balance problem worth two scoops.

☐ 3. **V5**

A sds on the back side of the boulder in a corridor. One very long move to the lip or crimp hateful right-hand sidepulls. A short V0 slab is opposite in the corridor.

X Boulder

Located 15 yards east of White Stripe Boulder is a big block with a distinct, north-facing overhanging corner.

☐ 1. **V0**

The killer, super low-angle slab on the south face. Entertaining no hands problems or super-casual warm ups.

North Face

A distinct overhanging corner with a flat boulder adjacent to watch the antics.

☐ 1. **Leroy V4**

Traverses the left blunt arête making up the overhanging corner. Pulls over onto the left face.

☐ 2. **Cherry Pie V6** ★

A contorted line that climbs out the overhanging corner and pulls over onto the right face. A great problem to watch your inflexible, technique-lacking friends flail on with alacrity.

☐ 3. **Fucker V4**

A low start climbing from right to left up the right arête of the corner.

Cherry Pie V6

West Face

A steep golden face with two problems and a very bad landing.

☐ 1. **Slot V1**

Climb the left side of the face off a giant jug to the arête. A squeeze-into-the-slot sds would be a tight affair and way harder. I said slot.

☐ 2. **O.S. V5**

A more attractive line is on the right of the north face and starts from a great matched edge then straight up the face or exit to the arête.

Hecla Heckler Boulder

Fifteen yards uphill (northwest) is a steep arête facing southeast.

☐ 1. **Hecla Heckler V4** ★★

The southeast arête from the big jug. Heads straight up the arête using holds on both sides of the arête.

☐ 2. **Chuckler V2** ★

On the short west face is a little problem with lovely edges.

Sharp Boulder

The big block just northeast from Hecla Heckler.

☐ 1. **V?**

On the right side of the southeast face is a corner system of questionable merit. Utilizes the low block under the main boulder.

☐ 2. **Cardboard Dog V6** ★

The arête/face on the northeast corner that starts on opposing sidepulls and makes a couple of tough moves to get through the steep start.

☐ 3. **Panama Red V5**

Just right of CD from a painful low start then up the thin, painful face.

☐ 4. **White Slabs V0s**

The slabs on the dark north face. Very bad landings.

THE IRRIGATION DITCH BOULDERS

Located 150 yards past The Group is a large talus slope of mostly crap boulders with a few damn good problems. Bring plenty of pads and a large sack for Shurfine.

JUGGA MUGGA BOULDER

At the beginning of the main talus slope, at the Y in the trail, look uphill (west 30 yards) and a bigger block rests with a crystal band running along the bottom of northeast face. Easily seen from The Group.

□ 1. South Face Slabs V0-V3

Three different, fairly entertaining slabs venture up the slabby, then vert, then slabby south face. The left side is easy and gets progressively more difficult on the right.

□ 2. V3

Climbs the southeast arête staying on the east face.

□ 3. Jugga Mugga V2

A great jug-hualish line on the northeast face starting on a jug and moving right through good edges.

DOUBLE ARÊTE

Just up the faint right trail 25 yards from the unobvious Y is a wide block with sharp arêtes (visible from the Y). The landings on these lines are horrific, if you even try them.

LOOKING DOWN ON YOU

As with any block in this maze of talus, you need to take your time and follow the directions very closely. From the Double Arête just past the Y in the trail, continue down river on the trail (65 yards total), which drops down over a couple of 3-4 foot rock steps and past a sign (Stay off Irrigation Ditch). Just before meeting up with the lowest trail (above the irrigation ditch), a clean block with a vertical wall facing the river and undercut south face is on the right (below a boulder with a white crystal dike on its east face).

□ 1. Minor Thing V1

Climb up the biggest edges on left side of the south face.

□ 2. Dance of the Caucasian V3 ★

The southeast arête can be climbed on either side. The south side is way easier and has actually been climbed, and can be done with a low start, on painful edges, to boost the grade (V7).

□ 3. East Arete V?

A blunt arete and blank face makes this undone line undone.

□ 4. East Face V0

Just above the chopped stump on the east face is a one-move wonder to big jugs.

WHITE DIKE

The block located directly above Looking Down on You.

□ 1. River Pirate ★ V0

The crack utilizing the arête. A V0 slab faces east and is directly right.

□ 2. Mutiny V3 ★

The right arête from a low start. Up the arête without flopping onto the V0 slab too early.

IRIE FACE

Sixty yards downstream from LDOY. Continue on the low fishing trail (above the ditch) and squeeze under and past a huge boulder nestled against the Irrigation Ditch (do not climb near the ditch–projects exist!). Irie Face is above the huge block by the ditch with a vertical southeast face that might produce extremely thin problems.

Feats of Strength V0

FESTIVAS

Thirty-five yards downstream from Irie Face. Continue on the fishing trail above the irrigation ditch and the boulder is on the right and faces east.

□ 1. V0

A warm up in the corridor on the west face.

□ 2. Feats of Strength V0 ★

Climb the double arête facing the river. Not the best rock in the world, but a darn neato problem.

□ 3. V2

The left side of the east face with a horrific landing.

□ 4. Airing of Grievances V2 ★

Climb the middle of the east face to a thin top out move.

□ 5. Newman V2

On the far right side of the east face is an edgy affair.

□ 6. V2s

An unnamed short boulder directly above Festivas in the walkway to reach the Butch Boulder.

BUTCH BOULDER

Located above Festivas 15 yards. A distinct traverse line splits the southeast face. A superb flat neighboring block makes Butch a great hang.

□ 1. Southeast Arete V5 ★

Heads up the southeast arête to big jugs.

□ 2. V7

A left to right frolic along the seam splitting the east face. Finishes on Get That Jug.

□ 3. Butch V6

In the middle of the east face start from a natural sit down on the adjacent block to the big jug then bust over the lip.

□ 4. Get that Jug V3 ★

Climb up the juggy northeast arête to, you guessed it, a jug, then more jugs.

Shurfine

SHURFINE

To reach this boulder from Festivas (Shurfine is visible downstream), skirt through the lowest boulders staying on the intermittent fishing trail above the irrigation ditch for approximately 60 yards. Shurfine sits close to the river. A left-facing dihedral faces the river and massive lines are right on the northwest arête and north face.

❑ 1. The Dihedral V?
Climbs the black dihedral on good locks.

❑ 2. V?
One of those giant, hard-as-shit lines for the youth of today.

❑ 3. Main Ingredient V?
A superb, proud line on the northwest arête with a tough start off a low corner then following a high seam on thin jams to continually better locks.

❑ 4. V?
The big-ass slab on the north face.

❑ 5. V?
On the left side of the south face is a thin one-move wonder.

VAPORIZER

A polished block resting next to the irrigation ditch and 10 yards upstream from Shurfine.

❑ 1. The Vaporizer ★★★ V3
Climb up the south arête from a stand start and move immediately right to slopers, then more slopers, then a sloper top out. A superb sloper problem.

TRIANGLE BOULDER

Resting against the south face of Shurfine is a triangular block with problems on the east face.

❑ 1. V?
Super bad landing. Climb the southeast arête from a right-hand pinch and left-hand edge.

❑ 2. V1
Straight up the east face on a discontinuous left-facing corner. A frightening little outing above a horrific landing.

❑ 3. V?
The bottom right arête on the east face. Starts pretty darn low and works the right arête without escaping into the slot.

❑ 4. Hidden Arete ★ V5
A hidden corridor is directly above Triangle Boulder with a steep arête problem above yet another crappy landing. Starts low on a super sharp left hand edge. Bring pads!

❑ 5. Steep Arete V3 ★
Directly above Hidden is a steep southeast arête above a small pit from a standing start. Start low on a left hand sidepull and move to the big shelf/edge for a V5.

WHITE ARETE

Above Shurfine's south face 40 yards is a small grassy meadow with a white block on the right side. Walk 10 yards downstream from the south face of Shurfine then head straight uphill 30 yards to the open meadow.

❑ 1. The Crotchety Arête V4
Starts low on the southeast arête finishing up the low angle slab.

SQUEEZE-BOX BOULDER

Above the White Arête approximately 35 yards. Squirt through the corridor left of the White Arête then head back to the right to a south-facing overhang with intersecting seams.

❑ 1. Squeeze Box V6
Start spread-eagled on thin edges in the intersecting seams. Move over the lip with bad feet and thin handholds on the slab.

Chul Lee on V5 Arête

AGNES VAILLE

A magnificent, lone, house-sized granite boulder sitting in a field of ponderosa pines. The problems on this lovely monstrosity range from a balancy warm-up to tall east-facing thin slabs, to huge lines on the west face. A couple of super-committing, undone variant lines on the southwest face await ascents. The Princeton Hot Springs should not be missed after a long session. Mountain hikes or bikes on the Continental Divide Trail (with ample bouldering possibilities near St. Elmo) can round out a trip.

Directions: This boulder is located past Mt Princeton Hot Springs. Head south of Buena Vista on Highway 285 for 6.0 miles from the intersection of US Route 24/US Route 285 and turn right on Chaffee County Road 162 (just past Nathrop). From the south (Salida) head north on US 285 for 9.6 miles from the intersection of US 285 and State Route 291. Make a lefthand turn on Chaffee County Road 162 at a sign for Mt Princeton Hot Springs/St. Elmo. Drive on Road 162, 8.8 miles, passing Mt Princeton Hot Springs to a right-hand pull-off for the Agnes Vaille Trailhead (sign). Walk up the trail approximately 350 yards keeping an eye out for the boulder on the trail's left side. The boulder rests 70 yards off the trail and is barely visible.

AGNES VAILLE BOULDER

East Face
A low-angle slab with numerous lines up the bullet stone and bullet holes.

☐ **1. V2** 🔵🟠
The far left side of the east face has one of the easiest lines that leads to a big rail at mid-height then heads slightly right. A direct start to the high rail is way tougher.

☐ **2. Left Bullet V5** ★★ 🔵🟠
Starts on the small, horizontal, sloping ledge at 5 feet and heads straight up through the left bullet hole. Bring a toothbrush for the horrifically minute holds.

☐ **3. Right Bullet V6** ★★ 🔵🟠
Climb the face right of the V5 and through the right bullet hole.

☐ **4. V2** ★★ 🔵🟠
Climb up the face directly below the high arête on progressively smaller edges to the arête and a scary final move.

North Face
☐ **5. V1** ★★★ 🔵🟠
Climbs up the right side of the north face on perfect right-facing mini corners. Balance out the top move to big jugs.

West Face
☐ **6. V5** ★★ 🔵🟠
Just around the corner from the V1 on the far left side of the west face is a long reach fest from a big sidepull/edge. Feels tougher the shorter and weaker you are.

☐ **7. V2** ★★★ 🔵🟠
Head up the low-angle ultra-classic dihedral to committing moves up high. The problem feels sketchier as the ground grows distant. Climb the sloping arête/ramp from a low start and finish up the tall face to make a good V6.

☐ **8. V4** ★ 🔵🟠
Right of the dihedral is an offset layback corner. Finish left on the same top-out as the dihedral.

☐ **9. Cock Fighting V4** ★ 🔵🟠
Same start as the previous V4 but venture up and slightly right on the 24-foot face.

☐ **10. V4** 🔵🟠
Keep heading right to the southwest face and climb up sharp, small edges to the big ramp then up and right.

The author on #10 V4

Scott Link on The Fissure V2

IRENES BOULDERS AKA IRON CITY

A small collection of boulders with five or six main blocks, surrounded by a plethora of diminutive fellow blocks, located near the old mining hamlet of St. Elmo. All told a dozen blocks have been muckled on. A great summertime and early fall destination as the forested alpine slope, altitude, and temperatures make for a very comfortable session.

Directions: Drive south of Buena Vista (the intersection of US Route 24/US Route 285) head south on highway 285 for 6.0 miles just past Nathrop to a right on Chaffee County Road 162. From the south (the intersection of US 285 and State Route 291 from Salida) head north on US 285 for 9.6 miles to the lefthand turn on Chaffee County Road 162, before reaching Nathrop. Signage for Princeton Hot Springs/St. Elmo. Continue to drive on Road 162 past Princeton Hot Springs, past Alpine to St. Elmo (17.7 miles). Go right on 292 Road past Iron City Campground and cemetery. Continue down the rough road (4x4 is best) for just under one mile to big granite blocks touching the road on the left and right.

A few small boulders are near the two main blocks and next to the dirt road. Problems range from V0 warm-up slabs to V5. More boulders are scattered along the mountainside to the west and north with problems in the same range.

The Author on a V3

The Author on LOS V1

THE FISSURE BOULDER

The obvious, biggest boulder just off the road and easily visible with a striking south face diagonal crack.

□ **1. V3**

The left arête on the south face. Straight up, utilizing the higher left crack of The Fissure, before the arête makes for a reachy V4.

□ **2. The Fissure V2** ★★★★

An all-time classic right-leaning crack that will surely bring a smile to one's face.

□ **3. V5** ★

The thin face right of The Fissure. Move up and left on progressively smaller hand and foot holds. An excellent crimp line! A V3 moves right from the same start.

□ **4. V3** ★

The right arête/face next to the chasm.

□ **5. Chasm Lines V0-V2**

Within the chasm/walkway that allows access to the north face are a couple of entertaining shorter problems.

North Face

Problems listed left to right

□ **6. V4**

The difficult little arête next to the chasm/walkway.

□ **7. V7**

The three-move seam with very little purchase for hands and feet. Try and get on from the ground for a double-digit problem.

□ **8. Fall V6** ★★

A superb (possibly more difficult than V6) line utilizing edges within the seam to make a high right move for a very sloping sidepull. A sds would certainly be double digit sickness!

Fissure Boulder

Fissure Boulder

Neighbor Boulder

Scott Link on Pointed Pain V4

NEIGHBOR BOULDER

The block resting against the west side of The Fissure.

□ **1. V0**

On the northwest face is a vertical, edge affair using the arête as one climbs higher.

□ **2. Pointed Pain V4** ★★★

The west face has an absolutely terrific sloping sidepull affair with big reaches.

□ **3. V4**

On the southwest face right of PP is a nice face on sloping edges and sidepulls. A low start makes a V5.

CHASM BLOCK

The smaller boulder making up the east side of the chasm/walkway has a couple of problems.

❏ 1. South Face V1 ◐

The short slab on the south face.

❏ 2. North Arête V3 ◐

The undercling/crack and arête on the left side of the north face. A V3 sloper problem can be done on the right arête.

THE SHACK

❏ 1. The Shack V2

A great low traverse found uphill 80 yards directly across the road from the shack that is passed coming to The Fissure.

LAST BOULDER

❏ 1. V0-V5

Uphill 70 yards from The Shack is a slab boulder then 65 yards east is a vertical boulder to play around on. No photos.

Sam Liebl on North Arête V3

Phillip Benningfield on The Shack V2

Mike Pont on Slab du Jour V2

SAN LUIS VALLEY AND PENITENTE AREAS

Bouldering in the San Luis Valley is a complete sensory experience. The views of the Sangre de Cristo Mountains, the afternoon and evening light, year-round good temperatures and seclusion all lend to enjoyable bouldering sessions. The welded tuff of Penitente and the Elephant Rocks presents a variety of pockets, highballs, and angles. Hidden Gulch, east of Del Norte, and the near endless canyons of the Elephant Rocks, see less traffic than the Penitente area. Much of the undeveloped rock is sub-par, but those wishing to find new problems could certainly ferret out some classics. The best areas to visit are Penitente Canyon, the Rock Garden, and the undeveloped Elephant Rocks.

Directions: From Saguache head south on State Route 285 for 17.2 miles (begin mileage at sign for Center and Del Norte). Turn right on Saguache Road G (Recreation sign for Penitente Canyon).

ROCK GARDEN DIRECTIONS

From Saguache head south 17.2 miles to a right turn on Saguache County Road G for La Garita and Penitente Canyon. Follow the paved road past La Garita to a right on Road 41G (also paved). From the right turn continue 1.4 miles to a dirt parking area on the left. Walk this trail/road 0.2 mile staying to the right at a split to a large, turnaround (undeveloped camping zone). Walk up the overgrown dirt road at the upper left side of the turnaround and look for sparse, small cairns that lead north to Earthmover and Visor boulders (approximately five minutes).

For the main Rock Garden Boulders drive a total of nine miles from Highway 285 (past the dirt parking area listed above) to an obvious lefthand parking area on 41G at the mouth of the Rock Garden.

PENITENTE CANYON DIRECTIONS

Penitente Canyon is reached by driving west for 7.1 miles (staying to the left on Road 38A at the fork with Road 41G). Penitente Canyon has a sign just off the right side of 38A. Turn right and drive down the dirt road 1.0 mile until it dead ends in a parking area. The boulders begin before entering the canyon and stretch well past the Virgin painting.

WITCHES CANYON DIRECTIONS

Follow directions to Penitente Canyon and continue on Road 38A 0.7 mile past Penitente to a right on a rough dirt road signed for Witches Canyon (very faded). Drive on this very rough road (2-wheel drive is very sketchy) for 1.2 miles then stay left downhill. Total is 1.4 miles to parking at the mouth of Witches Canyon. Walk through the gate (please close it behind you). All the boulders are found by using the gate as a landmark.

SIDEWINDER CANYON/BALLOON RANCH BOULDERS DIRECTIONS

These are located 0.7 mile past the Penitente turn. A sign for Sidewinder Canyon is off the right side of 38A. Drive down this rough dirt road (do not take the side roads). At 2.0 miles, 2.9 miles, and again past the 3.5 mile point, many fine boulders can be found. The Balloon Ranch Boulders require a 4x4 to reach as the road gets very rough after 2.5 miles.

ELEPHANT ROCKS

Elephant Rocks are located at 6.7 miles past the Penitente turn (Shaw Springs is the fourth dirt road south of FS 660). Turn right and drive 0.6 mile. The boulders are below the south-facing cliff across the drainage. For Sideshow Canyon drive 7.7 miles down 38A from Penitente and turn right on the 6th dirt road from FS660. Boulders are all along the main dirt road as well as in a side canyon (the 2nd faint dirt road off Sideshow Canyon).

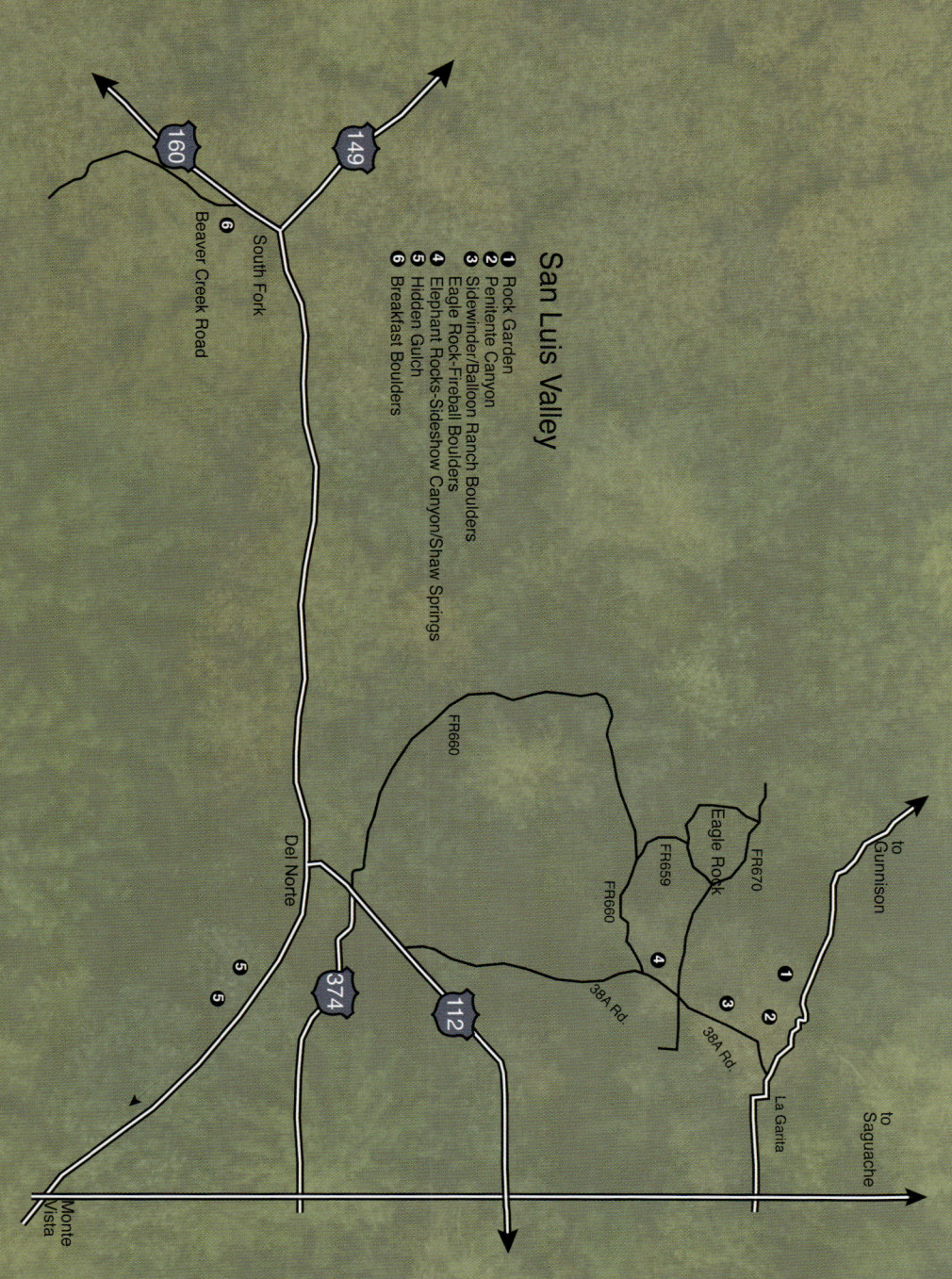

San Luis Valley

1 Rock Garden
2 Penitente Canyon
3 Sidewinder/Balloon Ranch Boulders
4 Eagle Rock-Fireball Boulders
5 Elephant Rocks-Sideshow Canyon/Shaw Springs
6 Hidden Gulch
6 Breakfast Boulders

THE ROCK GARDEN (OBSCURE BOULDERS)

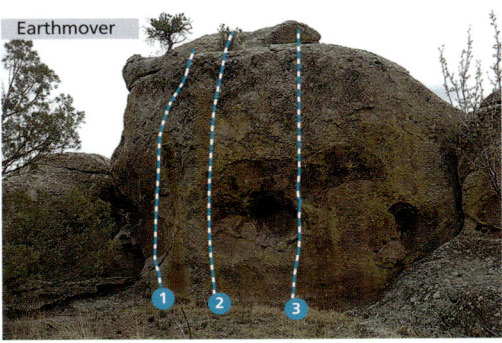
Earthmover

Frankly, the boulders and cliffbands around The Rock Garden and Penitente Canyon verge on absolute choss, but here and there lie some very, very worthy lines. Most of the boulders listed below reside in and around The Rock Garden. A few more obscure lines can be found between the two canyons and have fairly easy access. If the Front Range boulderfields are as crowded as a String Cheese concert, and you are desperately in need to boulder alone, these boulders only see traffic from soaring raptors or a lonely rattlesnake. Rest assured, there are twice as many completed problems as listed here: only the most prominent and higher quality lines are included.

EARTHMOVER BOULDER

A lichen-striped, northwest-facing boulder along a ridgeline with three decent highball-ish problems. While the quality may not reach into the stratosphere, the views and solitude make up for it without question. The back side of Earthmover has a couple of decent slabs.

❒ **1. Hammer V5** ★★
A vertical affair on the left side of the face starting off the flat platform, with a crux move from a sharp-edged bulb, finishing just left of the pine on top. A problem can be done to the left using all the bigger holds.

❒ **2. Nail V6** ★
In between Hammer and Earthmover is another thin face starting from a good left hand undercling and a hollow-sounding right hand pinch/edge and climbing straight up on awfully thin crimps.

❒ **3. Earthmover V5** ★
The middle problem up thin, sharp edges. Your fingers will hurt!

❒ **4. All Time Crack V6** ★★★★
A perfect crack in a left-facing corner located downhill (southwest) from the backside of the Earthmover approximately 70 yards. The ultra-clean crack faces east with a sloping landing. Bring a stack of pads and some serious gumption.

TIER BOULDERS

Across the large, flat meadow approximately 80 yards to the north from Earthmover (look carefully for cairns across the meadow as well as on the broken cliffband where the Visor is located) is a jumbled cliffband with pocketed boulders above the lowest tier. The problems are NOT visible from Earthmover, but trust me, they are there. The problems face north and west.

VISOR BOULDER

The most distinct, west, pocketed boulder on top of the lower cliff with north faces and a west overhang.

❒ **1. V0**
An easy line up the huge pockets on the left side of the north face.

❒ **2. Little Visor V3** ★★
Climb up the middle of the north face on good pockets to a longish reach for the top. A V6 (Brown Eyed Women) moves in from the right from the start of Fire the Still.

❒ **3. Fire the Still V8** ★★★
The all-time classic steep line up the northwest arête from a low start on an obvious large hueco for the right hand and a two-finger pocket for the left. Move up the arête on beautiful and painful pockets, find a miniscule sidepull, to a big reach/throw for small edge just below the top. Exit left.

Ned Harris on Little Visor V3

Andrew McClure on Fire the Still V8

❏ **4. The Sound of Wind V5** ★★★★
A line thought to be too loose, but an attentive eye unlocked a bomber sequence and now one of the best problems near Penitente. Start this classic, steep west-facing problem with the left hand on the same low hueco on Fire the Still and the right arête and journey up to excellent huecos to a couple of powerful moves slapping the right arête. Bring a spotter to protect against a brain-bashing landing on jutting rocks.

Pocket Boulders
Immediately left of the Visor are a couple of pocketed faces with excellent problems in the V0 to V2 (eastern-most block) range that make for good warm-ups.

The Meadow
Across the big grassy meadow from the Visor is a little smorgasbord of testy slabs.

❏ **1. Loose Liver V2**
North-facing, beautiful, burnt orange, right-leaning arête 15 yards before the Death Slab.

❏ **2. Death Slab aka Loose Bowel V2**
North facing 30-foot high slab up sidepulls to a questionable flake then muckle an underling over the bulge.

❏ **3. Slippery Serpent V3** ★★★★
One of the toughest V3s you will encounter and undoubtedly one of the most technical, most awesome, and most enjoyable. An east-facing friction testpiece up the left side of a wide offwidth.

❏ **4. V2**
Up the right open crack.

Slippery Serpent V3

The Rock Garden
This bouldering area's veritable smorgasbord of first ascent possibilities—it ain't called a rock garden for no reason—has long been overlooked. Rhyolite boulders range from squatty little slabs to super highball faces, ultra-classic cracks, stellar arêtes, and a handful of steep power problems. Only a fraction of the completed problems are included here. If you enjoy being alone and doing fun ascents this area has plenty of lines to choose from. The environment is well suited to early winter, spring, and fall sessions with spectacular views of the Sangre de Cristo Mountains and South San Juans.

Rock Garden Boulders
To reach the Warm Up Hueco Wall (WUHW), Ned's Highball (NH), and Slab du Jour (SDJ) walk up the main canyon trail for approximately 160 yards to the first side canyon on the left (a faint trail veers east). Walk 40 yards to a very faint trail and go right (south) with occasional cairns that lead to the first developed blocks along the canyon rim (Slab du Jour, et al). Walk uphill 60 yards to a black bulging face (The Killing Moon) with a large fir on the face's right side. Slab du Jour is in a hidden slot just around the west corner (where the fir is) and faces south.

From the top of Slab du Jour follow cairns east 110 yards to a distinct, 30-foot tall striped wall (Ned's Highball) on the northeast side of a small meadow (sheltered and warm on cold days).

To locate Warm Up Hueco Wall from Ned's Highball head due east following cairns, then northeast (up to the meadow above the cliffband). Follow numerous cairns across the meadow (total distance from NH is 275 yards). WUHW faces due south and is covered in huecos.

To locate the Envy Wall stay on the main canyon trail past the trail to Slab du Jour for another 80 yards (past a sport route on the right with copious amounts of chalk below an overhang). The approximate total from the parking area is 240 yards. Head left (southeast) uphill for 70 yards past big pines and through a little gully to the north-facing cliff line (cairns may be sitting on stumps). As soon as you get above the cliff go left to the first boulder (Envy Wall) with a tiny grassy hollow below the problems.

To locate Raptor Boulders head west from the parking area and up the hillside (please park here instead of farther down 41G) following intermittent cairns below the cliff line. You will be outside the canyon on the cliff line facing the road. Stay on the marked trails to avoid erosion. All problems are listed from the mouth of The Rock Garden headed west.

Slab du Jour
The first developed bouldering in the Rock Garden proper.

❏ **1. The Killing Moon V5**
On the big, black, dirty face left of the large fir tree. Climbs the tallest part of the northwest face through a big sidepull.

❏ **2. Pumpkin Chucking V6**
20 feet left of the Slab du Jour corridor is a tall scary thin face opposite The Killing Moon. The problem starts on two perfect jugs at chest height and moves up to a long reach.

❏ **3. Slab du Jour V2** ★★★★
Starts in the corridor at the base of the cliff. If you love steep slabs this line is unbelievable. Bring plenty of pads and at least one spotter for the top out. Another V2 is left.

Slab du Jour V2

Mike Frieschlag on Ned's Highball V3

☐ 4. **Flight of the Thresherman V5** ★★★★
The gorgeous line starting right of Slab du Jour in the open corner and exiting just right of the Slab du Jour top out. Dangerous.

☐ 5. **V1**
To the right of Flight is a shorter face with a right-angling mid-height crack.

☐ 6. **Let it Grow V2**
West from Slab du Jour approximately 30 feet is a vertical face with a low right-hand sidepull to a pocket then upwards.

☐ 7. **V?**
A difficult thin face left of LIG.

NED'S HIGHBALL ARENA
(AKA THE CYCLOPS BOULDER)
A line of tall problems above a gloriously good hang in a grassy meadow that faces south.

☐ 1. **Forever and Sunsmell V7**
On the far left blunt arête is a harder problem dealing with some looseness up high.

☐ 2. **Ned's Highball aka Cyclops V3** ★★
Climb straight up the 30-foot face past two distinct holes. Eight or nine pads should suffice.

☐ 3. **Hot Dog V4** ★★
The thin line right of Ned's Highball that ends in the upper groove. Not exceptional but gets done by those in the know.

☐ 4. **Adventure Land V1**
Walk south 15 yards from Ned's Highball past a distinct northwest arête (V?) to two very tall V1's before the cliff line peters out. The left problem climbs through an obvious large hand-size hueco and the right problem climbs the tall face a few feet right. That is all, otherwise it wouldn't be adventure.

WARM UP HUECO WALL V0-V2
Kinda high problems with a flat landing and super sunny exposure for the colder months. If you enjoy tooling around on a fine selection of holds this boulder will make you smile.

Trixie Tartasky on Hotdog V4

THE ENVY WALL

A fairly highball northwest-facing wall with many quality, undeveloped, scary problems in the vicinity. The two good problems on the NW face are solid for the grade, so you might pull harder than expected.

☐ **1. Envy V3** ★
The left side of the face past a nasty little nubbin.

Mike Pont on Envy V3

☐ **2. Jealousy V3** ★
Climb smack dab up the middle of the face on hard-to-discern edges to a right-facing layback.

RAPTOR BOULDERS

As with all the problems around The Rock Garden, the lack of traffic has left lichen on the problems. But, do not be fooled; the first-rate lines need no brushing and beckon one to climb up the lichen-striped faces. The Raptor Boulders have only been climbed a handful of times, so the low-angle lines will be a tad licheny. The vertical faces are ready and waiting.

You may not remember, but years ago The Rock Garden and Penitente Canyon were destination spots for hot-shot sport climbers. For some crazy reason, the sport climbers never realized that the short cliffbands would make for fine, oftentimes exceptional bouldering. Their loss is our gain. This long, convoluted cliff band offers more jaw-drops than a free Widespread Panic ticket giveaway.

THE SEAMLESS AREA

From the parking area walk west, outside the canyon, past the initial tall (30-50') cliff bands, approximately 175 yards, to a point where the cliff reaches an open meadow looking down into The Rock Garden. The Seamless Area is directly before the meadow at a tall gorgeous striking arête (too tall to boulder).

Seamless Area

☐ **1. V3**
The dirty, thin, technical, low-angle seam just left of Blinded by the Light.

☐ **2. Blinded by the Light V1** ★★★
The hand to fist crack that opens into a V-chimney the higher one jams. A great jamming problem. Did I say jam?

☐ **3. The Arête V1** ★★★
A classic 19-foot-tall blunt arête just right of Blinded. Two starts can be done. The easier version climbs the large rail on the northwest face or climb straight up the arête from the dirt (V2).

☐ **4. Mike's Face V1**
Ten feet around the corner from BBTL is a slab face immediately left of a right-facing corner with a splitter seam.

☐ **5. Seem V0**
A cruiser low-angle, right-facing corner with a nice seam to fiddle in.

☐ **6. V?**
The ultra-thin slab just left of the wide, chossy, crack in the corner.

☐ **7. Split V7** ★★
The stunning pocketed east face just left of the Peace Arête. The top out should be made in the middle of the face.

The author on Peace Arête V4

☐ **8. Peace Arête V4** ★★
The impeccable arête 20 feet right of Seem on the right of the striking east face. Top-out is on the right slab, before reaching the apex of the arête, to avoid loose rock.

FAIRIE GROTTO

This hidden grotto is directly behind Seem in a flat, shaded area with a giant ponderosa pine next to the entrance. To get all your pads into the grotto walk west to the first meadow (30 yards from Peace Arête) and go downhill (towards The Rock Garden proper) 25 yards then immediately left up and into the grotto. The left side of the grotto is low quality so no grades are given. The right side (west face) is higher quality.

WEST FACES

☐ **1. My Turn V5**
In the far back of the grotto is a thin face to a substantial throw for the lip.

☐ **2. Why V4**
On the next block to the right of the V5 is a terribly painful vertical affair up sharp edges.

☐ **3. V1**
Directly right on the next, taller block is a fun problem that moves through a distinct, sinker pocket after the starting moves.

☐ **4. ASOMH V1s** ★★★
To the right again are two 20-plus foot vertical faces.

☐ **5. Mikodin Cocktail V3** ★★★★
Probably the most distinguishable and classic problem at The Rock Garden! The pocketed, open corner is located left of the entrance to the Fairie Grotto on a small shelf above the open meadow. The problem requires more technique than pull and will surely test your stemming prowess.

☐ **6. V?**
The steep face directly opposite MC. Low quality top out.

NIMBLY BIMBLIES

This little smorgasbord of problems is located 175 yards west from the Seamless Area. Continue along the trail following cairns, trying to miss obstacles with your pads. The trail does not go in a straight line so be willing to walk up and down some. Please stay on the cairn-marked trail.

LITTLE NB AKA THE PIANO

A boulder detached from the cliff with a jug rail at waist-height, running along the west face. The problems here are V1 at the hardest but make for entertaining, albeit short, affairs. A quality flat hang is found on top.

☐ **1. Twisted Tree V2** ★
The rightmost problem on Little NB found right of the jug rail. Climbs the righthand layback corner and thin seam to a very long reach.

CHUCK'S ROOF

A smaller detached block directly down the hill a few yards from Big NB and Pipe Dream, east from Little NB a couple of yards.

☐ **1. Root of an Unfocus V9**
Starts with a sharp pocket for your right hand in the middle of the roof. Lurch up to an almost upside down pocket with the left, then over the little roof.

☐ **2. Renga V2**
Climb the blunt arête to the left of Root.

☐ **3. V1**
The south face's right arête. Kinda fun and safe.

Mikodin Cocktail V3

YOU'RE NOT THAT SPECIAL BOULDER

The next boulder below (downhill) from Chuck's Roof.

☐ **1. V5** ★★★
A terrifically terrifying and stupendous north-facing problem with an atrocious landing. Big moves to get situated on the slopers leading to jug finishing holds (a little ways back from the lip). Do not be fooled, this one requires a ton of pads and one damn good spotter.

☐ **2. V3** ★
A traverse from left to right on the west face of the same block. A great lowball problem with lovely slopers.

☐ **3. How Old are You Boys? V3**
The low angle 30-plus foot slab just west of #2. An opus to the slab masters of the world.

You're Not that Special Boulder

Big NB

The tall cliff band six yards south from Little NB with the obvious splitter finger crack. Problems are listed left to right.

☐ **1. Pipe Dream V2** ★★★
The open scoop facing north (towards Chuck's Roof) with a relatively bad landing. Exit right above Slap Happy.

☐ **2. Slap Happy V4** ★★★
The arête and crack immediately around the corner from Pipe Dream. A slopping top-out above a bad landing gets the juices flowing.

☐ **3. V0**
The low-angle, dual-corner slab opposite Slap Happy (by two-whole feet) with good slopers.

☐ **4. V5**
A few feet right of the V0 slab is a nefarious face that thwarts sassy comers. Starts on the northwest blunt, low-angle (with a small overlap) arête to vile holds.

☐ **5. Spill Some Wine V2** ★★★
The distinct north-facing crack located on Big NB. Climb this classic straight-on, all trad-style, or layback the splitter crack like a pumped sport climber.

☐ **6. Slabber V1**
A good line is found 10 yards to the right in the corridor (the downclimb leads through this corridor from the problems on Big NB). Climbs a vertical face above a low V-shaped overhang.

Slap Happy V4

Spill Some Wine V2

Long NB

The largest detached boulder on the righthand edge of the small open area westmost of all the Nimbly Bimblies.

Mike's Slabs

The 16-foot north-facing slab with a horizontal break at 2/3 height. Three problems head up the face with the thinnest slab on the left side of the face next to the arête. From left to right the problems are V3 (left), V2 (middle), V1 (right).

❑ 1. V0s 🌀

Five yards right from the right slab are a couple of easy, short warm-ups. One climbs the triangular block first encountered from the right slab then another one a couple feet right.

❑ 2. CIAOB V8 ★ 🌀

A pocket line is a few feet right from the V0s and starts from the big low jug to progressively smaller pockets. A stand-up start eases the pain of the two-finger pocket at eye level.

❑ 3. Instances of Silence V7 ★★★ 🌀🌀

A striking pocket line a few feet right of CIAOB. Stack lotsa pads, or stand on the shoulders of a dwarf, gnome, or other available tiny person. Pull on a sloping pocket or sharp edge with the right hand and reach way left into a good pocket, then scamper up to a right hand pocket. A slightly hidden left-hand crimp unlocks the beginning of this adventurous top-out, which is not for the faint of heart.

❑ 4. Trees on Rock V4 ★ 🌀🌀

On the opposite side of the Long NB from Instances of Silence. Climbs the thin, pocketed face utilizing the big left-hand layback to a flat jug at mid-height, then the biz.

Big Mouth Boulder

This distinct block with a roof/overhang/mouth feature is directly above (south) of Long NB.

❑ 1. V0 🌀🌀

On the far left side of the mouth (a wide overhang and use of a vivid imagination) is a casual affair moving left to right on a sloping rail/jug. Be careful exiting.

❑ 2. Twang V4 🌀🌀

On the far right side of the mouth is a tall vertical face adjacent to a smaller block/cliff. This highball is quite committing so bring ample paddage.

❑ 3. V0s

The boulder just right of Twang has a couple of safer, casual problems (north and west faces).

❑ 4. Slot Minimalist V? 🌀

A tight slot is directly below Twang with a tough sloping pocket traverse (right to left) on the boulder making up the left side of the slot.

Mike's Slabs

Andrew McClure on Instances of Silence V7

THE DUGOUT CAVE

Continue west following cairns from the Nimbly Bimblies for approximately 95 yards and a large overhang will be encountered. Probably the steepest problems found around The Rock Garden on a roughly 45-degree overhang, with a sort-of-safe landing zone.

☐ **1. Slinky Plus Escalator V11** ★★★

This hard problem does not have the best rock, but it does have some good rock. Sds on the arête and bust right into the cave on juggy (not so stellar rock) moves to a distinct finger rail, then up to the shelf, then back to the arête to top out. It's not over till it's over.

An easier problem (V4) starts low and exits early onto the slab at a right-hand pinch.

☐ **2. Kama V4** ★★

In the corridor making up the left side of SPE is a tall, gray, left-facing corner leading up the west face. Good till the last high hold.

☐ **3. The Big Picture V12?**

The problem is located 150 yards west along the cairned trail from The Dugout (past a large overhanging spire that faces east) on a large detached block and is described as one of the best lines in Colorado. Just look for a steep, colorful open scoop on the north face (facing the road) with a good landing zone and possibly not enough holds anymore.

Chuck Fryberger on the FA of Slinky Plus Escalator V11

The Big Picture V12?

Mike Frieschlag on Kama V4

THE DRUNKEN BUMBLER ARÊTES

These beautiful, neighboring twin arêtes are located approximately 250 yards past The Dugout Cave headed west on the cairned trail. Once again, do not think for a second the trail is straight as an arrow. Keep a sharp eye out for occasional cairns.

❒ 1. **In the Nick of Time V2** ★
The left arête from big jugs then move out the slightly sloping arête to an insecure top-out.

❒ 2. **V?** ★★★
The smooth right arête that gives new meaning to the word sloper. A gorgeous line that has very little, make that no friction for the hands.

DAWN TILL DUSK WALL

From the Drunken Bumbler Arêtes head back east on the same level for approximately 40 yards to a gorgeous west-facing pocketed wall with vile landings.

❒ 1. **Dawn V4** ★★
Leg breaker but a terrific line, starting down in the pit and moving up and left on great pockets and edges to a very committing finale above the uneven landing.

❒ 2. **Till Dusk V3**
The right line starting a little right of the lowest pit and finishing up and right on decent pockets. Yet another terrible landing.

THE CORRIDORS

This bushy area has some of the most aesthetic lines along the cliff line. From the Drunken Bumbler Arêtes head west another 60 yards to a bramble of bushes and two corridors separated by more bushes. Stellar hard rhyolite!

HIDDEN CORRIDOR

This shallow corridor is left of an undone roof above talus (there are only a couple along the cliff so it makes for a great landmark) and is defined by a 25-foot vertical wall facing northeast with a diagonal crack leading from right to left and impeccable pocket lines. Problems are listed as one stands at the mouth of the corridor.

Right Wall
The wall with the diagonal crack and tall (30-foot), pocketed undone face.

❒ 1. **V2**
The left arête a few feet left of the Smile Happy Crack. A big move reaches the top.

❒ 2. **Smile Happy Crack V2** ★★★★
Climb this kick-ass crack on big jugs at the start and not-so-good holds that appear substantial from the ground. An absolutely classic crack boulder problem!

❒ 3. **V?**
The face right of the Smile Happy beckons one to climb it, but the thin pockets and height are real deterrents. The arête right of this line does the same but, man oh man, you got to be a superstar without fear.

Left Wall
❒ 1. **V4**
Climb the blunt arête and pockets immediately left of the tree. A short V1 climbs up the face to the right of the tree.

In the Nick of Time V2

Drunken Bumbler #2

Dawn till Dusk

Andrew McClure on So Many Times V7

Trixie Tartasky on Groovy V3

WAVE CORRIDOR

This fine corridor only has two completed lines and is identi-fied by the smoothest rock on the cliff line with a large, thin 20-foot flake making up one side of the corridor. Lines on the flake have not been attempted, as the face is so thin it is hard to discern holds.

☐ 1. **End of the Day V1**
The left arête in the corridor with a tough little move to get situated on the undercut rock.

☐ 2. **So Many Times V7** ★★
Climb straight up the middle of the corridor from a hard-to-stick jump start on impeccable, smooth rock. V4 version stems between the corridor walls and starts on a matched edge.

☐ 3. **V?**
The crack right of So Many Times to the high arête or crack/seam.

☐ 4. **Panacea V2**
Located around the corner 20 feet from the Wave Corridor on a bench. If you are having a bad day, climb this laser cut arête. Start with the pockets and move up to a bomber edge and the top.

END OF THE LINE

Located 30 yards past The Corridors before the cliff makes an abrupt turn to the south.

☐ 1. **Mann's Warm Down V1**
Climb the far left side of the short black wall in a shallow left-to-right offset corner.

☐ 2. **Groovy V3** ★★★★
Located five yards to the right of Mann's Warm Down on im-peccable rock. The groove will be all to obvious after climbing the intersecting seams that lead to the big shelf 10 feet up. Top out straight up for a committing V6 highball.

☐ 3. **Ryan's Frightmare (Big Jim) V2** ★★★★

Continue around the corner to the south 20 yards from Groovy and a distinct tall open scoop will catch your attention. The line is directly above a flat landing in a small meadow. Bring some pads for this 20-foot tall problem that should not be missed.

☐ 4. **V2**
The bulge just left of Ryan's Frightmare.

Pat Wilde on Ryan's Frightmare V2

Penitente Canyon

This surreal canyon is best known for its incredibly short sport climbs and monks who always felt bad about their sins. There's also some fine, albeit limited, bouldering to be found. The hard rhyolite is incredibly bomber and adds a new twist to Colorado's repertoire of boulders. Many new problems exist up the left trail past The Virgin Boulder.

Parking Lot Boulders

DO NOT CLIMB ON THESE BLOCKS DUE TO DAMAGE DONE TO THE PETROGLYPHS. A FENCE PROTECTS THESE ROCKS!

Picnic Area

A hidden block with decent to bad rock. It is located by walking about 75 yards along a trail beginning at the picnic table. A nice bulge sits next to the trail with an aspen in front of it.

❏ 1. **V1**
On the west face is a lichen-covered slab. Not very good but another problem to tick.

❏ 2. **V3**
Start on painful crimps on the south face then head up the rounded slab.

❏ 3. **V0**
Just right of #2 on the southeast face is a jug at arms reach.

Tied-Up Boulders

A couple of problems on the left of the main trail leading into the canyon. The problems face the trail (north) and are located just before the notice board.

❏ 1. **V0** ★★
A crack on the left that is a little dirty.

❏ 2. **V1** ★
The pocket/edge wall to the right of #1. Terrible rock on top warrants a hasty retreat.

The Virgin Boulder

Trail Rocks

Trail Rocks

A cluster of boulders approximately 20' past the notice board on the left side of the trail. Great undone lines on the cliffband.

❏ 1. **V0s**
On the small boulders closest the trail are a number of V0s.

❏ 2. **V1**
On the colorful, overhanging boulder directly above #1 is a problem up the right arête (around right from the overhang).

The Virgin Boulder

An obvious block directly under the Virgin Mary painting. Simply walk into the canyon until the painting is visible.

❏ 1. **V1** ★
On the west face is a reasonable problem that begins under the roof and moves up and left.

❏ 2. **V3** ★★
On the northeast face (facing the painting) start matched on an edge six feet up then go to the lip. Not an easy top-out. Not pictured.

West Virgin Boulder

A short boulder that sits approximately 30 yards up the trail on the left from The Virgin Boulder. The problems face south.

❏ 1. **V2** ★
Starts below the guano then up a disheartening flake.

❏ 2. **V1**
The uneventful right arête from a low start.

West Virgin Boulder

WITCHES CANYON

It only took years of development and over 200 problems in The Rock Garden and Penitente area to finally feel the necessary itch to walk up Witches Canyon and realize there are literally a hundred more fun lines to be climbed. Problems in Witches tend toward tall vertical affairs on slopers, amazing huecos, and even cracks. The neighboring side canyons have unearthed more of the same as well as prime hueco lines and ultra-thin highballs.

The author on Quaking V5

BLACK WALL

A tall face off the trail's right side located just before reaching the first bolted routes in the canyon. Walk 150 yards northwest from the gate down the old roadbed to an obvious bouldering-size wall with a perfect flat landing.

1. Precision V6 ★

The far left thin affair on pockets and bad crimps. A tad committing like its neighbor.

2. Quaking V5 ★★★

Superb sloper problem roughly in the middle of the wall, starting from the lowest matched sloper to a good inset edge then up, up, up.

3. V3

Climb the exceedingly dirty seam if you really need to.

4. V3

On the far right side behind the tree is a highball hueco and edge-covered line with tip-toe moves at the top.

LITTLE NEIGHBOR BLOCKS

There are two boulders just past Black Wall (15 yards) and left of the first bolted routes. A couple of fun, safe lines at V2 and V3 can be done without scaring the shit out of oneself.

SHAPES BOULDER

A distinct laser-cut boulder located 50 yards past the Black Wall on the right with one thin problem.

1. V1

A slab line with tiny little holds to the upper left-leaning arête.

CRACK WALL

The most obvious wall in the canyon littered with highball crack problems right off the trail. 250 yards from the green gate (100 yards past Black Wall). All problems are highball and roughly V0-V4 (Make No Mistake V4 on right arête).

SLOT PROBLEMS

15 yards to the right of the Crack Wall is a hidden slot with short arêtes and vertical faces from V1-V4.

WITCHES YOU BITCHES WALL

A 20-plus-foot-tall vertical northwest-facing wall located on the left of the trail 60 yards past Crack Wall and up the hillside approximately 80 yards. A hoodoo sits on top of the cliffband and is easily visible from the trail.

1. V2 ★★★

The very tall left line up good edges and continuous toe dancing.

2. Witches You Bitches V2 ★★★

Classic line up the middle of the face on similar edges as the previous line and considered harder.

3. V1

Right line next to the seam.

Black Wall

Crack Wall

Witches You Bitches Wall

Triangle Stone

TRIANGLE STONE

A distinct low-angle triangle slab boulder 170 yards past Crack Wall on the right of the trail. A couple of V0-V1s can be done.

☐ **1. V2**
The left diagonal crack on the white face directly above the Triangle Stone.

☐ **2. V4**
The sketchy layback line right of the V2 through questionable rock up high.

☐ **3. On the Fence V2** ★★★
In the hidden slot above Triangle Stone is a spectacular and awfully dangerous hueco line. If you have the gumption and lots of pads and a friend to carry you out of the canyon then try this classic and committing line.

ROOF AREA

This section of rock is on the right side of the trail (450 yards from gate) and distinguished by big overhangs jutting out above the lower faces. Chalk cakes the biggest holds to very difficult top-outs on the first roof.

HIDDEN GROTTOS

Located directly above Triangle Stone but best accessed by taking the trail leading up hill from the Roof Area's first roof (past Triangle 40 yards) and pictured here. Walk uphill 130 yards through bushes and rock steps to a set of bolted lines (at 100 yards a classic and frightening V5 is to the left above a small access slot). The second bolted route has a couple of boulder problems around the corner. Follow cairns from the bolted route 40 yards to a hidden grotto above Triangle Stone. Numerous problems are here as well as two more grottos to the northeast (cairns may be present).

Roof Area-First Roof

Roof Area

2ND BOLTED LINE AREA

Not pictured.

☐ 1. The Fine Arête V7 ★★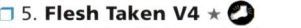

Just left of the bolted route is a blunt arête littered with decent sidepulls and a blank overlapping face. Good freakin' luck with the top-out.

☐ 2. Disagreement Man V3

The left huecoed line just around the right corner from the bolted route. Exit into Backtalk or take your life in your hands and exit straight up. Very bad landing through the steep start.

☐ 3. Backtalk V4 ★★

The right line close to the tree that starts off a surprisingly solid incut flake to a sloper crux. Good stuff!

HIDDEN GROTTO #1

An open area above Triangle Stone on top of the cliffband.

☐ 1. A Percent V0 ★★

The first and far left hueco line en-countered at the Hidden Grotto.

☐ 2. The Green Dream V2

★★★

A beautiful cruiser right hueco line up sinker holds to goods edges through the Swiss cheese or pull over the right bulge. A little tougher line can be done straight up between AP and TGD.

☐ 3. V?

Two very tall projects venture up the quality thin faces right of TGD. The right line starts low under the roof to the large open hueco…can be exited early to avoid scaring the living crap out of yourself.

☐ 4. 20 Percent V2 ★★

The big open hueco problem facing uphill and right of a squeeze chimney (the entertaining downclimb off this excellent little problem). Start down and low to the right for an added bonus.

☐ 5. Flesh Taken V4 ★

The same start as 20 Percent but figure out how to move up the offset seam.

Phillip Benningfield on The Green Dream V2

HIDDEN GROTTO #2

Walk around to the top of Hidden Grotto #1 following cairns.

❒ **1. Second Steps V0-V2**
Above Hidden Grotto #1 and easily seen is a fairly tall gray face with a couple of high slabs.

❒ **2. Slippery Slope V1**
A short problem to the right of Second Steps that climbs around an open hueco.

HIDDEN GROTTO #3

Follow cairns east from Hidden Grotto #2.

❒ **1. 80 Percent V3**
In the next (east) grotto from Hidden Grotto #2 is a very high west-facing gray slab on the left side of a long wall. Numerous other tall slabs have been done to the right of this highball.

BUCKET LIST BOULDERS

Continue along the old roadbed (in Witches Canyon) until it ends in a trail (475 yards past Crack Wall). Walk 90 yards on the trail to a bend to the right. Look back left and follow cairns up to the northwest facing an extended cliffline with nearly 10 problems to get all your juices flowing. Problems listed from left to right.

❒ **1. Pocket Line V2** ★★★
The first line encountered as you reach the cliffband. A big hueco is in the middle of the face.

❒ **2. Lichen Project V4** ★★★
A super tall slabby to vertical line requiring tons of commitment to reach the top.

❒ **3. Diaper Man V3** ★
Climb up the lefthand layback/groove to a big pocket out right…exit straight up for full diaper effect or exit right for ultra-soft sensations.

❒ **4. Something Shitty V2** ★
The face right of Diaper Man utilizing the blunt right arête.

❒ **5. Bucket List V0** ★★
On huge huecos from sds to high crimps.

❒ **6. Downhill Slide V1** ★★★
Climb up another tall face on superb edges. Two scooper!

❒ **7. Meet Your Maker V1**
The far right problem on the cliffband next to and using, if you need to, old fart, the green arête.

Mike Freischlag on Second Steps

Pocket Line

Bucket List Overview

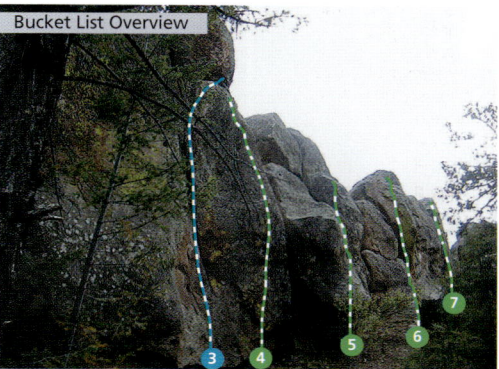

Ungenius Wall

On the trail just past Bucket List Boulders three bolted routes are encountered. Go right past these lines and up the gully/drainage for 150 yards to a cairn on the trail's left side. Go right (northeast) for 40 yards past a very tight slot (too tight for big pads to be worn) to a north-facing wall with a tall pine left of a big letter-slot hueco on the face.

❑ **1. Burning Bridges V6** ★

Ultra-thin gorgeous vertical face left of the pine.

❑ **2. V?**

A ridiculously thin pocketed face almost behind the pine.

❑ **3. Know it All V3** ★★★ 🪨

Superb classic line right of the pine that climbs through the letter-slot hueco.

❑ **4. V7** ★ 🪨 🔵

Right of KIA before the squeeze slot is a thin bulging face that keeps on going past an upper bulge.

❑ **5. Too Big for Britches V5** ★★ 🪨 🔵

Right of the main wall past the squeeze slot is a slightly over-hanging prow with hidden edges up high.

Names Boulders

Follow the numerous circuitous cairns from Ungenius Wall mainly north for approximately 190 yards to Luther's Boulder.

Ungenius Wall

Mike Freischlag on Too Big for Britches V5

Mike Freischlag on Know it All V3

Luther's Boulder

PB on Dennika Marie V2

LUTHER'S BOULDER

The coolest damn hueco-covered boulder with sweet cruiser lines with flat landings on the west and south faces.

❑ 1. **V0**
On the west face the far left line on the grass-covered ledge.

❑ 2. **Dennika Marie V2** ⬤ ★★
Start right of the grassy ledge either as a stand up or low right sds off good huecos to nice slopers in the open curved face.

❑ 3. **Luther V2** ⬤ ★★★
Just right of DM on nice huecos from a lowball start just cause the holds are so nice, but be aware there is one not-so-easy move to get set up on the vertical upper face.

❑ 4. **Big Luther V2** ⬤ ★★★
Up the steep prow on absolutely glorious huecos.

❑ 5. **V0s** ⬤
The not-so-safe hueco wall around the corner from BL on the south face.

❑ 5. **Dawnella V1**
Located 30 yards to the west from Luther's Boulder is yet another fun hueco line.

WHATEVER BOULDER

Located 20 yards to the west from Dawnella. A nice shorter block with three insignificant lines.

❑ 1. **Throw me a Stick V0**
The cruiser problem on the west face's left side.

❑ 2. **Whatever V2**
Climbs the steep scoop in the wall's middle.

❑ 3. **Corner Problem V1**
Far right huecos to crimps up high.

❑ 4. **Buzz Cockman V3** ★★
At the bottom expanse of the Names Boulders in a corridor is a terrific thin vertical face 30 yards below Whatever Boulder. The problem faces west.

Dawn Heigele on Throw me a Stick V0

Mike Freischlag on FA of Buzz Cockman V3

SIDEWINDER CANYON / BALLOON RANCH BOULDERS

The boulders are not actually in Sidewinder Canyon but the dirt road to reach the boulders passes by the turnoff for Sidewinder. This area includes the Balloon Ranch Boulders and a couple of small boulderfields that appear not to have been developed. Venture down this road if you love to do first ascents on quality rock. No grades are included for this area. Boulders can be found at 2.0, 2.9, and beyond 3.5 miles (Balloon Ranch Boulders). The road requires a 4x4 after 2.5 miles then quickly becomes flat and smooth.

ELEPHANT ROCKS / SHAWSPRINGS AND SIDESHOW CANYON

This may be the largest expanse of undeveloped bouldering in the state. The Elephant Rocks line the road for over a mile with numerous side canyons littered with rock. Two areas are included and all the problems listed are believed to be new ascents.

SHAW SPRINGS

Another set of boulders that appear unbelievable at first glance but turns out to be pretty damn crappy. The boulders sit below the south face of a broken cliff and stretch a couple of hundred yards. The easier problems in the V0 to V2 range have higher quality stone but most of the faces are loose and crumbly. With enough time and gumption a few more decent problems could be done on the better rock. Watch out for the not-so-friendly rattlers!

SIDESHOW CANYON

One of the last side canyons before the Elephant Rocks peter out. The problems are numerous and the quality differs as the walls top out. The weathered rock on top tends to be gritty and loose, while the low rock is pretty solid and pocketed.

SIDESHOW BOULDER

One of the many small cliffs on the right side of the main canyon (0.3 mile from the turnoff). This boulder is defined by a large open dihedral and by having chalk on it while the hundred other cliffs do not.

❏ 1. **V0**
The left slab on the left boulder.

❏ 2. **V1**
Climb the slab in the middle.

❏ 3. **V2** ★
Climb the bulge to the left of the chossy dihedral and finish on questionable holds.

ULTIMATE SIDESHOW BOULDERS

The problems in the side canyon are included to get some development started, as at least 50 more wait to be done. To reach the blocks turn left on the second faint dirt road after entering the main canyon (0.5 mile from the turnoff). Park on the knoll just after the Property Boundary sign for the National Forest.

FREAKSHOW BOULDERS

From the knoll walk to the southwest approximately 70 yards to the first side canyon. The problems face southwest. Problems are listed from left to right.

❏ 1. **Explosive Man V3** ★
The bulge left of Grit Spitter and just right of a tight dihedral. Use right-hand laybacks to an easy top-out. Another V3 begins just left before the tight dihedral and finishes up the same slab.

❏ 2. **The Grit Spitter V2**
The slab left of a filthy crack and right of Explosive Man.

❏ 3. **Here Comes the Skinny Man V3** ★★
On the right wall from Grit Spitter is a vertical wall with pockets. Climb the middle face. A harder problem is just to the right.

BREAKFAST BOULDERS

The Breakfast Boulders consist of the main Breakfast Boulder and a few satellite blocks. Many of the surrounding boulders are low quality but have a couple of fun problems. The blocks are nestled on a flat meadow and surrounded by pine trees, offering good summer conditions on excellent granite. Do not miss any of the problems on the north face of the Breakfast Boulder.

Directions: In South Fork begin mileage at the intersection of US Route 160 and State Route 149. Drive west on Hwy. 160 for 1.4 miles and turn left on Beaver Creek Road. Drive another 2.8 miles to the left turn (dirt road) to reach Million Reservoir (a sign is on the right before the dirt road). Go up the steep dirt road for 0.3 mile to a parking area. Walk southwest from the toilet then continue south—a faint trail leads to the boulders—for approximately 300 yards. More boulders litter the hillside to the south.

BREAKFAST BOULDER

The highest quality block in the area with excellent problems on its striped north face.

1. V1 ★
On the north face of the left block is a double arête. Start low and left and make one move to reach the right arête.

2. V5 ★★★
The best problem in the Breakfast Boulders. Begin on the left white jug and move straight up the face. A classic boulder problem!

3. V2 ★★
Just right is another white jug. Climb straight up. Pretty damn close to classic.

4. V3 ★★
Start on the low jugs above the little block and go straight up to a thin pocket top-out. Almost classic.

5. V0
The left slab problem on the southwest face.

6. V0
The wiggle seam slab problem on the southwest face. Dirty on top.

7. V1
Right of the wiggle seam is a pocketed slab. Filthy on top.

8. V3 ★
On the northeast face of the left block is a problem moving up to a broken piece of the face.

9. V4 ★
Right of #8 and left of the tree is another problem beginning in the layback then up to a difficult top-out. Dirty on top.

SMALL BOULDER

The small block directly across the trail from the Breakfast Boulder.

1. V1
The south face problem.

2. V2
The left side of the east face.

3. V1
A low start in the middle of the east face.

Naomi Guy FAing

Monte Vista's Boulder City

The expanse of rhyolite boulders near Monte Vista is an impressive sight. Every size and shape of burnt orange and terracotta hued boulder can be found, with all kinds of huecos, pockets, and edges. The quality of the bouldering does not always match the appearance, because the texture and fragility of the rock can be detrimental to flesh and psyche. Many of the boulders are house-size, but short safe problems exist; the landings tend towards flat, which is little relief on some of the 25-foot-tall journeys. If you are a spoiled brat (i.e., hate pain and blood) when it comes to bouldering, then avoid Monte Vista, but hardpersons will lap it up.

Directions: From Monte Vista take CO 15 south from the intersection of CO 15/US 160 for 12.2 miles. The road turns to dirt at the intersection of CO 15/FR 250. Take a right (headed west) and drive 8.3 miles passing through a small rhyolite canyon and past a National Forest sign. Go left on FR 2502A (the sign may not be present); FR 2502A is the second dirt road on the left after passing through the canyon. Drive 0.5 mile to the boulders on the left of the road.

V7

North (headed back down and above the road) from the Heart Boulder approximately 85 yards is a set of two boulders. Go to the uphill boulder's north scooped face. Climb the north-facing, steep set of good huecos.

The Bulb Boulder

Uphill approximately 25 yards from the V7 and behind tall pines is a well-featured pocketed boulder.

☐ 1. **V3** 🔵
The face just left of a stump. Climb the pockets through a bulge.

☐ 2. **V0** 🔵
A superb easy pocket problem on the south face starting from a big ol' hueco.

Heart Boulder

This is the house-size boulder first encountered down FR 2502A, with numerous large huecos big enough to sit in or squat under. The "heart" is evident when looking at the north face. Problems on this boulder tend toward big and bad-ass. Bring as many crash pads as you can.

☐ 1. **V4** ★★★
From a low start on the southeast face, climb out the white hueco then up the pocketed face to a casual top-out.

☐ 2. **Rebekah V5** ★★★ 🔵
Climb up and up and up the black stripe on the north face starting right of the undercut roof. Exit above the low roof on good edges to a bomber pocket. A direct start (V7) to this problem starts under the roof on the small huecos and traverses onto the face.

☐ 3. **Perfect 10 V3** ★★★ 🔵
Just right of #2, before the steepest part of the north face, climb up, up, and away on the pocketed wall. Many small edges can be used between the more obvious pockets to create ten excellent moves.

☐ 4. **Man in the Moon V3** ★★★ 🔵
Again start right in the steeper black rock and climb straight up the sharp edges and pockets. This line is perfectly spectacular—just like its neighbors.

Pat Wilde on Rebekah V5

Fireside Boulder

The smoke-stained boulder with a big firepit next to it, 10 yards north of Heart Boulder.

❑ **1. V0**
The line left of the overhang and firepit.

❑ **2. V1** ★
The line on the right of the overhang. Start off the hueco and go to good pockets.

❑ **3. V3** ★
On the back is a colorful, clean, pocketed face ending on a left-leaning arête.

Scoop Boulder

Uphill to the north 50 yards from Heart Boulder. The south-facing scoop is easily visible from Heart Boulder. Not pictured.

❑ **1. V3** ★
On the right edge of the scoop, climb up the rough pockets to a big dirty slab.

East Scoop Block

This massive boulder is located five yards east of the Scoop Boulder. The west face is an unmowed lawn of lichen. The east face offers clean lines with bad landings. The easiest downclimb is on the north face. Not pictured.

❑ **1. V2** ★★
Climb the left side of the southeast face on pockets.

❑ **2. V0** ★
The slab line left of the cleanest face and right of #1.

❑ **3. V3** ★★
Climb the clean face under the small roof on excellent pockets then pull over on small holds to a scary exit.

Substantial Slab Boulder

Directly above Scoop Boulder to the north 15 yards. A nice flat area, and a massive fir tree, is at the base of the problems.

❑ **1. V?**
Climb the west face on pockets.

❑ **2. V?**
The left, blunt, southwest arête. A hard start to gain the sinker two-finger pocket.

❑ **3. V0** ★★
The clean south slab left of the seam.

❑ **4. V0** ★
Climb the left-angling seam. The top is dirty—so climb under control.

❑ **5. The Slab V0** ★★
Just to the right of the huge fir is a 25-foot slab before the wall gets steeper.

❑ **6. V?**
Pull through the steep lower wall to the monster slab above.

❑ **7. V?**
Climb the extremely tall vertical southeast face.

Fireside Boulder #3 V3

Substantial Slab

Black Boulder

BLACK BLOCK

Located 20 yards east of the Heart Boulder. The best problems reside on the east face. Many other problems exist beyond those listed.

❏ 1. **V2** ★★
The left side of the east face, before the arête. Perfect landing.

❏ 2. **V1** ★★
Climb just right of #1 on good edges. Perfect landing.

❏ 3. **V5** ★★
A hard problem starting just left of the low hueco and making two hard moves at the start. A low start boosts the grade to V?+.

❏ 4. **V2** ★
Climb the left side of the scoop facing the dirt road. Excellent pockets to a friable exit.

WARM-UP SLAB AREA

The Warm-Up was one of the early developed blocks and as the years pass the neighboring boulders have revealed numerous fun problems, with the potential for plenty more. This flat area has become the newest camping zone.

WARM-UP SLAB

A low-angle boulder located 30 yards east of the Black Block. All problems on the west face are V0.

❏ 1. **V1** ★
Directly behind the Warm-Up Slab is a small block with two V1 problems.

SMOOTH BROWN BOULDER

Located above The Root Canal, 40 yards to the east. The upper massive boulder making up the conglomeration has numerous projects on the north and east faces that require plenty of pads. No photo.

❏ 1. **Smooth Brown V2**
Absolutely perfect slab facing west (towards the road) below massive upper Smooth Brown Boulder. A V1 is just left.

❏ 2. **Make it Your Bitch V4**
Crimpy west face 25 yards uphill from the uphill side of the Smooth Brown Boulder.

DIAGONAL SEAM BLOCK

A big boulder located 80 yards uphill from the Warm-Up Slab. A distinct diagonal seam splits the brown west face. No photo.

❏ 1. **V3** ★★
A great warm-up traverse from right to left along the seam and exiting before the north face.

❏ 2. **V2**
The line before the wall overhangs the adjacent boulder. Long descent across a dirty slab.

❏ 3. **V0**
The problem just right of #2. Same award-winning slab descent.

PETRA BLOCK

This mixed-quality block is located 40 yards east of the Warm-Up Slab. A gorgeous lichen-covered arête faces northwest with a wide wall stretching to the south face.

❑ 1. **Allesandrina V1** ★★
Climb the beautiful northwest arête, starting off the block. A low start adds quite a punch to the festivities.

❑ 2. **V5** ★★
Just right of #1 is a pocketed face to a hard move to reach the lip.

❑ 3. **Petra V4** ★★
Climb the black south face on positive edges and a great pocket.

❑ 4. **V3**
The scooped face to the right of Petra.

ROAD BLOCK

The boulder sitting directly below the Petra Block a mere 10 yards. The pocketed west face (facing the road) has problems. Not pictured.

❑ 1. **V6** ★
Climb the gold face straight up at the left end of the diagonal seam.

❑ 2. **V4** ★
Starts right of #1 then heads straight up and left of the obvious loose flake.

BLACK AND TAN WALL AKA THE STREAKED FACE

A long black east face littered with numerous problems. Located 120 yards uphill (northeast) from the mini mud cliff, 100 yards east of the Heart Boulder area. Problems listed left to right.

❑ 1. **Forever Becoming V6** ★★★★
The beautiful southeast golden arête just right of the high overhang. Superb moves on quality pockets.

❑ 2. **The Ribler V2** ★
Just around the east corner (right) from FB. Think slot!

❑ 3. **V4** ★★
Right again on tight pockets through undercling…two starts to the same exit.

❑ 4. **V3**
Above the log landing is a low start on big pockets.

❑ 5. **V3**
The corner before Right Streak.

❑ 6. **Right Streak V2**
A jump problem on the shield right of small low corner. Big jugs up high.

I WANT IT BLOCK

Located directly below the Black and Tan is a decent thin block.

❑ 1. **Left Arête V?**
Too thin to handle.

❑ 2. **I Want It V3**
Southwest face on pockets. Loose flake.

Mike Freischlag on Black and Tan Wall V4

Black and Tan

The Ribler V2

THE HUECO AREA

Another vast expanse of good blocks located 0.3 mile down FR 2502A from Heart Boulder, or a short three-minute walk. The blocks are just off the road on the left.

THE ROOT CANAL

A distinctive boulder with a small tunnel through the entire base (the boulder looks like a tooth). The block sits 25 feet from the dirt road and has problems on every side. The downclimb, which faces the road, is a chore at V0—loose and licheny.

❏ 1. **Triage V2** ★★
On the west face is a pocketed problem with one painful lock-off.

❏ 2. **The Nasty Downclimb V0**
The only way off the boulder besides pitching 12 feet onto pads. A loose flake marks the start and end.

❏ 3. **V1** ★
The slab affair to the right of #2 and before the silken tan and red face.

❏ 4. **V7** ★★
Climb the thin pocketed face left of the southeast arête.

❏ 5. **V6** ★
Climb straight up the east face on pockets and the area's sharpest edges. The top-out has massive jugs.

❏ 6. **V?**
The east arête on small pockets.

❏ 7. **Lolita V4** ★★
Climb up the middle of the north face to an obvious edge and pocket, then move right to bad edges and an insecure top-out.

❏ 8. **V4** ★
The harder V4 line starting from the bomber pocket on the northwest corner and exiting up the same minute edges as Lolita.

❏ 9. **V1** ★
Directly across the road from Root Canal is a maroon face, with a big pocket at mid-height, facing the road. A hueco problem (V2) sits just to the left on an adjacent boulder and is much harder from a sds.

❏ 10. **V1** ★
On the boulder just south of Root Canal is a short problem out the hueco, off a bomber edge and tiny pocket. One move to the top flop-out.

❏ 11. **Kia V4** ★★
Found on the northwest arête 20 yards to the north of Root Canal (on the way to the Hueco Boulder). Start low on the sloping hueco with tiny pockets then move over the lip to the right slab face.

❏ 12. **Commit V2** 🔲 🔲
Directly uphill 35 yards from Kia facing east is a tall outing that follows seams above a ramp. A massive project is just left.

❏ 13. **Mikes Giant Slabs V0-V4** 🔲
To the east a few yards from Commit is a south-facing slab with problems topping out around 20-25 feet.

❏ 14. **Brown Eye V2** ★★
Found 25 yards west of Root Canal. Climb the west face's eye.

❏ 15. **Finger Thumb V3** ★
Found 20 yards west of Brown Eye. Climb the south seam. A V1 climbs the dirty southeast slab to the right.

Eric Pals on #6

Eric Pals on Kia V4

#9 V1

Brown Eye

Finger Thumb

Roadie Boulder V9

ROADIE BOULDER V9

An immaculate 45-degree southeast-facing, pocketed overhang 12 yards downhill from Brown Eye and close to the dirt road.

Across the road from the V9 is a set of two boulders.

❏ 1. **V1**
North face problem starting from a low hueco and exiting left.

❏ 2. **V4**
Start on the right side of the big hueco and surmount the hueco roof with spread eagle skills.

❏ 3. **V3**
The vertical wall right of the big hueco on micro-pockets to a high-ish sloping gray pocket then the top.

THE HUECO BOULDER

From Root Canal walk uphill to the north 40 yards past Kia and a slabby boulder (many V0s can be done, with a nice flat top to hang out on). The problems on the Hueco Boulder face southwest and begin in a huge overhang.

❏ 1. **White Guilt V4** ★★
The left hueco on the steep southwest face. A hard start, off the hueco's left side, to a huge ledge.

❏ 2. **Monika V6** ★★★
Start with the right hand in the white hueco and the left hand in the lowest undercling. Move up and over the lip to the big pockets and a harrowing slab finish. The Bathtub direct start is V9 and begins as low as possible in the inverted bathtub.

❏ 3. **V0s**
Fifteen yards to the northwest is a slew of low-angle V0 slab problems on two blocks that are easily visible from Hueco Boulder.

White Guilt V4

YASMINE'S BOULDER

Just up the hill to the north from Hueco Boulder is an obvious overhanging arête.

☐ 1. Cliché V4 ★★
Climb the golden face left of #2, utilizing the bomber edges and some questionable laybacks.

☐ 2. Yasmine's Arête V5 ★★★
A near-perfect arête route, except for the pain in the tips. Starts low on the arête to good pockets then a scary throw and top-out.

☐ 3. V0s
The excellent pocketed slabs around the corner on the north face.

☐ 4. V0-V3
More problems exist on the south side—but the rock hurts soooo bad!

☐ 5. DYC V3 ★★
The north-facing hueco left of Cliché. Starts low on lovely bat dung.

Pat Wilde on Cliche V4

Pat Wilde on Yasmine's Arête V5

THE REVEREND

Yet another big boulder sitting up the hillside from Root Canal. Walk north 100 yards past a couple of enormous blocks. The problems reside on the northeast face and rarely see the light of day. The downclimbs require patience (or a little endurance to downclimb #1).

☐ 1. Created by God V0 ★ 😊
Climb the left side of the face starting on pockets or a sharp edge to the biggest jugs on the block. Finish up the cruiser edges to the top. This is the easiest downclimb.

☐ 2. Loved by All V3 ★ 😊
Climb up the middle of the face starting on a good pinch then into the right-facing mini-corner and the top pockets and edges.

☐ 3. Feared by Satan V5 ★★ 😊
Start the same as #2 then move right to a good layback and bomber jug. The straight-up exit slab is a serious affair (no holds visible to the naked eye) but fortunately the line exits immediately right of the exit for #2.

The author is Feared by Satan V5

Hueco Warm-ups

THE HONEYCOMB V1 ★
Down the gully to the left (east) of The Reverend approximately 25 yards. The problem climbs through—you guessed it—a honeycombed face.

HUECO WARM-UPS
Head uphill and to the right 70 yards from Root Canal (a little right of the enormous blocks separating Root Canal and The Reverend). The wall is littered with numerous huecos and the problems face the dirt road. Every line on this wall is a blast!

☐ 1. **V3** ★★
The left problem. It slaps over the lip from a good two-finger pocket.

☐ 2. **V2** ★★
Climb the problem just right of #1.

☐ 3. **V2** ★★
Start in the right side of the larger huecos to monodoigts and a balancy top-out.

☐ 4. **V3** ★★
The rightmost pocketed face in the small corridor.

LESS THAN DESIRABLE BOULDER
Directly down the hill from Hueco Warm-up wall and 40 yards east from Root Canal is a large rectangular block.

☐ 1. **V2** ★★
Climb the thin southeast arête.

☐ 2. **V0**
A couple of dirty V0 problems climb the southwest face.

The Honeycomb V1

NED'S WONDERLAND OF ROCK

Another 40 yards east from Less than Desirable are two blocks with extremely nice problems on short north-facing overhangs. The boulders are a few yards from the dirt road.

UPPER NED

The block farther from the road than Lower Ned.

❏ 1. **V4** ★★
A low start on the north face and left of the corner. Climbs to a shallow pocket and bad edge then to the top. A dynamic problem is just right.

❏ 2. **V3** ★★
A low start on the northwest face, then up good edges and pockets.

LOWER NED

The block closer to the dirt road.

❏ 1. **V4** ★★
Another low start on the north face, up through great edges then pockets.

❏ 2. **V4** ★★
Just right, start low to a throw to the ramp and a long reach over the top.

❏ 3. **V4** ★★
Start off the ramp and move right to the left-facing mini-ramp with a pocket and exit.

❏ 4. **V3** ★
Climb the west arête.

❏ 5. **V0**
Climb the southwest face left side up the slab.

NED'S POCKET WALL

Yet another big boulder that looks like all the others. Walk east approximately 60 yards (do not go uphill) staying in the open meadow (go up before reaching a large boulder with dirty seams and possible chalk). Then walk straight uphill 20 yards—the V3 faces uphill. No photo.

❏ 1. **V0**
Climb the dirty east face.

❏ 2. **V3** ★★
Climb the short, pocketed northeast face. If you like shallow two-finger pockets you'll dig this.

GOLDEN FACE BLOCK

A perfect golden west face with an impressive left-trending arch. Walk 60 yards east across the hillside (do not go up) from Ned's Pocket Wall.

❏ 1. **V3** ★★ 🪨 💧
Climb the seam on the left side of the west face.

THE ELDO CONTINGENT'S AREA

Fifty yards straight uphill from the Golden Face is an alcove with three sides. An extremely tall left wall is undercut at the base with a wide chimney separating it from a gorgeous arête. A shorter clean face is right of the arête.

❏ 1. **Eric's Arête V5** ★★ 🪨 💧
Climb the huge arête right of the wide chimney.

❏ 2. **V0-V3** ★
On the shorter block right of #1 is a selection of problems moving around the corner.

Lower Ned #3

Golden Face Block

Eldo Contingent's

Eric Pals on the Hone Stone's Bernholtz's Arête V6 Photo by J. Houck

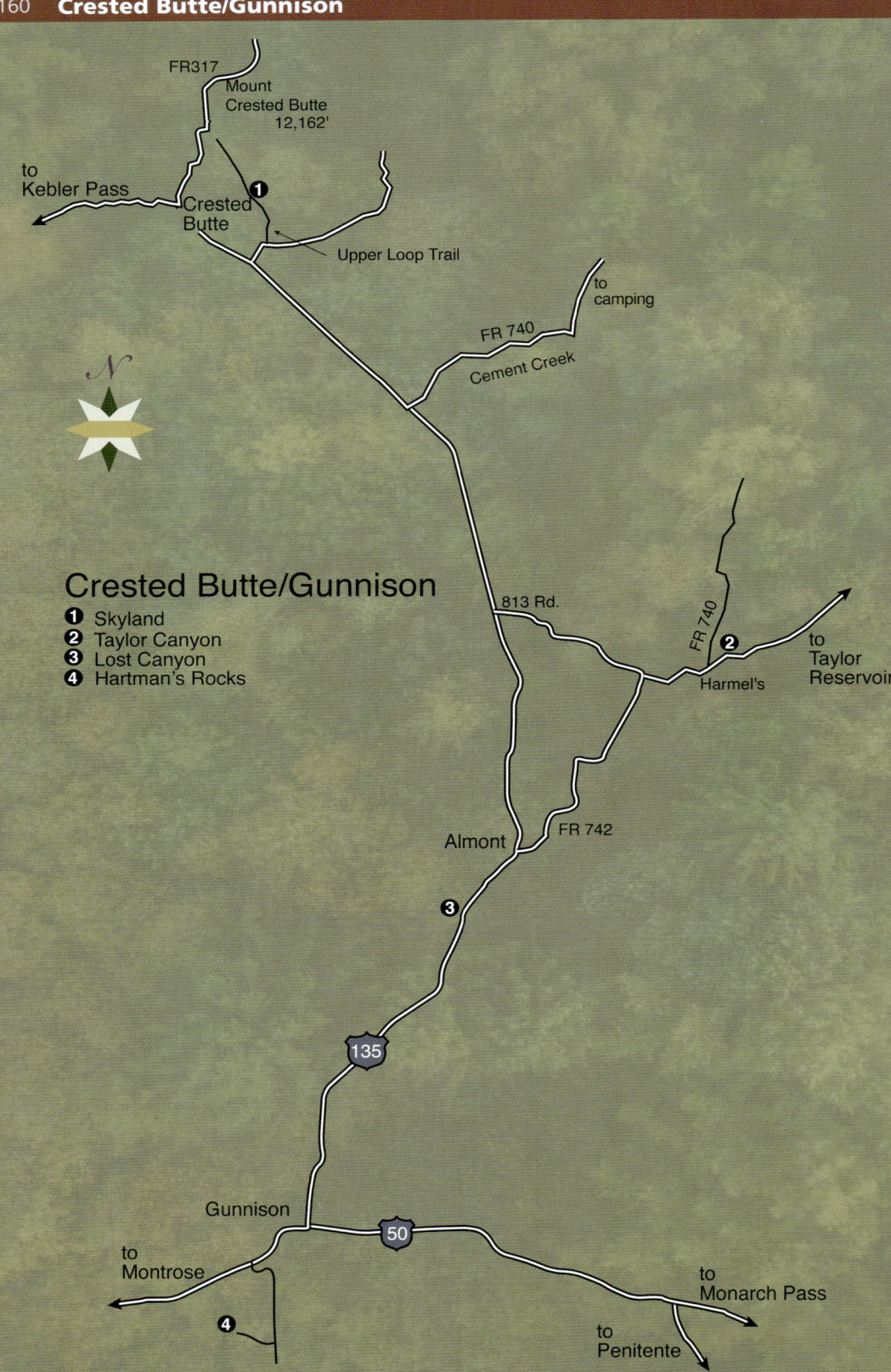

FR317

Mount
Crested Butte
12,162'

to
Kebler Pass

❶ Crested
Butte

Upper Loop Trail

to
camping

FR 740

Cement Creek

N

Crested Butte/Gunnison

❶ Skyland
❷ Taylor Canyon
❸ Lost Canyon
❹ Hartman's Rocks

813 Rd.

FR 740

❷

to
Taylor
Reservoir

Harmel's

Almont   FR 742

❸

135

Gunnison

50

to
Montrose

❹

to
Penitente

to
Monarch Pass

CRESTED BUTTE/GUNNISON

SKYLAND

On the lower western flank of Mount Crested Butte lies a cluster of spectacular granite boulders. Nestled in aspens and alpine meadows, these boulders have easy access and a beautiful panoramic view. Many classic problems climb the immense faces on dead vertical terrain or substantial overhangs. With problems ranging from V0 to V11 many challenges await the highball aficionado. Those who enjoy contrived problems and traverses won't be disappointed either. Be sure to climb on the High Times Boulder—arguably one of the best in the state.

Directions: From Crested Butte's four-way stop sign continue towards Mount Crested Butte. Take a right on Snowmass Road (no sign—only one for Hunter Hill) at 2.3 miles from the four-way stop. Turn right on Hunter Hill Road immediately after turning onto Snowmass Road and drive 0.5 mile to a parking area where the road bends. Take the Upper Loop Trail south for at least 15 minutes to the boulders.

Note: the boulders are listed from south to north.

WARM UP ROCK

The farthest south area with two boulders just off the Upper Loop Trail. The well-chalked lines are reasonable problems that get the juices flowing. The northeast face (not facing the trial) has terrific jug haul problems from V0 to V3.

Warm Up Rock

❒ 1. **Mahone V5** ★★
Just left of the tree on the west face is a sit-down start that moves through two good pockets to a long reach and the sloping top. A traverse from right to left on the west face is V2.

❒ 2. **Hell's Ditch V2** ★
On the left side of the south face is a sit-down problem that ascends a faint black-lichen streak on minuscule crystals or a long reach to the top.

❒ 3. **Micro V1** ★
Climb just right of #2 to the small slot below the lip then an easy top-out. A good variation off the left-hand undercling all the way to the top is V1.

THE SPICE ROCK

To the south of Warm Up Rock, only a few yards, is a lone block with Spicy (V5)—a traverse of the east face to the south face. Not pictured.

PORTRAIT AREA

From the backside of Warm Up Rock walk into the aspens 25 yards to a trail leading to the left (northwest). Take this trail for 100 yards to another intersection. Go right uphill (north) a little over 100 yards to two huge boulders with a tall jug-haul face on the downhill (south) side of the first block encountered. There are problems all over both boulders and only the most traveled (i.e. good ones) are included here.

PORTRAIT OF AN ARTIST BOULDER

❒ 1. **V0** 🌀 🌀
The jug-haul facing south and first encountered from the hike up the hillside.

❒ 2. **V2** 🌀 🌀
Ten feet right of the V0 is a nice face that can be done utilizing good left hand holds or bypassing the better left edges and moving straight up on less than ideal holds.

North Face
Problems listed from left to right.

❒ 3. **V1**
The crimpy open corner just right of the slot separating the two boulders.

❒ 4. **V2**
Super sloping starter holds on the slightly less than vertical face just right of the V1 problem.

❒ 5. **Portrait of an Artist V5** ★★★
Excellent sloping problem facing uphill (northwest) on the boulder's far right side. Start real low on the lowest edge below the higher corner, or off the excellent incuts at crotch level for a tad easier problem and move up and right away from the corner.

Andrew Null on Portrait of an Artist V2

RED SKY BOULDER

The block adjacent to the Portrait Boulder. A tight-squeeze corridor separates the boulders.

West Face

☐ 1. **Red Sky V6** ★★

The awesome, obvious, highly chalked problem residing above the ankle-breaking talus. Start low for the full grade (V10) or bypass the initial squatty sit start for a hard V6 problem. Bring your pads!

☐ 2. **V?**

Immediately left of Red Sky is a newer, thin, sloping edge/gaston problem much harder than Red Sky.

Southeast Face

☐ 3. **V4** ★★

On the far left side of the southeast face (next to the slot) is a sloper shelf to start to a bad crimp then up and right to a good incut edge.

☐ 4. **V5**

The shallow pocket affair just right of the V4 with a big throw to the high shelf. A V2 is immediately right.

☐ 5. **V3**

Start off the sloping hueco on the wall's right side and go for the top.

Northeast Overhang

A couple of problems venture out the steep face. Only one is clean.

☐ 6. **V3**

On the far left side starting from a pinch and moving up the seam to a good edge then the arête.

☐ 7. **V11** ★★

This new addition to the already stellar bouldering at Skyland introduces the most difficult face climbing in the aspens. From the uphill side of the Portrait Area walk east and north for 175 yards on a nearly non-existent trail to a faint drainage with historical trash (metal cable) lying on the ground then straight uphill (north) to a massive block with a couple of new lines. The V11 follows sloping edges through the steep section of the wall (landscaped landing zone). A V3 slab is to the left and more projects are right on both sides of the aesthetic arête. A highball V2 is on the next boulder to the east.

THE WAVE

Uphill to the northeast from Warm Up Rock, approximately 75 yards, is a 15-foot tall boulder with excellent slab problems on the southwest face.

☐ 1. **Slab Masters of the Universe V2** ★★

Start seven feet left of #2 and climb straight up.

☐ 2. **Slabs Kick Ass V2** ★★

The awesome slab in the center of the west face. Climbs past the dung-like covered edge at nine feet up to either atrocious handholds or a dyno to the lip.

☐ 3. **Jagged V0** ★

Begin on the lower right and traverse the thin, fin-like lip of the boulder to the left and an easy mantel finish.

The Wave

Kurt Frye on The Wave's Slabs Kick Ass V2

Sam Sommers cruising Slab Happy V3. Photo by Sarah Nicholson

THE WEDGE

Found southeast from The Battleship approximately 25 yards. This block offers overhanging arêtes and a couple of easy slabs. Walk north on the trail from Warm Up Rock until Joint Rock is on the left and The Battleship is on the right, in the aspens.

❏ **1. Slab Happy V3** ★
Start the same as #2 and move left to the east arête then up the slab. A sds is V5.

❏ **2. Captain EO V4** ★
Climb the north arête, staying to the right.

❏ **3. Left V2** ⏱ ◉
A superb tall problem in an open corner with long reaches between good edges.

❏ **4. Middle and Right V0** ⏱
The two problems right of Left are excellent low-angle affairs and great warm-ups.

The Wedge ① ② ③ ④

JOINT ROCK

The huge boulder on the left side of the trail after a short stroll from Warm Up Rock. The problems on this 23-foot-tall block are all committing and first class.

❏ **1. Big V4** ★★★ ⏱
Climbs the left arête of the west face to the midway point then pulls onto the easy north slab. The Long Shot (V5) is a classic of classics that starts as a sit down to Big and continues up the overhanging west face to a fun dyno and, fortunately, a reasonable top-out after 20 feet of climbing.

❏ **2. Escape Hatch V2** ★ ⏱
Climbs the right side of the west face from a low start and pulls onto the dirty slab less than halfway to the top. The Filth Pig (V6) is a terrifying extension of Escape Hatch that continues up the dirty arête.

❏ **3. Blunt Boy V1** ★★★ ⏱
Classic. Climb straight up the 23-foot tall south face.

❏ **4. Mister Twister V2** ★★ ⏱
Just right six feet is an alternative start to #3 that eventually ends the same as Blunt Boy.

Joint Rock

① ② ③ ④

THE BATTLESHIP

Directly across the trail from Joint Rock is a massive monolith in the woods before entering the swamp. Only four problems have been done on this block with a few new desperate problems waiting in the wings.

☐ 1. All Hands on Deck V5 ★★★

A great overhanging traverse beginning off a block below the lip that skirts the right side of the west face and finishes around the corner.

☐ 2. Anchors Away V2 ★

Starts on a big jug above an ankle-breaking stone and muckles through the offwidth on the south face.

☐ 3. Tropic of Capricorn V7 ★★

On the right of the blank orange face is a line of thin sidepulls and edges. Climb in from the left on terrible holds. It eases up the higher one gets. A V6 starts on the low, fragile, right jug and finishes to the right. Not pictured.

HICK ROCKS

A few yards north of The Battleship is a small conglomeration of short boulders with a few eliminates and sds problems.

☐ 1. 16 Horsepower V4 ★

Starts on the far left side next to an adjacent block. Climb right and finish left of #2's top moves.

☐ 2. Electric Hoedown V5 ★★

A sds on the blunt arête that moves left to the layback arête for the right hand with good edges for the left hand, then the top.

☐ 3. Still Feel Gone V4 ★

Begin in a low small pod to the right of #2 and traverse left to the orange lichen. Go straight up to the top off a right hand pinch.

☐ 4. V6 ★★ ●

The far right problem on the east face.

SUPERNATURAL BOULDER

A lone problem approximately 15 yards northeast from Hick Rocks.

☐ 1. V9 ★

The problem starts low in an overhang on a big bulbous hunk of granite to bad gastons and immense amounts of pain. Finish to the right on excruciating edges and bad feet. The problem looks like a three star but the pain keeps it at one star.

The Battleship

Hick Rocks

Supernatural

☐ 2. Supernatural V10 ★ ●

A super classic hard problem on impeccable granite! Instead of venturing right head straight up with good crimps for the left hand and not so good holds for the right. Make sure to bring an attentive spotter and a couple of good pads for the back slapping block.

☐ 3. The Wilder Arête V10 ★★

Just around the corner to the left from Supernatural is a double-digit problem which heads up the north arête from a real low start on terrible sloping holds.

Wilder Arête

HIGH TIMES

Approximately 25 yards west of Hick Rocks resides an awesome 19-foot-tall boulder with ultra-classic lines on the east face. Reasonable slabs brush shoulders across the west face. The star system for these problems does not do them justice.

❏ 1. **Machine Head V5** ★★
A traverse across the east face from #2 to #5.

❏ 2. **Left El Skyland V3** ★★★
An unbelievable highball problem on the left of the east face. Begins in a bomber undercling and climbs through the left-facing dihedral to massive jugs and an easy top-out.

❏ 3. **Center El Skyland V4** ★★★
Six feet right of #1 is a spectacular 19-foot problem that climbs bomber edges to an incut flake. The top-out requires a long reach from a flat jug to a bulbous hold over the top.

❏ 4. **The J Crack V5** ★★★
Five feet right of Center is a right-facing corner/ramp that leads to hard-to-find edges and a scary flop finish. The most committing problem on the east face.

❏ 5. **Right El Skyland V2** ★★★
Begin on the far right of the east face and climb up huge edges to a hueco. Move right to the blunt arête and a giant jug. The final moves are a little tenuous.

❏ 6. **Casual Corner V1**
On the north face is a left-facing dihedral with good holds. A V2 variation climbs the slab to the left without using the dihedral.

❏ 7. **Off Ramp V0** ★★
The downclimb. Climbs the middle edges of the north face.

❏ 8. **Cheeky Monkey V1** ★
Climbs the blunt west arête. A true slab just to the right is V3.

HONE STONE

The northern most developed boulder at Skyland. Walk north past the High Times boulder for a minute. A large block on the left side of the trail sits in the meadow. Many outstanding problems are found here.

❏ 1. **Atomic aka Tick Fever V7** ★★★★
Climbs the middle of the south face through a sharp pocket to opposing sidepulls then a vicious slope finish on the slab. A V9 direct start climbs from a sit using the thin left-angling edge to reach the starting holds on Atomic.

❏ 2. **Bernholtz's Arête V6** ★★★
An ultra-classic problem that climbs the overhanging southeast arête. The start uses a two-finger pocket then an arête pinch to gain the pocket on the top. Finish by moving right to a good edge. A sit-down start called The Weeping Warrior checks in at V8.

❏ 3. **The East Slabs V1** ★
A number of reasonable slabs begin by pulling over a small bulge or into a scoop.

❏ 4. **The Southwest Slabs V1–V6** ★★
A number of slab variations climb the varying angled faces. The problems on the left (west) face are far more difficult.

❏ 5. **V5**
A problem left of Atomic and starting on the steep face then groveling onto the slab.

Hone Stone

THE SHIELD

A massive orange and gold block to the northeast about 20 yards (across the Upper Loop Trail) from the Hone Stone. Not pictured.

❏ 1. **V2**
Climb the left side of the huge burnt orange face.

❏ 2. **V?**
A big tall problem done by a big tall climber. Up the face right of #1.

The author on Right El Skyland V2

ZACH'S CAMPGROUND

This collection of boulders sports a couple of entertaining problems hidden away in the woods above the Upper Loop (closer to the Mt. Crested Butte cliffs).

Directions: The blocks are uphill and northeast from The Shield approximately 100 yards. A distinct trail can be taken from The Shield (20 yards northwest from of the Hone Stone) headed northwest then back northeast (look for faint game trails).

❏ **1. V5** ★★
The new line on the first boulder encountered from the faint trail. The problem begins in the open dihedral with a jump start to a good flat jug then hard moves to the finishing slab. A direct start will up the ante substantially.

❏ **2. V0**
The easy left-angling arête right of the open dihedral.

❏ **3. V6** ★
Hard left-to-right traverse on the back of the boulder.

❏ **4. V3** ★
A sds on the blunt arête right of the traverse's end.

❏ **5. V5**
Climb the left arête (to the far left of #1) using the right-hand face holds left of the low-angle dihedral leading to the boulder's top.

❏ **6. V0**
The low-angle dihedral, which is one of the easiest ways to downclimb the block.

❏ **7. V3** ★
Just left of the main block is a lone fin with a clean, slightly overhanging face starting from a low start. The arête to the left is an easy V0.

TAYLOR CANYON

A granite laden canyon with many multi-pitch routes and, fortunately, some fine bouldering. The developed boulders are found at the base of Harmel's Second Buttress—the largest cliff within spitting distance of Harmel's Resort. A small, although ample boulderfield supplies the majority of problems in the vicinity. Many other boulders exist farther up-canyon as well as just up the dirt road leading to North Fork Campground.

Directions: From US Route 50/135 intersection in Gunnison take State Route 135 to Almont (10.2 miles). Follow the right fork (Gunnison County 742) toward Taylor Reservoir for 7.5 miles. The boulders are found below the granite cliff on the left side of the road and directly behind the sign for North Fork Campground.

THE SUGAR CUBE

The largest square boulder at the base of The Second Buttress. It is also the closest to the North Bank sign.

❏ **1. Slabs Rule V2** ★★
Maybe not! This is real slab climbing with bad feet and atrocious holds that torture unknown muscles.

❏ **2. Average Arête V0** ★★
Not really an arête. The flake system on the south face. Great for stretching.

❏ **3. White Grease Streak V0** ★★
On the east face is a crystal dike with good edges.

❏ **4. Out of Bounds V1** ★
Just right of #3 is an eliminate that climbs the upper right arête without using the ledge.

❏ **5. Gloomy V3** ★
A traverse of the boulder's north face starting on an obvious low jug and going right on slopers. A complete traverse of the boulder without using the top holds is Rock Around the Block (V5). Not pictured.

THE UFO

Closer to the cliff a few yards from The Sugar Cube is a small overhanging block with a nice traverse.

❏ **6. The Butter Hole V3** ★★
Start on the far right fin then traverse left then up before reaching the adjacent boulder. A nasty V4 called Final Frontier mantels the sloping lip halfway into The Butter Hole.

The Sugar Cube

The UFO

THE SLOT BLOCK

To the north of The Sugar Cube approximately 20 yards is a golden face with two technical problems. Not pictured.

❐ 7. **Snug Slot V4** ★★

Climb the east arête utilizing a bad finger jam to start. Finish up slopers and an unstable top-out.

❐ 8. **Something Must Break V4** ★

Just right of #7 is a sit start below a rock scar. Start on a good sloping edge then gaston like the dickens up to progressively better edges.

THE APOCALYPSE AREA

On the base of the second butress lies a 65-foot left-to-right traverse. It is located just past the wooden fence. Many eliminates can be done along the traverse.

THE PILLAR

A distinct tall boulder found up the campground road 80-odd yards on the left. A tall slabby side faces downriver and a steeper side upriver.

❐ 1. **V4** ★★

The slab that climbs the detached flake.

❐ 2. **V7** ★★★ 🔵

Easily the best looking problem in Taylor Canyon! Climb the slightly overhanging face left of the wide crack to a good edge at mid-height then throw to a flat ledge.

THE GUTTER

Located 0.2 mile down North Fork Campground road on left. A small spot (a car a couple yards from cliffband) might fit. The name of the cliff does not do it justice; it only provides an obvious name since a drainage pipe is found on the left side of the wall. The Gutter has 50 feet of solid granite and too many problems to list—a great place to get a pump. Problems range from V0 to V8 (harder as one moves right). A good sandbag V5 traverses the wall from left to right. A V3 slab is on the right of the wide chimney. Best not to top out—unless you like to solo on less-than-ideal rock.

BONZAI BOULDER

Also reached by parking 0.1 mile past One Mile Campground (just upcanyon from North Fork Campground). Park on the right just past a cattle guard then walk up the road 30 yards then down and across the river (low water only). Bonzai is visible on the far bank.

❐ 1. **V0-V3** ★★

A selection of problems on the north face from straight-ups to a traverse. Not pictured.

❐ 2. **V2** ★★

Climb the northwest arête from a low start.

❐ 3. **V6**

Climb the ultra-thin seam right of #2 to sharp edges.

❐ 4. **V0**

The dirty west seam right of #3.

❐ 5. **V1** ★★

Climb the west slab found before the left-angling arête of #6.

❐ 6. **V4** ★

Climb the southwest arête starting from thin edges on the south face then moving into the sloping arête.

The Pillar

The Gutter

The Gutter

BONZAI EAST FACE PROBLEMS

❐ 7. **Bonzai Straight Up V9** ★★

Start on lowest layback and slap up the blunt bulge on slopers and bad sidepulls.

❐ 8. **Bonzai Left V6** ★★

Same start as #1, but move right then head straight up before the seam, leading to the tiny pine. Expect slopers and bad edges.

❐ 9. **Bonzai Right V5** ★★

Same start as #1 then move right and climb up the seam, exiting on holds right of the tiny pine.

MM10 BOULDER

Located 0.1 mile past mile marker 10 on the right side of the highway (10.1 miles from Almont). A large pullout is present. This area is also a good spot to gain access to the opposite side of the Taylor River and many attractive boulders (very low water only).

The scattered boulders near MM10 see very little to absolutely no traffic. The first boulder has a couple of decent face climbs (V0-V3) on the east face and is only 30 yards from the highway. Other blocks can be found upriver in the woods and would require some concerted cleaning.

LONE PINE CAMPGROUND

Located 14.6 miles up Taylor Canyon from Almont on the right. A stellar block sits in campsite #12 (get this site and you can boulder to your heart's content). More small boulders are close by but the difficulty of #12 Block (V0-V7) will probably keep you busy for an overnight stay or two or three.

LOST CANYON

A ridge of Dakota Sandstone that faces south and east and caters to the V0 to V6 connoisseur. The incredible amounts of holds—in every shape and size—lends the area an abundance of contrived problems. Considering the orientation of the cliff and its easy access from the highway, bouldering can be done year round—even in the Gunnison Valley's harsh winters.

Pete's Wicked Traverse

Directions: Drive north on State Route 135 from the Highway 50/135 intersection in Gunnison for 7.5 miles. On the left side of the road is a long band of sandstone higher up the hillside. Park below the ridge in a pullout on the left (west) side of the highway. The pullout on the right with the mailboxes should not be used unless absolutely necessary. Stay well out of the way of the mailboxes if parking on the right! From the pullout a steep trail heads to the ridge.

PETE'S WICKED TRAVERSE

The detached part of the ridge that is seen after reaching level ground from the steep trail.

❏ **1. Pete's Wicked Traverse V5** ★
Starts on the left overhang and traverses right across the entire face.

❏ **2. Extra Stout V2** ★
Begin on the left-facing double flakes and climb up without using the big sidepull on the right of the small roof. The top-out is dirty.

❏ **3. Lard Ass V6**
A contrived problem nine feet right of #2 that traverses left very low from the jug at the base of the long flake system over to the double flakes on #2 then out right. Of course the big sidepull on the right of the small roof is off.

❏ **4. Average Ale V1** ★
Eleven feet right of the big flake system and right of the right-facing dihedral is a straight-up problem. A sit down start boosts the problem to V2.

The Cave Area

THE CAVE AREA

Twenty-five yards north of Pete's wall is a large roof beginning four feet off the dirt. A large carpet scrap is usually in place. Note: Many of the problems in the cave begin on the same hold—a twelve-finger edge that faces north and is called the starting hold in the following descriptions.

❏ **1. Atrocity Exhibition V5** ★
Begin on the starting hold and move left under the roof then out to the lip. Do not use the good jug on the lip but two small crimps to the right then a pinch for the left to get on the vertical face.

❏ **2. Unknown Pleasures V4** ★
From the starting hold make a huge reach straight out to the flat jug on the lip then up the face. A slightly harder variation matches on the flat lip jug then goes all the way to the sloper straight up from the jug without using any intermediates.

❏ **3. The Cave Lap V7** ★
On the north face of the cave (white rock) a circular, up and down problem can be done from the starting hold. Not shown.

❏ **4. BB Shot aka Bob's Dyno V3**
Two successive dynos from the pockets above the starting hold: first to an incut rail below the two-finger pocket, then to the rail above the pocket.

❏ **5. Flying High V6** ★
From the rail at the end of #4 dyno all the way to the distant corner up and right.

❏ **6. Nuerobashing V3** ★
Contrived and fun. From the starting hold climb right to small holds below a jug in the back of the big chalked bulb, then up the face without reaching around the arête.

THE MAIN HANG

Just past The Cave Area is a 200-foot vertical traverse with easy eliminates. No photo.

The Web Wall

THE WEB WALL

Past The Main Hang is a tall section of the ridge measuring 15 feet high. It is south facing and constitutes some of the highest bouldering at Lost Canyon.

❐ **1. Mortimer V1**
Just left of #2 is an uneventful problem that exits up and right on the ramp.

❐ **2. Spider Monkey V2** ⋆
Begin seven feet left of The Web and climb up bomber pockets.

❐ **3. The Web V1** ⋆⋆
Climb straight up the wall just left of the white streak. Super fun.

❐ **4. Caught in the Web V4** ⋆
A traverse of the wall from right to left and ending by climbing up before the slot.

FAT BOTTOM

An undercut section of the ridge that reminds the locals of buttocks. A south-facing buttocks is found about 50 yards north of The Web. Just left of Fat Bottom is a wall with interesting dynamic problems from V1 to V5.

❐ **1. Rank V5**
The sharp crimps just right of the crack. Of course, the left wall is off, no matter how much one's tips bleed.

❐ **2. Pit Full of Patchouli V4** ⋆
Start just right of the crack and climb right to the blunt arête and up on Fat Bottom Hippie Chicks.

❐ **3. Fat Bottom Hippie Chicks V3** ⋆⋆
Begins low and right on a flat jug then moves left on slopers and up the blunt arête. Hard for the grade.

❐ **4. Stinky V5** ⋆
Climb #3 to the arête but continue around to the crack.

Fat Bottom

TWEAK WALL

Almost at the north end of Lost Canyon is a 16-foot-tall wall with three distinct lines that climb the right wall of the open dihedral. A mere 15 yards north of Fat Bottom.

❐ **1. Glory Digger V5** ⋆
Begins just right of the corner on two bad underclings and climbs up tiny edges and eventually sinker pockets.

❐ **2. Celebrated Summer V7**
Same start as Glory Digger but climb right to a shallow pocket then up—off-routing the crack to the right.

❐ **3. The Old Timer Arête V0** ⋆⋆
Climbs the southeast arête on the dark brown rock.

THE LAST STOP

The final wall a few yards north of Tweak Wall, before the landings become hundred foot rolls down sage covered hillsides. Not pictured.

❐ **1. Last Stop V0** ⋆⋆
The blunt arête and the last good problem at Lost Canyon.

Tweak Wall

The Groove V1

Super Model V5

HARTMAN ROCKS

A few miles southwest from Gunnison is the best-smelling bouldering area in Colorado. The sagebrush expanse of inter-mittent granite outcrops has endless bouldering possibilities, and can satisfy the hungriest first ascentionist. Every year new areas are discovered and developed. Excellent side benefits of Hartman are the superb views of the Elk Range, the San Juans, and the Collegiates as well as terrific mountain biking. Pick up a map at Rock and Roll Sports that shows the trails, and loca-tions of additional bouldering areas.

Directions: From the intersection of US Route 50/135 take Hwy. 50 west towards Montrose for l.6 miles to the brown sign for Hartman Rocks Recreation Area. Turn left on CR 38 (Gold Basin Road) and drive around the fence that borders the airport runway. Stay on this road for 2.4 miles—driving past a dirt factory.

For Super Model Area turn right at the sign for Hartman Rocks Recreation Area and go up the big hill (Heart Attack Hill). The second right past the cattle guard has a parking area in a cul-de-sac.

For Bambie's Area continue on Gold Basin Road for 5.5 miles crossing over a cattle guard where the road turns to dirt. Park on the left just after the cattle guard. The Bambie Trail heads west directly after the cattle guard.

SUPER MODEL AREA

There are only a few problems at Hartman Rocks that are both beautiful and worth the flesh loss; the immaculate Super Model is one of them! The area around Super Model has a number of fine, short problems as well as others listed in *Colorado Bouldering*.

Directions: Follow the directions above. From the cul-de-sac walk down the hillside to the west and hit a dirt road. Go right down the steep road 100 yards veering left (a 4x4 truck can make this easily) around the rock formation and continue on the road past a sign (#4 on the right for a mountain bike trail). Look to the left for a cluster of pines and boulders (the begin-ning of the Super Model Area). Super Model is located west from the pines and small blocks (Groove Boulder) 30 yards.

SUPER MODEL BOULDER

A gorgeous north face with thin edges leading to a horizontal crack near the top. Tall slabs can be done on the west face at V0-ish.

☐ 1. **Super Model V5** ★★★ 🌐 🌀
Climb the gold and tan face on very thin edges to an easy top-out.

WEST BLOCK

The westernmost boulder of the three.

☐ 1. **Eric's Vicous Sloper Problem V4** ★
The west block in the cluster, located a few feet from Groove Boulder. A sds matched on the left sloper then up to a sharp set of edges.

☐ 2. **V0**
On the west face is a casual slab.

NAMELESS BOULDER

The middle block of the three, with problems on the west face.

☐ 1. **V1**
A crappy little edge affair on the far left of the west face.

☐ 2. **V3** ★
Climb left from the right-angling crack up thin edges to a pebble at the top.

☐ 3. **V2** ★
The right problem starting from the crack then muckling onto the sloping arête.

☐ 4. **V0**
A bad problem starting off the incut edge left of the tree to the jug at the top of the face.

GROOVE BOULDER

The easternmost block of the three.

❏ **1. V2** ★

Climb the west face up good sharp edges.

❏ **2. V3** ★★

From the black pebbles on the left side of the southeast face slap up the groove and exit straight up.

❏ **3. The Groove V1** ★

When you figure out how to climb the groove, the problem is easy. Starts with the right hand on the dike and the left on the sloping black pebble.

BAMBIE'S BOULDERS

As with any area at Hartman Rocks there are boulders and cliff-bases littered with problems (many unrecorded due to sub-par rock). Bambie's Boulders certainly vies as one of the better areas to climb at, with its easy approach, decent quality, and a wide variety of problems to get all the juices flowing.

Directions: Hike up the Bambie Trail (a singletrack trail) following a barbed wire fence on the right and continue through a small aspen grove then past short pinnacles on the trail's right side. Right after the pinnacles pass a small block on the trail's left side. Walk 25 yards and look up the hillside on the right for the Hard Mantel Boulder (total distance from the road is 250 yards). To reach the main Bambie's Boulders area, walk west past the Hard Mantel Boulder up a very faint trail over slabs to the upper tier of rock (125 yards). To reach Whatever Dom Wants continue past Hard Mantel on the Bambie Trail for 80 yards (past a cliff band with a low roof above white rock) to a boulder on the right of the trail with "Lilly" scraped on the face. Take the drainage 30 yards past "Lilly" to the west and uphill approximately 50 yards to a west-facing boulder (Whatever Dom Wants).

HARD MANTEL BOULDER

A block 20 yards off the trail's right (west) with a distinct crack through a roof on the east face. Problems have not been done on the northwest face. Not pictured.

❏ **1. Hard Mantel V5** ★

Climb the face below the crack and top out using the crack. A burly affair turning the lip.

LOOK MA BOULDER

A distinctive lichen-covered block that has a large east-facing visor hanging out from the upper tier of rock. Approximately 125 yards west above Hard Mantel Boulder.

❏ **1. Look Ma V2** ★★★

No kidding! The fall from up high on Look Ma could be catastrophic. Climb the southwest face above a jumble of rock on small edges to the horn on the right blunt arête then the top.

❏ **2. Don't Look Ma V3**

On the northeast face is a harder problem above yet more tumbled rock.

THE WORM AREA

Located on the same tier as Look Ma Boulder and 20 yards to the north.

❏ **1. The Worm V0**

This 30-plus-foot problem is located just uphill 20 yards from Look Ma Boulder and faces Look Ma Boulder. A good warm-up, facing southeast, on questionable rock.

❏ **2. V0** ★

The left problem that climbs into excellent patina rock. Downclimb the gully between this problem and The Worm.

The Worm Area

❏ **3. V0**

The crack to the face and patina rock. Continuing up the crack is also V0. Same downclimb as #2.

Located just to the southwest from Look Ma in a lower tier is a short block with a problem up the left side and a traverse.

❏ **1. V2** ★

Climb from a sds up the left side to sharp edges and slopers.

❏ **2. V5**

Traverse the lip of the boulder either way for a painful and difficult outing.

The next four problems are located to the southeast from The Worm, 15 yards along a set of separate boulders leading to the east. More lines can be done to the north on numerous small blocks.

❏ **1. V2** ★

Climb the left arête to small edges on the face and an easy slab finish.

❏ **2. V3** ★★

Climb the right side of the block from a left-hand sidepull and right-hand edge to the slab finish.

❏ **3. V2** ★

The tall face found directly right and above the previous two problems on a tall block in a passageway. Climb the left side of the extremely tall face.

❏ **4. V2**

The right exit up the tall face avoiding the friable flake up high.

❏ **5. V3** ★

Directly above the tall face is a slightly overhanging boulder with a left-leaning seam.

❏ **6. V2** ★

The west-facing crack found west of The Worm and around the corner. Very tall, and dirty on the exit. A V1 climbs right of the crack. Not pictured.

HIGHBALL CRACK WALL

The next six problems are on the lowest tier, about 20 yards west from The Worm. Walk past the west-facing V2 crack and down to the west to a set of tall cracks, facing northwest, above a short slab. The lichen on the wall is very colorful. Any fall from high on the cracks would most likely result in a shattered something, perhaps a pelvis.

❏ 1. **V0** ★
You will break your leg if you pitch off this dihedral on the left side of the crag.

❏ 2. **V3**
Climb the face just right of the dihedral. The first ascentionist stated these words 15 feet up the problem: "Don't break! Don't break! Keep going!" The problem looks magnificent but needs a cleaning.

❏ 3. **V1** ★
The first left-leaning crack right from the dihedral. The lower slab still juts out on this problem.

❏ 4. **V1** ★
Just to the right is an easier crack problem.

❏ 5. **V5** ★
From a low start off a big sloper (just right of a mound of bat guano) dyno up to a right-facing corner then continue up.

❏ 6. **V0**
The dirty crack right of the V5.

❏ 7. **Whatever Dom Wants V5** ★★★
If you knew who Dominique was you'd be submissive too. Climb the southwest face up secure sidepulls to a horrifying belly-scraping top-out on slopers. See the Bambie's Boulder introduction for directions.

LILLY BOULDERS

Just 20 yards west off the Bambie Trail (80 yards past the turn at the Hard Mantel Boulder) is a boulder with "Lilly" scraped on it. Two blocks sit on opposite sides of Lilly with problems on them. Not pictured.

❏ 1. **V4** ★
On the south boulder adjacent to Lilly is a problem on the west face. Start from a flat jug then around to an edge on the north face then the top.

❏ 2. **V5** ★
Climb the overhanging south arête 15 feet north of Lilly.

❏ 3. **V0** ★ ⬤
This problem truly has a bad landing! Climbs the south-facing dike 30 feet above and west of Lilly.

Unnamed climber on #2 at the Highball Crack Wall

Jonathan Houch ascends Whatever Dom Wants V5

Ross Perrot at Society Turn

TELLURIDE

This old mining town, turned trendy ski resort, is home to extensive and varied bouldering. Three high areas offer a plentiful supply of problems: the Mine Boulder area, Society Turn (with its sloping pleasantries), and the awesome sandstone of the Ilium Boulders. For those wishing to escape the crowds, the Bear Creek Boulder—with its two mile approach—is a safe bet. The views, from scenic mountain valleys to busy highways, are as diverse as the stone.

Telluride
1 Ilium Boulders
2 Society Turn
3 Mine Boulder
4 Bear Creek Boulder

MINE BOULDER

This heavily-travelled boulder has some of the most spectacular views in the state. With Bridal Veil Falls to the southeast and Telluride down the valley, this popular boulder isn't lacking scenic vistas. The pebbled stone easily has a hundred variations to choose from. The curious can venture east on an overgrown trail to other more obscure blocks.

Note: This boulder is on land owned by the nearby mine. Respect the landowners at all times.

Directions: Drive east out of Telluride until the pavement ends. Continue on the gravel road past the Pandora Mill for 0.4 mile (the road goes left then immediately right to the Mine Boulder).

Southwest Face

This is the vertical face first encountered from the gravel road.

❏ **1. V0** ★★
Climb the left black streak on smaller pebbles than found on most of the other problems.

❏ **2. V0** ★★
Start in small pockets and climb up through the biggest pebble and huge pockets.

❏ **3. V0** ★★
The right side of the southwest face before turning the corner. A bomber undercling is at mid-height.

❏ **4. V2** ★★★
Climb the left side staying close to the arête. The top-out is casual.

❏ **5. V4** ★★
Just right, partially in the black streak, are crimpy pebbles to an easy top-out.

❏ **6. V2** ★★★
Start in the hole at chest height and go up and slightly left. Easy ending.

❏ **7. V2** ★★
Just right of the hole on good-sized pebbles. Good holds on top.

❏ **8. V2** ★
Right again up the short side of the south face.

❏ **9. V5** ★★
Traverse the south face from right to left, ending by going up the right side of the southwest face.

BEAR CREEK BOULDER

This huge boulder is located up the hiking trail two miles from the south end of Pine Street. The trail is now closed to motorized vehicles. The Wasatch Boulder is past the Bear Creek Boulder up the Wasatch Trail. Not pictured.

SOCIETY TURN

This area easily makes Morrison seem like a remote, pleasant bouldering area. The constant hum of traffic makes it hard to bear. There are two distinct bouldering areas on this small cliff band. The lower area smells and looks like mounds of guano; yet it climbs well. The upper area offers some interesting, although dark, movements out of a fire-blackened cave. If contrived bouldering in an unpleasant setting floats your boat, then pack your bags for the Society Turn.

Directions: From Telluride drive down valley (2.9 miles from the baseball and soccer fields), almost to the intersection of State Route 145 where it heads to Ophir. Directly east of this intersection is Last Dollar Road. Go up this road for 0.2 mile and park. The cliff is directly across the road and easily visible on the hillside.

Society Turn

ILIUM BOULDERS

This is the most extensive bouldering area near Telluride and surely the best. The sandstone blocks have a perfect texture, the problems are varied, and the setting is stellar. The full spectrum of techniques is available to the curious boulderer including a multitude of slabs, contrived overhanging problems, and cracks.

Directions: Headed towards Telluride on State Route 145 from down valley (Placerville), take the South Fork Road turnoff to the right. This turnoff is at the base of the long hill climb to reach the upper valley. From the South Fork turnoff drive 1.5 miles to pullouts on the right (a little past a large boulder sitting next to the road). A distinct trail on the opposite side of the road leads to the boulders, which are just beyond the powerlines.

BOULDER 1

The southernmost block reached by taking the north-south trail to the southern block. It can also be reached straight up from the road on a distinct trail after a mere 100 yards. Long traverses can be done to circumnavigate almost the entire boulder. This boulder has broken.

❑ 1. **V4** ★
Straight up the west face starting on the low shelf.

❑ 2. **V2** ★★★
A sds on the southwest face.

❑ 3. **V0s** ★
The straight-up problems on the south face.

❑ 4. **V3** ★★
Traverse the south face around to the west face (right to left).

❑ 5. **V0s**
East face straight-up problems. Fun slabs on bomber edges also serve as the downclimbs.

❑ 6. **V1** ★★
The north face crack/seam.

❑ 7. **V1** ★★
The right crimpers on the north face. Just left of the trees.

BOULDER 2

Located approximately 35 yards to the north on the trail from Boulder 1. It is actually two blocks, one resting against the other.

❑ 1. **V0** ★
Climb the west slab of the eastern block on good edges and pockets.

❑ 2. **V0** ★
Climb up the northwest face of the west block starting in the large pockets.

❑ 3. **V3** ★★★
A traverse of the west block from the south face left to the west face underclings or slot jugs up high. Finish on the northwest face's huge pod.

❑ 4. **V0** ★
Climb the right arête on the south face on opposing sidepulls.

❑ 5. **V2** ★★
On the eastern block is a sds on the southeast arête. One can also bury oneself deeper for a lovely lay-down start.

Boulder 1

Boulder 2

Boulder 3

BOULDER 3

Found approximately 30 yards north of Boulder 2. Also reached by a trail starting at the road and heading straight into the aspens and blue spruce.

❑ 1. **V0** ★
Climb the southwest corner on small positive edges.

❑ 2. **V4** ★★
Just right on the south face is a one-move-wonder to reach high edges. It begins from a left-hand layback and right-hand crappy hold.

BOULDER 4

The most extensive selection of contrived problems for the Ilium Boulders. It is located north about 40 yards from Boulder 3. A wide crack splits the south face.

☐ 1. **V0** ★
Climb the huecos left of the left-facing corner.

☐ 2. **V2** ★
Just left of the low roof is a slab problem on sloping dishes and small edges.

☐ 3. **V3** ★★
A sds on the west face starting on the lowest undercling and going left to a flat jug before cutting right to the downsloping arête. A V5 left variation begins on underclings to an upside-down pocket, then finishes the same as #3.

☐ 4. **V0**
The wide south face crack.

☐ 5. **V0** ★★
The slabby south face right of the crack.

☐ 6. **V1** ★★
Climb the seam on the left side of the east face.

☐ 7. **V5** ★★
Traverse the east face right to left, then move up the south face using thin edges and precise footwork.

☐ 8. **V1** ★
Ascend the northeast arête from a low start on a triangular-shaped hold.

☐ 9. **V3** ★★
A sds left of the crack in an overhanging alcove. Many variations can be done in this alcove.

☐ 10. **V2** ★★
The overhanging crack on the north face.

BOULDER 5

A mere 10 yards north of Boulder 4.

☐ 1. **V2** ★★
Begin as a sds on the southwest face starting on a low flat jug.

☐ 2. **V1** ★★
Start on the south face and move left and finish around the southwest corner.

☐ 3. **V4** ★★
Traverse the entire boulder from the south face to north face staying on the face below the top holds.

☐ 4. **V0s** ★
A couple of slab problems can be done on the north face.

BOULDER 6

Another whopping 15 feet north of Boulder 5. A distinct crack splits the southwest face.

☐ 1. **V1** ★
The left side of the north face using the arête.

☐ 2. **V2** ★★
The right side of the north face on bad underclings and micro foot edges.

☐ 3. **V2** ★★
Climb the overhanging crack on the southwest face.

☐ 4. **V3**
Starting on opposing pinches, climb up the south face not using the incut flake. The problem is V1 with the flake.

Boulder 4

Boulder 5

Boulder 6

North Boulders

Continuing north on the trail a few more problems can be done on the sporadic blocks. These blocks see very little traffic in comparison to the main boulders.

☐ 1. **V1**
The first boulder north of Boulder 6 on the left side of the trail has a low juggy traverse on its southeast face.

☐ 2. **V?**
A thin gritty problem on the next boulder north (on the right side of the trail).

☐ 3. **V0**
The gray slab at the far north end of the boulders.

☐ 4. **V0** ★★
Downhill from the gray slab is a small block with two arêtes meeting up high. Pinch the duel arêtes to big top-out holds.

Sub Boulders

Uphill, to the southeast approximately 40 yards, from Boulder 4 is a tall block with an orange and black west face. The problems below are not pictured.

☐ 1. **V2** ★
The zigzag traverse on the west face. Best downclimbed, as the left arête is filthy.

☐ 2. **V2** ★
A low start on the south face's left side.

Continuing southeast on the trail past the orange and black boulder (approximately 30 yards) is a nice block with diagonal pockets on its southwest face.

☐ 1. **V2** ★★
A sit down start on the west face, traversing up and right on bomber pockets.

☐ 2. **V0s**
A couple of problems are on the east face.

North Boulder

North Boulder

Derek Wolfe on the Road Boulder Dihedral V1

DURANGO

Durango bouldering consists of three well-traveled areas: Turtle Lake, The Boxcar, and Dalla Mountain Park (Sailing Hawks). Sailing Hawks, a longtime discreet area, has been purchased by the City of Durango from Jake Dalla and is now open to the public without access issues. Mr. Dalla, in his infinite wisdom, has shared his longtime private park (Jacob's Ladder) with everyone so we all can have fun like he did as a child. Please respect this sacred area by being respectful of others and keep in mind Mr. Dalla's extremely generous philanthropy. Rest assured there are plenty of sandstone blocks shaded by tall pines and far more problems than listed here. If the short, pleasant hike is too much, simply go to Turtle Lake or the old-time classic Boxcar, superb venues on their own!

Directions: Sailing Hawks: from US Highway 550 that splits Durango drive to 25th Street and go west at the Big O Tires store. Drive on 25th past the middle school and past Birkett Drive to a large pullout on the right clearly marked for Dalla Mountain Park. Park here and walk up the dirt road for a few minutes (750 yards) to the first hairpin and a take a distinct trail straight uphill where the trail intersects yet another old roadbed and go left a few yards to another trail headed straight uphill towards the cliffs hidden behind large ponderosa pines (staying on the second roadbed headed west will reach Ellen's, Euro, The Alley, and Cigarette boulders. Continue uphill to a distinct square block (Warm-Up Boulder) littered with holds and chalk just below the cliffs. At this point there is a trail system skirting the cliff base. Go left and within a minute chalked boulders begin to appear in the forest and continue as one walks farther west.

Durango

1 Turtle Lake Boulders
2 Sailing Hawks
3 The Boxcar
4 East Animas

THE BOXCAR BOULDER

A one-in-a hundred boulder! If the state was full of Boxcars there wouldn't be a reason to ever use a rope. Just like the Turtle Lake Boulders, this block has perfect texture. The only downfalls are that the best problems face east (bad morning sessions in the summer) and the incessant noise from Highway 550 is more annoying than elevator music. But don't dare miss these exceptional problems.

Directions: Headed north on US Route 550 from Durango and before leaving town turn left into the Centura Health Mercy Medical Center. Park at the far north part of the lot and walk due west up a steep dirt path. Go north for about 200 yards and the boulder is trailside on the left (west).

Note: The parking is sketchy at the Health Center. Towing is possible. Either get dropped off or use the Hampton Inn parking lot.

SOUTH FACE

Problems are listed left to right.

❒ 1. **V0** ★★
Climb the left-facing crescent.

❒ 2. **V2** ★★
Nine feet right of the crescent is a problem starting in a little pod and going straight up.

❒ 3. **V2** ★★★
Traverse the wall from right to left. A harder variation can be done by traversing the low holds across the face.

EAST FACE

Problems are listed left to right.

❒ 4. **V4** ★★★
A 14-foot problem that climbs the southeast arête off a low sloping hold. The top-out holds are not particularly comforting.

❒ 5. **V3** ★★★
The big right-facing dihedral on the east face. 17' tall.

❒ 6. **V3** ★★★
Just right of the dihedral is a big flake. Start there and finish on the V3 to the left. Good top-out holds.

❒ 7. **V3** ★★★
Just left of the black streak, finishing to the right. Bomber top-out holds are welcome on this 17-foot tall problem.

❒ 8. **V2** ★★★
Just right of the black streak is a straight-up problem. The beginning moves are difficult with an uneven block to land on.

❒ 9. **V4** ★★
Climb the overhanging arête on the right side of the east face. A lovely mantel top-out with an atrocious landing is in store. Bring a spotter and a pad for this one!

Neil Kaptain on The Boxcar   Photo by John Sherman

Sailing Hawks

Sandstone boulderfields in Colorado do not come finer or in a sweeter setting than Sailing Hawks. If anyone argues the point simply laugh and head to the ponderosa-shaded blocks in a premier city park. Two-scoop and ultra-classic lines dot the hillside alongside contrived overhangs, epic traverses, and filthy choss blocks.

Tsunami Boulder

From the first road continue uphill to the crest of the steep hillside (before reaching the 2nd roadbed) to a distinct side trail and go right to reach Tsunami (350 yards south).

❒ 1. **Tsunami Relief Arête V7** ★★
Sloper fetish fiends come one and all. This sorta safe sloper line will amuse anyone who hates edges.

❒ 2. **Tsunami V3** ★
Go out the roof.

Warm-Up Boulder

A superb starter boulder with more ups, traverses, and contrived problems than is necessary for a thorough warm up. Problems range from V0 super-cruiser hueco jug hauls to V3 circumnavigating traverses.

Tsunami Boulder

Warm-Up Boulder

Triangle Boulder

Triangle Boulder

A great small boulder located 140 yards to the north (then west) from Warm-Up on a distinct trail. Down in a pit between two blocks and left of the main trail.

❒ 1. **Something Wicked this Way Comes V4** ★★
Start at head height sidepull/edges and move left then up. V6 from a sds in crack.

❒ 2. **Journey of Foreigner V5** ★★
Low start same as SWTWC but stay right without the arête. V6 sds.

❒ 3. **Laser V4** ★★
Climb up the right arête.

Little Sandy Boulders

Thirty-five yards north past Triangle Boulder are three boulders on the left side of the trail.

❒ 1. **V2**
North facing slab on trail that moves to the arête then up.

❒ 2. **V2**
Sit start and move up the west arête.

❒ 3. **Afternoon Monsoon V5**
The northeast arête on the next boulder that starts from the undercling.

❒ 4. **V0s**
The crack left of AM, also in the corridor.

Little Sandy Boulders

BLEEDING LIP BOULDER

Located a couple of yards past Little Sandy on the right side of the trail.

❏ **1. V2**
Climb up the south corner then traverse left on pockets. Pull over early or continue left to white rock.

❏ **2. Bleeding Lip Traverse V6** ★
Slopey traverse on the northwest overhang starting from a low hueco. Pumpy. Given a V6 grade for the full traverse. A short traverse comes in at V2.

❏ **3. Wave V5**
The steep arête just right of BLT. From a sds on little crimpers to high arête.

PETRIFIED BOULDER

Twenty-five yards past Bleeding Lip. A massive block that overhangs the left side of the trail. Plenty of low sit starts, contrived problems, and big pumps.

❏ **1. Petrified Arête V3** ★
As almost any line at Sailing Hawks, do a sds and climb the east arête to the crack with a tree growing out of it.

❏ **2. Al Montana V10**
Horrendously thin edges just right of PA starting from a sds on an undercling.

❏ **3. Global Warming V8**
Again to the right (12 feet from PA) from a sds in a seam/slot then up left slightly. V6 headed up to the right from same low start. V7 moving further right then up.

❏ **4. V3**
Start in gold rock above the block on a sloper sidepull to a pocket and pinch.

❏ **5. V0**
Just right, climb up the left-facing corner from a low start.

❏ **6. Petrified Prow V5** ★★
Right from the V0 and before the big corner/scoop is a nice line to a high pocket.

❏ **7. Desert Sun V3** ★
Climb up the right-facing scoop to a big move for the lip. V6 moving right through a gold patch.

❏ **8. Classicnessitude Arête V3**
As the name implies a good problem up the arête right of the DS scoop. And it starts actually standing on two feet!

❏ **9. Darkness to Light V1**
On the far right side of the north face is a juggy crack leading through a low overhang.

❏ **10. The Rib V5** ★
Sds at the crack and move out to the right arête or straight up the overhang without the crack.

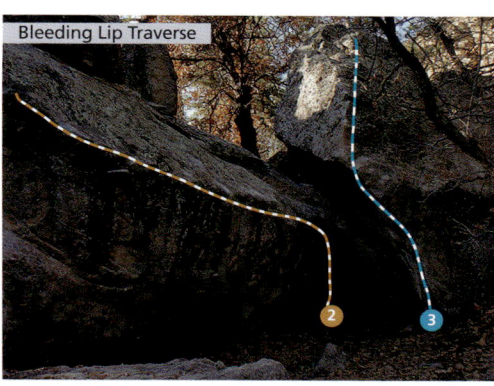
Bleeding Lip Traverse

Petrified Arête V3

Petrified Prow V5

The Rib V5

SKULLY

Ten yards from Petrified to the left (northeast) as one faces the big overhang is a super block with a couple of great lines.

☐ 1. **Skully Direct V3** ★★★
Classic line up prow/scoop. V5 low start or V6 from sds on boulder to the left.

☐ 2. **Mulder V3**
Climb the low arête right of SD and exit onto slab.

SUNDAY STROLL BOULDER

Eighty-five yards west from Petrified is a smaller side trail (take it). Go 40 yards to the west then north. Problems face west and north (Sunday Stroll).

☐ 1. **Sunday Stroll V6** ★★★
Super classic line on the north face from a sds on left hueco and right edge.

☐ 2. **Abolish Monday Mornings V3**
Sds to the right of Sunday Stroll on a detached pillar with a terrible landing.

☐ 3. **Sunday Driver V3**
Around the corner to the right, go up good edges to a large top rail.

☐ 4. **No Traffic V3**
A small boulder above (northeast) from Sunday Stroll block with a shallow left-facing corner and surprisingly balancy line.

LEGACY OF THE KID BOULDER

A superb block located 85 yards past Sunday Stroll on the main trail. Take a right side trail to the northeast for 35 yards to the block. Legacy is visible through the woods from Sunday Stroll.

☐ 1. **Legacy of the Kid V9** ★★
The hardest line on the block. Starts as a sds and moves up and through the tan streak. A V6 has the same start but moves left to exit.

☐ 2. **Nipple Ripper Traverse V5** ★
A traverse across the southeast face. Start at the far left corner and climb through Legacy. A V3 is around the corner from the start.

☐ 3. **Last Tango in Durango V6** ★★
On the west face is a clean golden face with a problem climbing through crimpy/slopey holds. A V3 has the same start but busts up the arête.

☐ 4. **V5**
Climb out the roof on the north face from a sit start. Harder variants can be done into the neighboring lines.

Legacy of the Kid

Skully

Sunday Stroll

Last Tango in Durango V6

WHITE ROCK

Ninety-five yards past Legacy the trail hits a white boulder on the right. Not the best stone but problems can be done.

White Rock

EURO BOULDER

The biggest baddest boulder in the woods of Sailing Hawks. Walk past White Rock a short distance to a split in the trail. To the right are numerous other boulders (Girl, Three Slices, the Sanctuary, etc.). Euro has incredibly long traverses, tons of highballs (toprope anchors exist), some with leg breaking landings, and super tall slabs. There are countless problems ranging from V0-V13. Euro can also be reached from the lower trail system where Ellen's, The Alley, and Cigarette Boulder are found. At an obvious 4-way intersection located approximately 500-plus yards from the trail leading to Warm-Up, go right (uphill) for 175 yards to the boulder.

South Face
Problems listed left to right

☐ **1. Sacred Traverse V10** ★
A long traverse of the south face from left to right.

☐ **2. Golden Arm Traverse V11** ★
Traverse around the whole dang boulder. An even harder variation (V13) does a super lowball traverse across the south face then continues around the block.

☐ **3. Glory Arête V9**
Follows the far left arête or venture slightly right close to the black streak for a V7. Another V7 then a V6 are right of the black streak.

☐ **4. V8**
There are two of these highballs on the left side of the south face. Both lines climb up and through the white rock left of the left-facing corner.

☐ **5. Magic Potion V5** ★
Head up the left-facing corner and exit by moving right.

☐ **6. Urango V8** ★
Climbs the face right of the corner and moves into the black rock. A V10 called Duran Problem climbs straight up from the same start.

☐ **7. Jumping Jack V7**
A jump start if you couldn't figure that out, which starts a few feet right of Urango and exits by moving up and left. A V5 moves out right.

☐ **8. Richard Simmons Total Body Workout V3** ★
Sds under the steep bulge and moves through yummy pockets. A V5 has the same exit as the previous V5.

☐ **9. Reverse Population Growth V6**
To the right of RSTBW with a low start through the roof.

Northwest Face
You would do best to bring a ton of pads, a few spotters or better yet, DO NOT FALL!

☐ **1. V0**
The lower-angle north side of the leftmost arête.

☐ **2. Addicted to Material Goods V5** ★
Right of the northwest arête is a hueco start to a corner. Highball like everything on this monstrous block. Two V6s start a little to the right and finish the same.

☐ **3. V2**
Climb the crack. Variants can be done to the left V4 or right V7.

☐ **4. V7**
Climb up between the black streaks through the horizontal.

Euro Boulder South Face

Euro Boulder Northwest Face

☐ **5. V4**
Not recommended. Climbs the jugs just right of the gray/black streak. A couple more problems in the same range climb up the face to the right before the right arête.

☐ **6. Fear and Chaos V8**
Climb the far right arête and don't fall!

Big Ass Boulder

About 185 yards past White Rock is a trail on the right. Take it for 25 yards to a massive block with highballs facing the main trail from V0-V4. Nuff said.

Girl Boulder

Eighty yards past Big Ass is a small (safe) block on the right side of the trail with a couple of V0s.

Figure 8 Boulder

A hundred yards from Girl Boulder to the north is a fine block next to the trail.

❏ 1. **Figure 8 Traverse V3**
Sds on far left and move right across the entire face.

❏ 2. **The Authority V4**
Near the end of the traverse find a pocket and go up. A V3 is right.

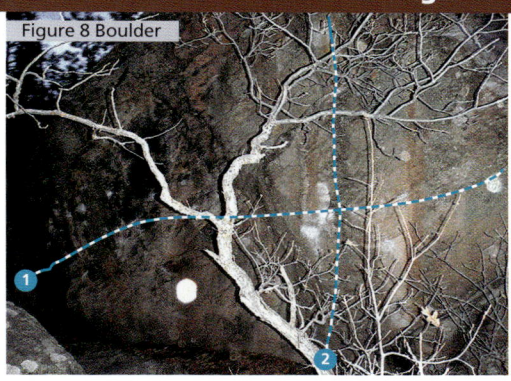
Figure 8 Boulder

Black Arête

Thirty-five yards past Figure 8 is a side trail on the right. Take it for 30 yards back to the east to a nice overhanging arête. Not pictured.

❏ 1. **Black Arête V7**
Sds and climb through overhang then up arête.

❏ 2. **Eco-conscious V4**
Climbs near and through the black streak a few feet left of BA.

❏ 3. **V1**
The offwidth, for shits and giggles. More left if ya want.

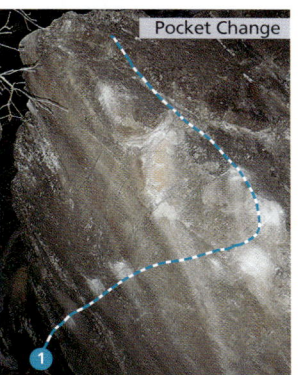
Pocket Change

Three Slices

Forty yards past Black Arête are a couple of boulders on the right side of the trail. Not pictured.

❏ 1. **V0-V1** 🌲
Sit start if you have to and go up any of the first three cracks.

❏ 2. **Three Slices V5** 🌲
A stand start, yea! To the right of the right crack are some chalked holds and the arête. Go up to a sidepull then up some more. Fun.

❏ 3. **Country Cardio V4** 🌲
Climb the right arête on the second block. A V2 traverses through the crack with the same top-out.

Pocket Change

Located 45 yards past Three Slices. Take a righthand side trail for another 35 yards east to a superb hidden zone of exceptional problems on splitter rock. This zone has a couple of all-time aesthetic lines with perfect landings.

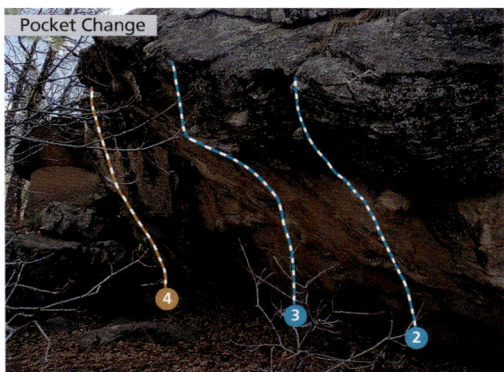
Pocket Change

❏ 1. **Pocket Change V3** ★★
This line looks cool and climbs great through the obvious pockets to the right arête. A couple of V5 variants can be done on the same face by eliminating some pockets and top-ping out early or doing the arête sans pockets.

❏ 2. **Desert Rain V5**
Around the corner from Pocket Change is a lowball (sds) start off two huecos then up through the roof.

❏ 3. **Pockets of Perception V3**
Sds on two pockets left of DR and climb up then left of the black streak. A V5 starts left and finishes the same.

❏ 4. **Under the Sea V6** 🌲
The name might be fitting but climb up the far left arête.

❏ 5. **Agent Orange V9** ★★★
An absolutely stellar line that looks like it would fit in perfectly with Font problems. Start standing, not sitting for a change, on opposing holds and up the slopers. A V12 starts lower with the right hand actually on the underbelly of this gorgeous block.

❏ 6. **Code Name V5**
Around the left corner, start sitting and traverse right along the sloping lip.

❏ 7. **Golden Arête V8** ★
Fifty yards north from Agent Orange is a spectacular arête. Do it from a low start (undercling for the right) and get a double-digit V11 slap/sloper-fest.

THE SANCTUARY AKA THE ROOM

Walk 420 yards northwest past the Pocket Change area to a side trail on the right. Walk 30 yards to a natural doorway then into the Sanctuary.

□ 1. The Lorax V7
Starts low and left and moves right through crimpy holds. V3 straight up the dark ramp/arête. Dirty top-out!

□ 2. Once-ler V1
Inside The Room on the right (north) wall. Climb the corner/flake. Sds is V3.

□ 3. V5s
On the opposite side (south face) of The Room are two V5s in lighter colored rock. A little dirty on top.

Once-ler V1

KEYSTONE CAVE BOULDER

Go left (west) before heading uphill to Warm-Up Boulder for 50 yards then uphill (there are a couple of trails leading to the boulder visible from the old roadbed) then head uphill for 50 yards to a big boulder with a large cave on the north face.

□ 1. Recession or Depression V7 ★
On the left side of the south face climb up to a crescent then up some more.

□ 2. Gang of Three V4 ★
To the right of ROD is a flake. Use it and go up past the horizontal.

□ 3. Gift of the Valkyrie V4
The arête between the south and east faces. Bring some Depends!

□ 4. Historical Conquests V5
Climbs up the white east face and engages one instantly in the feeling of fear.

□ 5. V2
A couple of V2s are on the far left side of the north face overhang. Enjoyment without the fear factor of the taller south and east face lines.

□ 6. V4
On the right side of the north overhang, start low on a good hold and move up and left to finish. V5 staying to the right after the start.

Keystone Cave Boulder

ELLEN'S BOULDER

From the trail headed uphill to Warm-Up Boulder head north and west for over 200 yards going past Keystone Cave (300 yards before the intersection headed uphill to Euro Boulder) to a lefthand trail. Take this trail for 25 yards to the west to reach two extremely huge blocks. Problems on these big blocks range from V0-V8. Not pictured.

□ 1. Ellen's Arête V8
Sds on the far right of the first block encountered, above ground blocks, and crimp like hell through sharp pebbly edges to a tall finish. V5 by exiting right after the starting holds.

THE ALLEY

On the bottom trail (2nd old roadbed) system before heading uphill to the Warm-Up Boulder head west past Keystone and Ellen's to the 4-way intersection that heads uphill to Euro Boulder. Go another 200 yards west. Take the right hand trail for 30 yards to reach The Alley, which is a corridor between two large blocks. There are more cruiser V0s than necessary with a couple of harder lines up to V2.

CIGARETTE BOULDER

180 yards north from The Alley to a righthand trail. Walk 50 yards up this side trail to reach this exceptional smaller boulder.

□ 1. 50-foot Smoking Ban V6
Same start as Cigarette but finish left.

Cigarette Boulder

□ 2. Cigarette Problem V4 ★
Sds on flake and through the big slot to the nice upper face. A V6 moves left after the flake through thinner holds.

□ 3. Stand and Deliver V5 ★
Sds left of the flake and then move back into the finish for CP.

TURTLE LAKE BOULDERS

The perfect sandstone of the Turtle Lake boulderfield is a great place to have an awesome session with problems of various styles from slabs to steep. Situated in a dense scrub oak stand, the shade and orientation of the blocks allow for pleasant summer sessions. Be sure to check out the east overhang of the Road Boulder and the problems on the Big Boulders.

Directions: From downtown Durango turn left on 25th Street (between Big O Tires and Firestone). This turns into Junction Street (CR 204). Drive 2.9 miles to a right (north) and turn onto CR 205. Drive another 1.1 miles to a dirt pullout on the right side of the road. The first Turtle Lake boulder can be seen sitting on the opposite side on the road.

A. ROAD BOULDER

This is the block sitting closest to CR 205. A trail to the other boulders begins next to this.

❏ 1. **The Dihedral V1** ★★
The open dihedral facing the road.

❏ 2. **V2** ★★
The pebbly east face beginning on a low pod.

❏ 3. **V3** ★★★
From the east-face pod traverse right on big, flat jugs then onto the north face's pockets. A good V1 climbs from below the north face pockets and finishes up the pockets.

❏ 4. **V2** ★★★
A sds on the east face that climbs through the yellow rock on slots. Many variations can be done.

B. PENNY BOULDER

Just west from the Road Boulder, approximately 25 feet, is a golden north-facing boulder.

❏ 1. **Penny Candy V1** ★
The west face on diagonaling edges.

❏ 2. **V0**
Climb the gray slab on incut pockets.

❏ 3. **My Two Cents V1** ★★
Just left of #2 is an arête problem.

❏ 4. **10 Cents Short of a Dime V1** ★★
Climb the sloping edges on the north face.

❏ 5. **There's a Lesson Here V4** ★★
This problem is on a separate block ten yards northwest from the Road Boulder. Begin low on an incut edge and slap to the arête, then move up and left on difficult laybacks. No photo.

C. NORTH BLOCK

This boulder is northwest 45 yards from the Road Boulder. Take the left path 25 yards after the Road Boulder to a short block with a black northeast face.

❏ 1. **Golden Year V1**
Climb the gold and white east face.

❏ 2. **V0**
The left side of the northeast face.

❏ 3. **V0**
The right side of the northeast face.

Road Boulder

Road Boulder

Penny Boulder

North Block

Turtle Lake Boulders

A. Road Boulder
B. Penny Boulder
C. North Block
D. Big West
E. Big East
F. Eastern Block

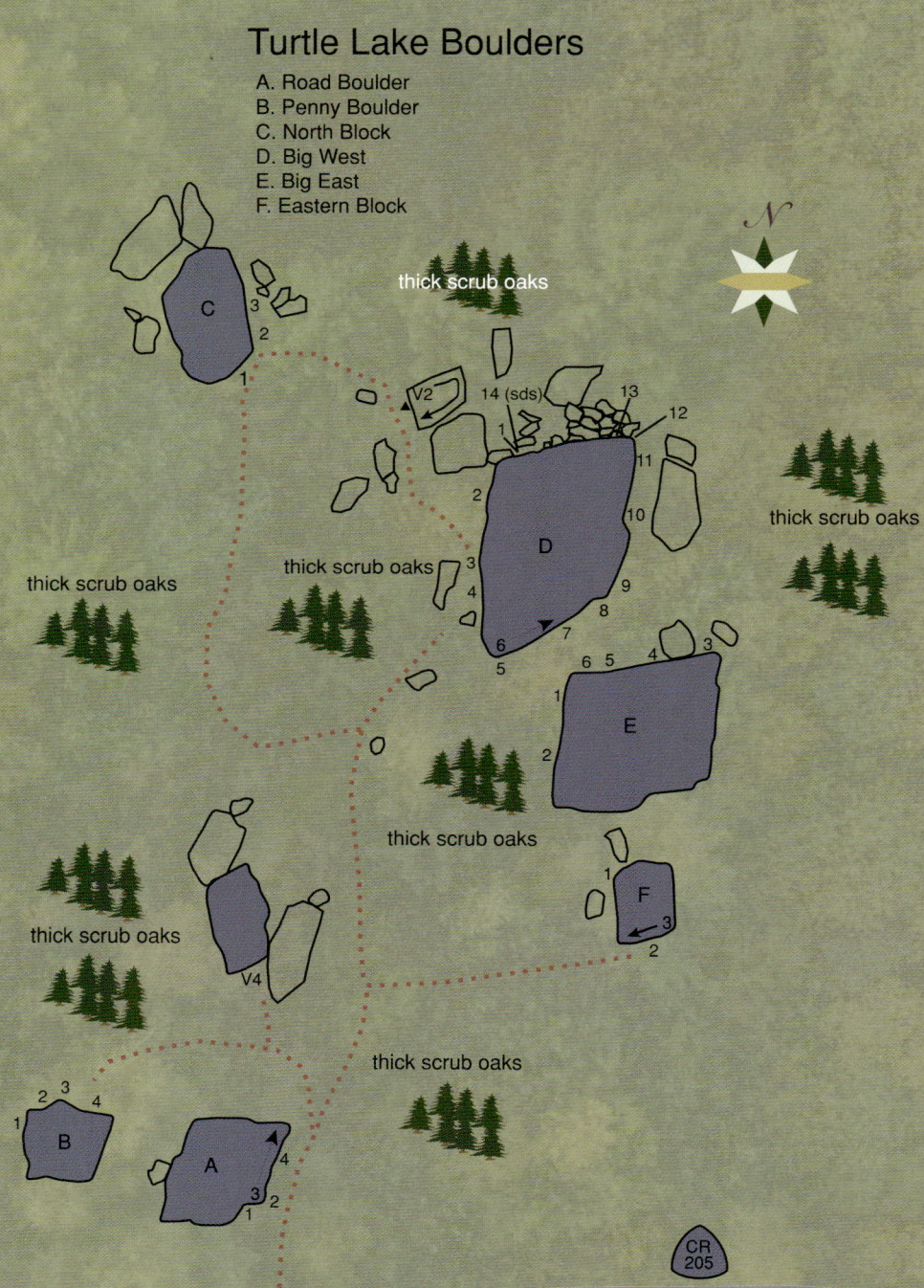

D. Big West

The massive boulder on the right side of the trail from the Road Boulder. Take the right path 25 yards after the Road Boulder to a huge block.

❑ 1. **V2** ★ 🔵
A sds in a hole on the north face.

❑ 2. **V1** 🔵 🟢
Climb the right diagonaling wide slot on the left side of the west face. Dirty on top.

❑ 3. **A Brief History V3** ★★★ 🔵
This problem kicks ass! To the right of #2 and behind the tree is a tall face.

❑ 4. **Center El Turtle V6** ★★ 🔵
Again right is a thin crimp face starting below a small bulbous hold at eight feet. The crimps get worse as one gets higher.

❑ 5. **Western One V4** ★★
A traverse of the west face left to right. Start before (right) of the small boulder adjacent to the wall.

❑ 6. **Fade Away V4** ★
The left side of the south face staying on the blunt corner.

❑ 7. **Beckon the Call V8**
Many variations up to V11 exist in the overhang along with Beckon the Call (V8), which starts as an sds on an undercling and moves out and left on edges and bad pockets.

❑ 8. **Monkey Hang V4** ★★
Traverse across the lip on huge jugs and heel hooks from #5 to #7.

❑ 9. **The Wonder V4** ★
A one-move power problem at the right edge of the overhang. A roll onto the slab finishes the route.

❑ 10. **V0** ★★★ 🔵
Climb the low-angle slab on the far right of the south face. This route exceeds 25 feet.

❑ 11. **V0** ★★★ 🔵
On the east face is another tall gray slab that climbs diagonaling ramps for over 25 feet.

❑ 12. **V2** ★★★ 🔵 🟢
Climb the open scoop on bad laybacks to good pockets. Very bad landing!

❑ 13. **V1** ★★ 🔵 🟢
Right of the scoop, just before the arête, is a problem starting in a left diagonaling slot. Also a terrible landing.

❑ 14. **V6**
A sds on the north face's left arête.

Big West

Big West

E. Big East

The companion monster boulder just east of Big West. The south face of this boulder is covered with V0s as well as the best downclimbs. On the east are serious highballs from V6 on up.

❏ **1. V2** ★
The left side of the west face. Utilizes the arête.

❏ **2. V0** ★★★
Climbs the middle of the west face on an offset seam moving up and right.

❏ **3. The Fin V6** ★★
On the far left side of the north face. Starts on bad underclings to a big throw. The top-out is harder exiting left (V7). The SDS is V11.

❏ **4. V6** ★★
Start standing on the adjacent block in the middle of the north face. Long reaches and a strong will to live are mandatory.

❏ **5. Bird Hole Left V6**
Start right of #4 then up with the right hand to the bird hole.

❏ **6. V3** ★★★
This problem is on the right side of the north face and stays left of the arête.

F. Eastern Block

This short block is just a few yards southeast of Big East.

❏ **1. V2** ★
A sds arête that uses a thin layback.

❏ **2. V3** ★
Straight up the south face is a dynamic problem beginning on bad underclings.

❏ **3. V4**
A right-to-left traverse through underclings.

Big East

Big East

Eastern Block

The author on Bird Hole Left V6

THE DIAMOND BLOCK

Ninety yards north from Big East is a superb block with a steep west face and deluxe slab on the south face.

☐ 1. Midnight Rider V3 ★ 🌑 🌑

A low-angle slab with delicate moves getting situated well as finishing.

☐ 2. Ship's Prow V2

Move up the west arête on fairly sloping grips. V4 sds.

☐ 3. West Face V2

A number of variations can be done here with a long traverse from the far left to get more of a pump.

TEEPEE BOULDER

Again, head north uphill for approximately 200 yards past two small blocks to a boulder with a ramshackle wooden teepee erected near the west face.

North Face

☐ 1. V4 ★

Start on opposing sidepulls and jump to a good jug.

☐ 2. V2 ★

The right arête on the north face that utilizes good sidepulls

to move up.

West Face

Problems listed left to right.

☐ 3. V4

On the far left side is a tough vertical affair with a longish reach to the top grips.

☐ 4. V2 ★

An easier vertical outing is just right.

☐ 5. V3

A crimpy rig in the middle of the west face.

☐ 6. V1 ★★

The far right face/arête that is an excellent warm-up.

The Diamond Block

Teepee Boulder

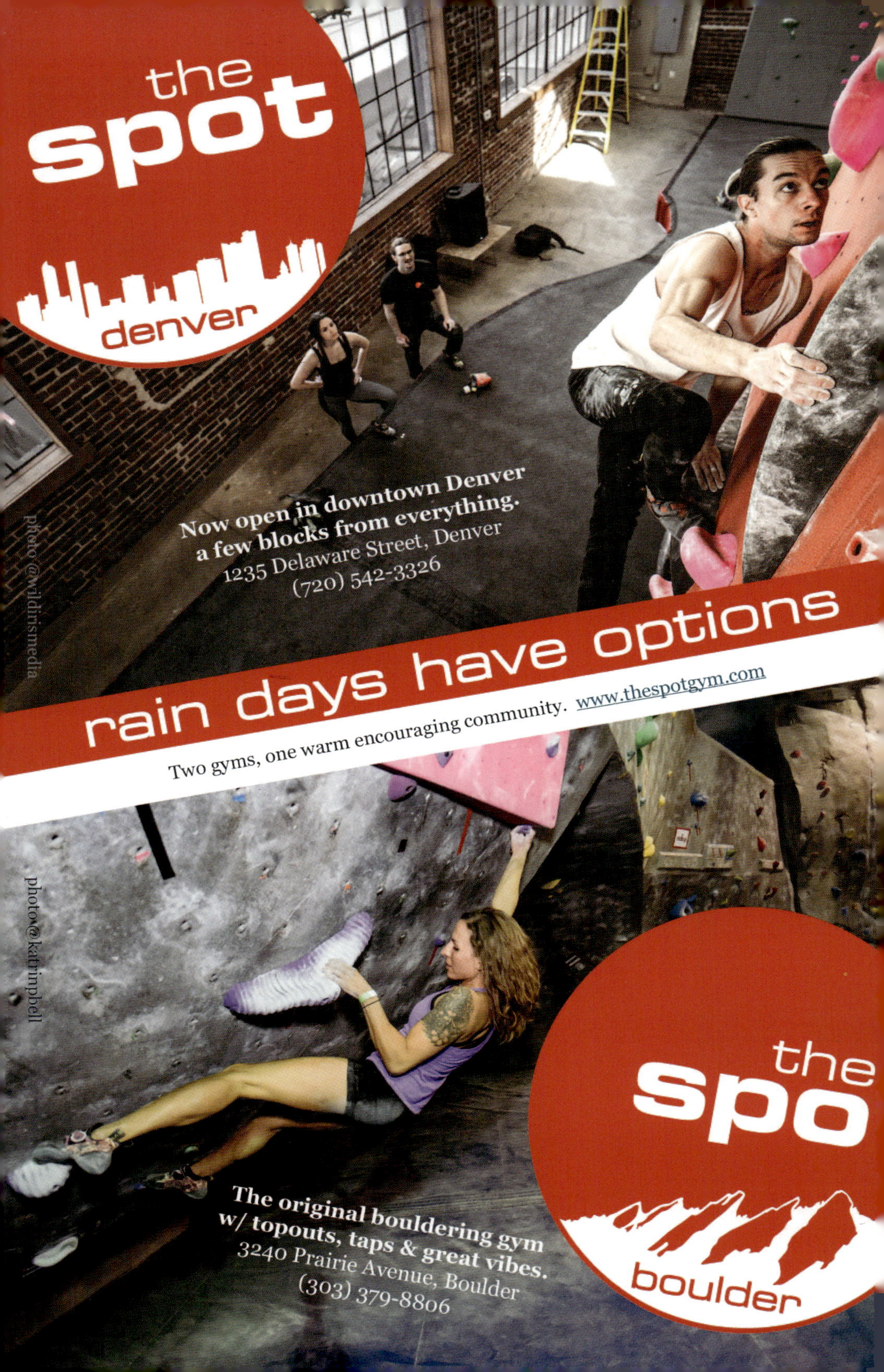
the
spot
denver
Now open in downtown Denver
a few blocks from everything.
1235 Delaware Street, Denver
(720) 542-3326
photo @wildirismedia
rain days have options
Two gyms, one warm encouraging community. www.thespotgym.com
photo@katrinpbell
the
spo
boulder
The original bouldering gym
w/ topouts, taps & great vibes.
3240 Prairie Avenue, Boulder
(303) 379-8806

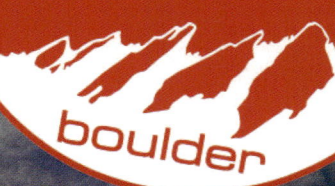

The author cruising up the Telephone Boulder

NEW CASTLE

This bouldering area is limited and small compared to its closest neighbors, Redstone and Independence Pass. Nonetheless, it offers a few outstanding problems on solid sandstone. With a landscape of tall junipers and sage, and a tendency for mild temperatures, these boulders can be climbed throughout the year. In all, the boulderfield offers about ten climbable boulders and great diversity. From vertical classics like Trabaharder to sloper problems such as Stinkin' Lincoln, these boulders exploit nearly every technique.

Directions: From I-70 exit for New Castle (#105) and drive 1.2 miles through town to 7th Street (CR 245). Go right and follow the road out of town (this is a major speed trap area—speed limit 15 mph). At 2.4 miles, take a right on CR 241 (East Elk Creek) and drive 0.35 mile. Park on a small pullout up the road on the right and walk back down the road and up a faint, zig-zagging trail. Skirt the water pipe at the far right end of the road and walk straight uphill. The first boulder encountered on the hillside has a telephone pole sticking out of it.

Note: The dry, fragile landscape demands treading lightly. Stay on the existing trail.

A. SHADY CHARACTER
The first boulder seen as one approaches the water pipe. Before walking to the end of the road look across the pipe and a somewhat hidden boulder can be seen 15 yards east of the pipe.

☐ 1. **One V5** ★
A low start on a glued flake. The leftmost problem that climbs the rounded arête.

☐ 2. **Two V6** ★
A sds to the obvious overhanging groove.

☐ 3. **Three V7**
The right face which was done before a chiseler took tools to the rock. A lot easier in its present sorry state.

B. TELEPHONE BOULDER
After crossing the water pipe where it disappears underground walk straight uphill. This boulder has seen little development due to the improved quality of the higher boulders. A few V0s to V2s can be done on this block.

C. INTIMIDATOR BOULDER
Just up the hillside from the Telephone Boulder is a square boulder with a multitude of problems and contrivances.

☐ 1. **V0**
The leftmost problem found directly behind the tree on the west face. A V1 sit down can be done to this problem.

☐ 2. **Intimidator V2** ★
Starts sitting down on a three-finger pocket then up the arête.

Shady Character

Telephone Boulder

Intimidator Boulder

☐ 3. **Jeremy's Problem V4** ★
Just right of #2 is a sds that climbs slightly right.

☐ 4. **Intimidating Traverse V7** ★★
The traverse from left to right across the boulder's two climbable sides.

A. Shady Character
B. Telephone Boulder
C. Intimidator Boulder
D. Holloway Boulder
E. Eukanuba Boulder
F. Stinkin' Lincoln

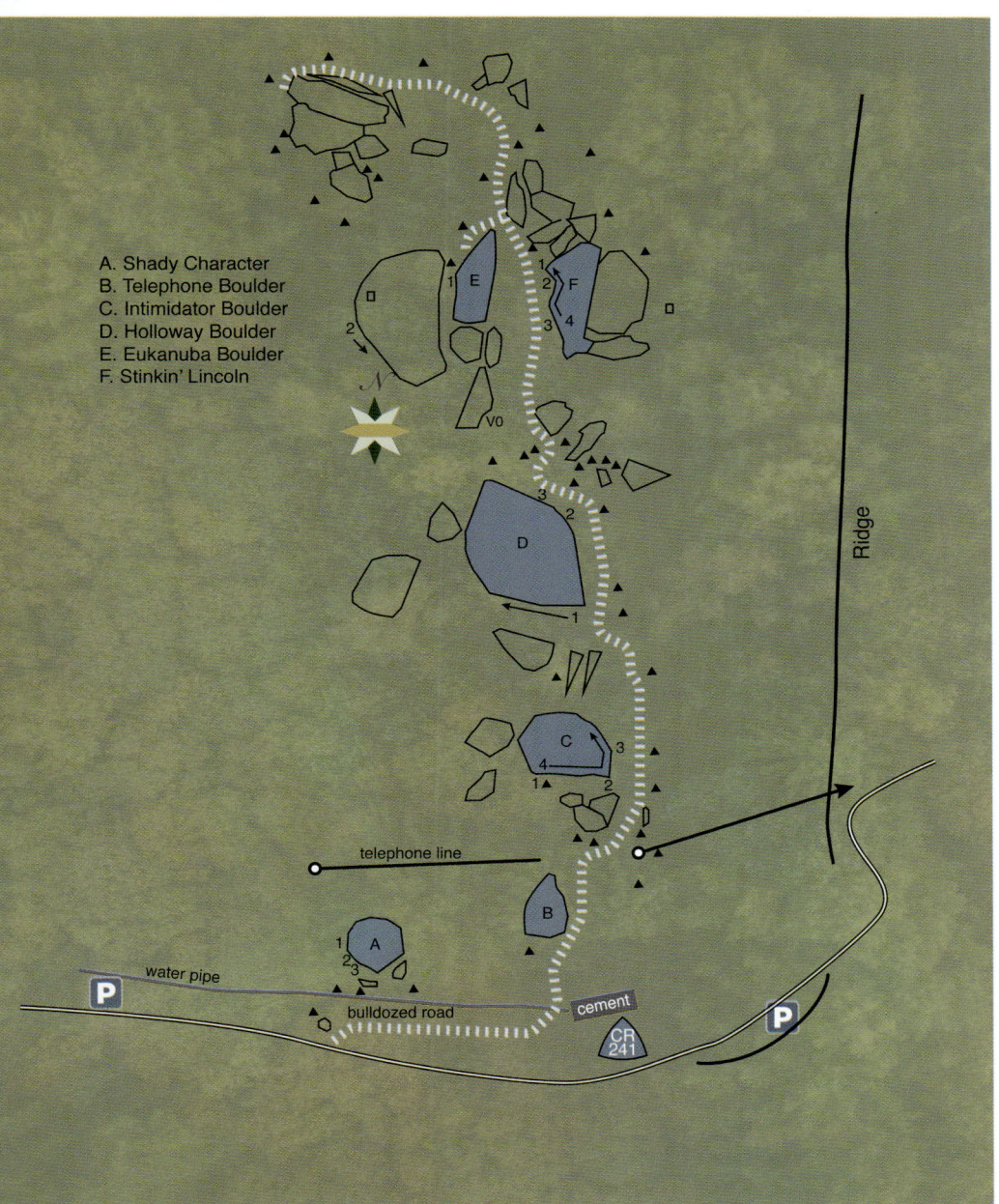

D. Holloway Boulder aka Poor Man's Bleau

Just east of the Intimidator Boulder. Walk straight up the hillside to a nice block with steep traverses on the east and west faces.

☐ 1. West Face Traverse V6 ★★★
Start low and right on a good hold and traverse left with an early exit on a jug. A V8 bypasses the jug exit and continues left for the remaining few feet.

☐ 2. Scott's Arête aka Assboss V8 ★
Start sitting down and climb the southeast arête up and right not using the holds on the left slab.

☐ 3. Lightning Foot Jones V3 ★★
Starts just right of the arête as a sds on a flake. Climb up and right on the short face.

☐ 4. World's Smallest Problem V0 ★
On the hillside, before reaching Stinkin' Lincoln, is a short problem that faces southwest and start sitting down. A whopping two whole moves.

E. Eukanuba Boulder

Just north of Stinkin' Lincoln is the hillside's tallest boulder with a classic problem on its north face and V1 slabs on the south face.

☐ 1. Trabaharder V9 ★★★ 🌀
One of the best problems in the state for aesthetics and movement. Climb a series of left-facing sidepulls up and left above an adjacent juniper. A tad dangerous getting situated on the slab. A V10 direct start is named Positioning.

☐ 2. Lippy V0
Directly behind Trabaharder is a short block that provides easy viewing of the repeated failures on Trabaharder. Lippy traverses the lip of the north face.

F. Stinkin' Lincoln

A short boulder found uphill approximately 30 yards from the Holloway Boulder. A V-shaped roof on its left side defines it.

☐ 1. Left Lincoln V4 ★★
Climb the left most arête without using the right wall.

☐ 2. Center Lincoln V1 ★★
Begin in the V-shaped roof and stem up and right on good holds.

Holloway Boulder

Eukanuba Boulder

Stinkin' Lincoln

☐ 3. Stinkin' Lincoln V5 ★★★
A classic sloper problem to the right of Center that starts as a sit down.

☐ 4. Stinkin' Linkage V7 ★★★
A superb traverse of the boulder from right to left. Start on Stinkin' Lincoln and go left all the way through the roof and finish on the slabby east face.

Chiseled Arête V3 Photo by Phillip Benningfield

UNAWEEP CANYON

This vast canyon may well hold the largest concentration of boulder problems to be done in the state, even though one in twenty boulders is unclimbable. The soft Dakota sandstone blocks dot nearly every drainage, plateau, and hillside along a six-mile stretch of road. With a low elevation and infrequent shade trees, summer bouldering is near impossible, but the remainder of the year can be very rewarding. Rest assured that the areas mentioned are not all inclusive, as new problems are developed on a regular basis by boulderers from all over the state.

Directions: From Grand Junction take US Route 50 south to Whitewater. Turn right on State Route 141 (a scenic byway) and drive to the canyon, which begins as sandstone ridges and eventually turns to granite multi-pitch cliffs. All areas are listed in miles from the intersection of Highway 50 and Highway 141.

Best Boulder Problem in Unaweep is located 0.8 mile past the cattle guard (2.8 miles from the intersection of US 50 and State Route 141a). Park on the right side of the road just past a guardrail in a spot big enough for three cars. Walk back down Highway 141 40 yards over a large culvert with stone walls. Head east (uphill) on the left side of the culvert approximately 150 yards following a very faint trail with a couple of cairns. The best problems face uphill (east).

Bat Cave Area/The Slum is located 1.3 miles up canyon. Park in a steep pullout on the right directly before the bridge. Walk up the trail, which begins over the barbed wire fence at 250 yards. Stay on the left trail until a landscaped trail leads to the ridgeline. The wall is southeast-facing. To reach The Slum continue on the trail 350 yards past the small drainage. A smaller trail leads left 150 yards to reach the boulders. The Slum is a tight chasm behind the first set of large boulders.

Rock Shop is on the right side of the canyon at 1.9 miles. Park and cross the creek to reach this long traversing wall.

Texas Boulders/Cancel Christmas
This area is located 3.3 miles up the canyon on the right (just after the cattle guard). Take a right-hand dirt road to parking on either side of the creek. Texas Boulders are found by walking north above the dirt road from the parking (on the west side of the creek) for approximately 150 yards. The blocks are directly above the cattle guard on Highway 141.

Cancel Christmas is found by walking along the dirt road southwest for a few minutes (stay on right-hand road). Approximately 100 yards past an old wooden drainage in the dirt road, head uphill to the west 80 yards. The boulders are found on the south end of a large meadow.

Rock Garden is located up canyon at 4.3 miles on the left. A dirt road veers sharply back from Highway 141. Park immediately after exiting the highway.

Bone Park is located on the right side of the highway at 5.0 miles. A distinct rectangular boulder (Fossil Boulder) sits in the open meadow surrounded by a dirt road.

B.C.'s Western Boulders
These are located at the righthand pullout at 5.0 miles (Bone Park Area, with Fossil Boulder). A good place to camp. Additional directions included with boulders' descriptions.

Hole in One Boulder is located on the left side of the canyon at 5.8 miles. It is a lone block approximately 35 yards from the roadside.

The Black Wave/Brain Area is located on the right side of Highway 141 at 7.1 miles. A dirt road leads directly to The Brain.

Grand Valley Overlook Boulders
This collection of blocks is located 8.1 miles up SR 141 on the right. A large pullout is obvious with a sign for Grand Valley Overlook. The boulders are visible to the west across the creek from the pullout. Walk on a trail across the creek then take the dirt road 150 yards to the west.

Liquor Store Boulder
Same directions as Grand Valley but turn onto the left-hand dirt road at the beginning of the GV pullout. Park immediately then walk straight uphill 75 yards to a distinct traverse boulder.

Mike Freischlag on #3 V4

BEST BOULDER PROBLEM IN UNAWEEP

BOULDER

That's right, the best damn boulder problems in Unaweep are on this east face. The stone is solid (for Unaweep), the view is real nice, and the landing is sand. And, if that's not enough, the Best Boulder Problem ranks as one of the hardest lines. Problems listed left to right across the east face:

❏ **1. V?** 🌀
The left arête with a back-breaking block on the east face. Sounds too good to be true.

❏ **2. Two Smoking Klems V3**
Can you say sandbag? The humungous dyno from the big huecos. Being short will be a detriment on this problem.

❏ **3. V4** ★★★
Straight up the middle of the east face from the sinker pockets to the huge rail then up. This line defines the best part of the boulder.

❏ **4. V2** ★★★
The right to left traverse across the big rail. A fabulous problem on tasty holds.

❏ **5. The Best Boulder Problem in Unaweep V7**
★★★
A complete traverse of the wall from the farthest right holds to the huge dyno. 'Nough said.

THE BEST BUDDY

75 yards to the north from The Best is another east face littered with fun problems. The south face down climb is easily seen from The Best. Problems listed left to right.

❏ **1. Daisies and Butterflies V2** 🌀
On the blunt southeast arête is a gripping problem: not scary but a good grip is crucial.

❏ **2. Raindrops to Waterfalls V2** 🌀
Just to the right is a fine line that moves into the leftmost edge of the big rail running across the east face, then up.

The Best Buddy

Daisies and Butterflies V2

❒ 3. **Traverse V2**
The right to left traverse across the east face on the big rail. Sounds familiar.

❒ 4. **V4**
On the far right of the big rail are two gorgeous edges. Head straight up to the sloping holds and a straight up a frightening top-out or move right and finish above the dihedral for a safer exit. Top-out holds are very questionable on this problem.

❒ 5. **V?**
The dihedral, with questionable top-out holds.

❒ 6. **V1**
Straight up the hill 20 yards to the east is a low-angle slab facing north.

❒ 7. **V?**
On the west face is a bear-hug problem to a left leaning arête. Terrible landing zone.

#3 V2

BAT CAVE
The large southesast-facing overhang wall at the terminus of the landscaped trail 250 yards from from the barbed wire fence at the parking area. Some blatantly chipped holds grace the right side of the overhang.

❒ 1. **V5** ★
A traverse from right to left starting on the sloping flake low and right. Finishes past the steep wall and corner on the west face. Many eliminates can be done to boost the grade.

❒ 2. **V5–V7** ★
On the wall's right side are some contrived problems that pull out the roof on chipped edges and slots. A real classy set of problems.

Bat Cave

JUNIOR CAVE
Located 25 feet to the right of Bat Cave. A V6 traverse goes either way across the cave. No photo.

THE SLUM
Easily seen from the main trail to the south from the Bat Cave. Walk along the main trial another 350 yards going south. A small path goes left 150 yards towards the blocks. Behind the first boulders is a hidden corridor.

❒ 1. **V7** ★
Traverse right to left within the corridor beginning from small crimps and moving left.

❒ 2. **V7**
Straight-up problems within the corridor on friable rock with atrocious landings. Not recommended.

The Slum

ROCK SHOP
The long traverse area that faces the road. An excellent area for a pump as well as contrived problems from V1 to V10. The only downfall to the area is the shortsightedness of a boulderer who thought chipped pockets would add to the natural problems.

❒ 1. **V7**
The main traverse of the wall that begins on the left side above a dirt mound. Traverse right or come into the dirt mound from the right for the same grade.

TEXAS BOULDERS
Named for a large boulder shaped like Texas, with a toprope anchor for a southwest-facing crack problem. Some boulders in the vicinity have anchors but can be bouldered with a couple of pads.

Rock Shop

ANCHOR BOULDER

A large block with excellent warm-ups on the south face. Toproping anchors are present. The downclimb is on the east face.

❏ 1. **V0** ★★
The left problem on the south face. Good holds abound.

❏ 2. **V1** ★★
The middle line up the tallest part of the face.

❏ 3. **V0** ★
The right line on the south face.

HORIZONTAL CRACK BOULDER

A gritty block found 25 yards west of Anchor Boulder.

❏ 1. **V?**
The left line on the east face.

❏ 2. **V3** ★ 🌙
The right line. Start on good pockets to a sloping right-hand edge then to the top.

CORRIDOR BLOCK

A tall boulder found 39 yards to the north through a corridor from Anchor Boulder. Problems are on the northwest face. The downclimb is in the corridor.

❏ 1. **V3** ★★ 🐾
The arête dividing the north and west faces.

❏ 2. **V3** ★★ 🐾🌙
Climb the west face with an initial long reach. The higher holds are a little questionable.

❏ 3. **V0** 🐾🌙
Climb the crack right of #2.

Anchor Boulder

Horizontal Crack

Cancel Christmas East

Corridor Block

Cancel Christmas Block

A huge block with problems on the west and east faces. The boulder just northeast has a couple of V0s.

East Face

❏ **1. V3** ★★
The left set of pockets to the lip.

❏ **2. V4** ★★
Climb the middle of the face from good pockets then right hand up to another pocket then the top.

❏ **3. V3** ★★
The right line starting off a good pocket to the high pocket on #2.

West Face

❏ **1. Cancel Christmas V6** ★★
A committing line starting just left of the small boulder at the base. Excellent pockets lead to a difficult reach to gain the top.

❏ **2. The Grinch V3**
A low start adjacent to the boulder on the right of the west face. The holds are questionable.

Cancel Christmas West

ROCK GARDEN

The only boulderfield on the left side of Hwy. 141 with a concentrated number of problems. The problems stretch well down the dirt road as well as above the parking area. A white smiley face is spray painted on a rock directly before the lefthand pullout.

FACES BOULDER

The first boulder encountered from the parking area. Found just off the right side of the dirt road with a beautiful, tall south-facing wall.

☐ **1. V2** ★ 🌐
The gritty face left of the southwest arête.

☐ **2. V3** ★★★ 🌐
The south face problem that climbs excellent edges.

☐ **3. V1**
The southeast arête. Not too exciting.

☐ **4. V4**
The short sds problem that is just southeast from Faces.

CHISELED ARÊTE

Uphill and east approximately 20 yards from Faces Boulder. The name does not indicate the strong hand of a chipper.

☐ **1. V3** ★★
The left side of the clean arête. A V4 can be done to the right before #2.

☐ **2. V5** ★★
The right side of the perfect arête.

☐ **3. V0** 🌐
A number of easy slabs can be done on the east face.

☐ **4. V3** 🌐 ⚫
A highball problem is about 20 yards southeast from the Chiseled Arête. It climbs the black west face on less than ideal rock. Not pictured.

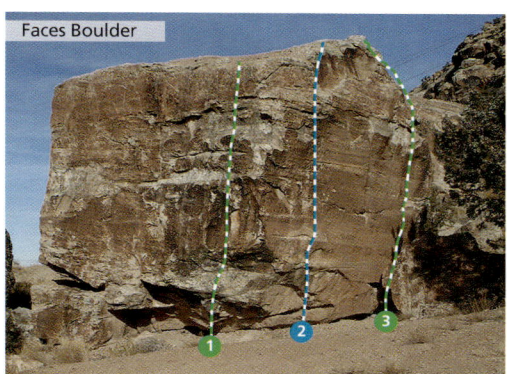
Faces Boulder

Chiseled Arête

Mike Freischlag on the V0 slab of Chiseled Arête Boulder

GASH ROCK

This chasm is located to the south from Faces Boulder approximately 25 yards.

❏ 1. **V2** ★★
The problem faces east and is on the left side of the wall. A bolt is on top.

DECEPTION ROCK

A short block just up the dirt road on the right from Faces Boulder.

❏ 1. **V4** ★
A sds power problem pulls through the overhanging south face.

Note: The next boulders in the Rock Garden are located further down the dirt road from Deception Rock.

ORANGE CRUSH ROCK

A colorful block on the right side of the road approximately 65 yards from Deception Rock and before reaching Broken Boulder.

❏ 1. **V4** ★★
The middle of the north face on crimps, which follows a black streak.

❏ 2. **V2** ★
The right side of the north face on sloping pockets. Finish straight up or right. Two different starts.

BROKEN BOULDER

This is the huge boulder sitting alone in the left meadow after passing Orange Crush Rock. Look not for a broken boulder, but for a boulder that will break you. Three tall problems climb the south face.

❏ 1. **V2** ★ 🌀
The tall face on the left side of the south face. Somewhat fragile.

❏ 2. **V2** ★★ 🌀
Climbs the middle of the south face in a right-facing corner.

❏ 3. **V1** ★★ 🌀
The right side of the south face. Climb above the ledge at eight feet.

❏ 4. **V0**
The east face slab/ramp.

❏ 5. **V2** ★
The northeast arête. A thin traverse can be done into the arête from the right to boost the grade.

❏ 6. **V3** ★★
The north face problem up laybacks.

❏ 7. **V2** ★
The right arête of the north face.

Gash Rock

Deception Rock

Orange Crush Rock

Broken Boulder - South Face

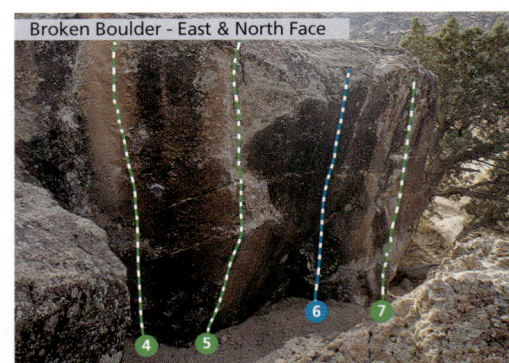
Broken Boulder - East & North Face

COLORED BOULDER

The multicolored block on the left side of the road approximately 200 yards past Broken Boulder. The east face has a number of V0 to V2 problems. Problems aren't labeled.

STRIPED ROCK

The last black and burnt orange boulder approximately 135 yards past Colored Boulder on the left side of the road.

☐ 1. **V1** ★
The left side of the east face is ascended via sharp crimps.

☐ 2. **V1** ★
Just left of the arête on the east face.

☐ 3. **V2** ★★
The right side of the northeast arête.

☐ 4. **V7** ★★
The north face crimp problem with a big move to finish.

POLE ROCK

The small block 30 yards past Striped Rock on the right side of the road. Not pictured.

☐ 1. **V1**
The left side of the arête on the south face.

☐ 2. **V3** ★
The right side of the southeast arête.

☐ 3. **V0**
The line left of the white streak.

BONE PARK

The first area on the right after the Rock Shop (3.1 miles). The Fossil Boulder sits 25 yards off the highway.

FOSSIL BOULDER

The tall, rectangular boulder sitting alone in the giant dirt road/pullout area. A fossilized bone is on the east face (please do not climb on the fossils).

☐ 1. **V1**
On the south face is a right-facing then left-facing dihedral system.

☐ 2. **V0** ★
Jug hauls on the east face (faces the highway).

☐ 3. **V5** ★
A traverse that climbs around the entire boulder.

VICTORIA'S SECRET

The boulder located approximately 80 yards to the northwest of Fossil Boulder. The problems are on the overhanging backside (unseen from the Fossil Boulder). Not pictured.

☐ 1. **V2** ★★
The left problem on the northwest face.

☐ 2. **V3** ★★ 🔘
Straight up above the fire pit on the northwest face.

☐ 3. **V5** ★ 🔘
From a low start on the west face climb up and left on bulbous slopers to good crimps then jugs.

☐ 4. **V3** ★ 🔘
Same start as #3 but move up and right above the tree stump.

☐ 5. **V1**
The south face problem almost within the gap between the adjacent boulder. Not pictured.

Colored Boulder

Striped Rock

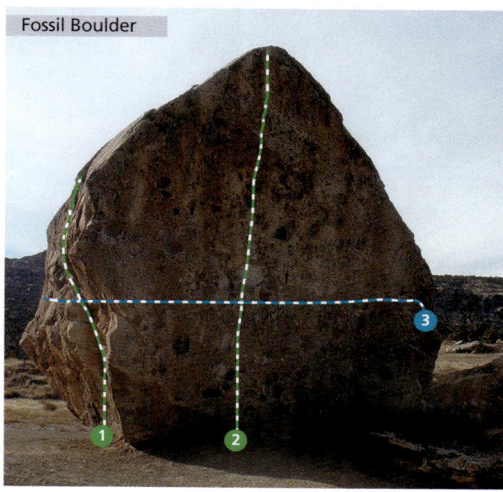
Fossil Boulder

PLETHORA BOULDER AKA RIGHT GONAD

The overhanging block approximately 130 yards to the west from Fossil Boulder. The block sits just off the right side of the highway. Classics!

☐ **1. V6** ★

The huge dyno off the shelf and undercling on the left side of the southeast face. The top-out is quite hard.

☐ **2. V6** ★★

Climbs up the discontinuous seam off layaways to a jug. Hard top-out.

☐ **3. V5** ★★

Start on the incut edge at head height and reach the sloping pocket below the lip then over. A good variation V6 begins left and low and exits the same as #3 by traversing in using pockets left of the high sloping pocket.

☐ **4. V4** ★★

The same start as #3 but finish right in the open groove.

☐ **5. V4** ★★★

Just right of the arête is an awesome dynamic problem. Begins on a great undercling pinch.

☐ **6. V5** ★★

A traverse starting on the lower left of the east face and finishing up the pod problem (#7).

☐ **7. V5** ★★

Starts below the large pod on underclings and gains the pod. Finish up the sloping, left-angling arête and pull onto the slab.

LEFT GONAD

The block just left of the Plethora Boulder. The vertical wall facing the highway has three problems.

☐ **1. V0** ★

The straight-up problem off an awesome pocket to a good ledge.

☐ **2. V4** ★

Climb up the holds surrounding the seam.

☐ **3. V5** ★

The traverse on the southeast face from right to left.

HOLE IN ONE BOULDER

A lone boulder up the highway 0.8 mile from Bone Park on the left. It sits approximately 35 yards from the roadside.

☐ **1. V3** ★★★

Climb up the distinct one-holed south face. A superb problem on bomber stone.

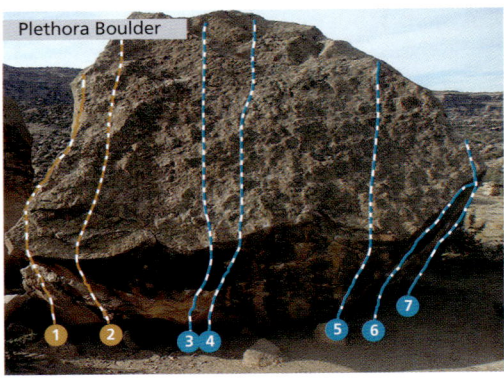

Plethora Boulder

Left Gonad

Hole in One

B.C.'s Western Boulders

This area is easy to find by following a superb trail marked with cairns every 10-20 yards (don't expect all the cairns to be in place due to heavy bovine traffic). A collection of blocks found on the west side of the creek from the Fossil Boulder (the obvious block standing a stone's throw from Highway 141 with bone fossils on its east face). From Fossil Boulder walk southwest to a trail marked with cairns (follows a drainage to the creek). Cross the creek then uphill to a cow-trail intersection and go left approximately 100 yards to Artifact Boulder. Big Black Boulder and the Upper Boulderfield are found by continuing west on the marked (cairn) trail. Big Black is approx. 200 yards west and the Upper Boulderfield is 75 yards below the cliffs and on the west side of a dirt road.

Artifact Boulder

Somewhat of a novelty for Unaweep since the boulder has a near-horizontal roof on its south face. Problems on this block vary substantially in quality. Cows and their detritus seem attracted to it like moths to a flame. South face problems range from V1 to a V6 traverse. Detailed descriptions are left out.

Big Black

A beautiful lone block with decent quality problems along the north face (many contrived lines can be done). Problems on the east face are tall and V0. North-face problems are listed from left to right.

❑ 1. **V0** ★★★ 🚌
An excellent line on the left arête. One of the better lines in the canyon.

❑ 2. **V2** ★★ 🚌 🌙
Just right of #1 is a super-long reach from the starting holds to incut holds.

❑ 3. **V3** ★
From thin edges left of the crack climb straight up on ever-thinning edges. Not pictured.

❑ 4. **V0** ★
The crack on the right side of the block. Not pictured.

Upper Boulderfield

A collection of beautiful blocks sporting maroon and black stripes. This area is undoubtedly one of the funner in the entire canyon with ten or so climbable blocks nestled in the same zone. Problems listed range from incredibly tall V0 slabs to short V6s; many more nearby lines can be found and done.

Slabular Block

This is the first big boulder encountered, with a great south-facing warm-up slab. A comfortable flat rock sits adjacent to take the mandatory naps and get refreshments.

❑ 1. **V0** ★ 🚌
The left side of the south face, up big holds.

❑ 2. **V0** ★★ 🚌
Climb the broken seam up the middle of the south face.

❑ 3. **V1** ★ 🚌
Directly right of the seam, climb not-so-obvious holds to the top.

❑ 4. **V2** ★ 🚌
The blunt right arête, before the flat boulder. A hard start then eases up.

❑ 5. **V3** ★ 🌙
Sitting on the flat block climb up the sloping holds.

❑ 6. **V1** ★
Climb the face just to the right of #5.

Artifact Boulder

Big Black

Slabular Block

West Boulders

Two blocks that sit just to the west of the Slabular Block.

First West Boulder

☐ 1. V2 ★★
Climb the northeast slab and hope for the best when you reach out left. A safer exit can be done to the right.

☐ 2. **West Crack V0**
The short crack facing the Second West Boulder.

☐ 3. V0
Climb the west arête and don't fall!

Second West Boulder

A shorter version of First West Boulder. The north side has numerous sit-starts.

☐ 1. V2 ★★
The leftmost problem on the north face. A sds makes it V4.

☐ 2. V6 ★
A sds just left from the offset seam and #3. One big move to get the ass off the dirt.

☐ 3. V4 ★
A low start in the offset crack. It's V0 from a stand up start.

☐ 4. V0 ★
The south face has a couple of nice V0 affairs.

Southern Block

A lone boulder south from Slabular Block a mere 40 yards. No photo.

☐ 1. **Let The Chips Fall Where They May V0**
Climb the fragile east face.

☐ 2. V2 ★
Climb the left-leaning sloping ramp to a dirty top-out. V4 from a low start.

Eastern Blocks

A couple of lone problems can be found to the east of Slabular Block 25 to 40 yards away.

☐ 1. V3 ★★
The jump start problem of the area. The first move can rebut the easily swayed, but this is a problem well worth a couple of failed jumps.

☐ 2. V2s
There are a couple of reasonable problems on the easternmost boulder before the open field area. One is vertical in a corridor. The other faces the field and starts steep to an easy top-out.

The Black Wave/Brain Area

This scattered selection of boulders is NO LONGER the last developed area in the sandstone part of the canyon. Many problems on some of the more frightening faces await ascents..

The Brain aka Dr. Seuss Cave

The first boulder on the left after exiting the highway on the dirt road. About 40 yards from the road. The problem faces southwest.

☐ 1. **Psycho Boy V6** ★★
A dynamic problem that starts on two-pocket underclings and throws to the lip.

First West Boulder

Second West Boulder

Bucket Cave

Found approximately 40 yards downhill (west) from The Brain. It has problems on the overhanging northwest face and a dark brown south face.

☐ 1. V3-V5 ★
Many sds problems can be done throughout the overhang.

☐ 2. V4 ★★
Traverse either way across the northwest face.

☐ 3. V4
A sds problem on the south face that climbs up and right on sloping edges and jugs.

Black Wave Area

Found by walking south from The Brain past a huge overhanging, west-facing arête that sits next to a drainage. Continue south over the next ridge for approximately 200 yards, staying on the west side of the highway. The Black Wave is just past Big Red Boulder.

Big Red Boulder

A huge red block a little over 30 feet northeast from the Black Wave.

☐ 1. V4 ★
The red and black striped northwest face. Starts on a left-hand layback and climbs up through the black stripe.

☐ 2. V1
A dirty problem climbs the overhang on the east face.

Black Wave

The boulder just southwest from Big Red. It has a clean, black east face.

☐ 1. V4 ★★
Climbs up the far-left side of the Black Wave beginning in the layback crack and going through the limbs of a nearby juniper

Bucket Cave

Bucket Cave - south face

BLACKED-OUT BOULDER

Found closer to the highway from the Black Wave approximately 20 yards to the southeast. The problems are on the east face.

☐ 1. **V1** ★
Climbs the sharp flakes on the left side of the east face.

☐ 2. **V2** ★
Just right of the large sharp flake is a straight-up problem.

☐ 3. **V3**
Starts right of the plus sign on a pinch nipple and trends left.

☐ 4. **V1**
Just right of the nipple climb up and right.

Big Red Boulder

GRAND VALLEY OVERLOOK AREA

Whether or not these boulders are newly developed does not matter; these are easily some of the best problems Unaweep has to offer. The rock is pretty good and the lines have very aesthetic movements. Besides, the boulders are so damn easy to find all your mental energy can be used to figure out sequences.

CHINESE ALGEBRA BOULDER

The name says it all. Found next to the dirt road.

Black Wave

☐ 1. **V1** ★
Climb the left side of the northeast face starting from a low fin and edge.

☐ 2. **V2** ★★
Climb the line just right of #1 from a right-hand undercling and thin left edge. Then climb straight up to progressively better edges.

☐ 3. **V2** ⬤
Climb the right side of the northeast face eight feet left from the arête. The holds on this one are less than desirable.

☐ 4. **Chinese Algebra V6** ★★★
Low start on the left side of the west face, then to bad slopers leading out to the right. A tough mantel problem exits after reaching the sloping lip.

☐ 5. **V3** ★★
The right line out the overhang on the west face.

☐ 6. **V1** ★
Climb the brown rock on the far left side of the south face. A traverse can be done into this problem from the right.

☐ 7. **V1** ★
Climb the thin edges right of the juniper from a low start.

☐ 8. **V0** ★
Climb the arête just right of #7.

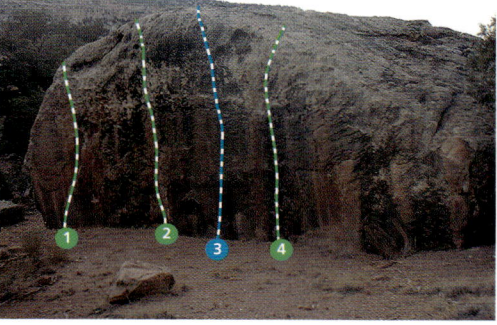

Blacked-Out Boulder

Grand Valley Overlook Boulders

S Crack Block

A tall boulder found 40 yards to the north from Algebra. The south face is clean and burnt-orange.

◻ 1. **V1** ★
Climb the traverse on the northeast face then top out. Bad feet at the end of the traverse.

◻ 2. **V0**
Across the south face are many casual tall V0 slabs.

◻ 3. **V2** ★
Climb the southeast arête, with a long reach to gain the high finishing holds.

◻ 4. **S Crack V1** ★
Climb the crack on the southeast face.

◻ 5. **S Seam V3** ★★
The right crack on the east face.

◻ 6. **V?**
The dirty, fragile righthand problem before the tree.

Boxcar Boulder

Found 30 yards uphill to the north from Algebra. The gorgeous southeast face is undercut on the left side.

◻ 1. **V?**
Start at overhang on the left side of the southeast face and pull onto the face then up.

◻ 2. **V4** ★
Starts off a ledge on the left before the undercut roof.

◻ 3. **V3** ★
Climb the middle seam on the southeast face with a boulder to land on.

◻ 4. **V4** ★
The ultra-thin seam right of #3 that peters out then opens up at a mono.

◻ 5. **V0**
Climb the right arête on the southeast face.

◻ 6. **Racing the Sun V2** ★★
Climb the left side of the north face from a triangular hold to bad sloping edges.

A few shorter boulders are located 20 yards below the Boxcar. Problems range from V2 to V5.

Arête Boulder

This distinct block has two fine arêtes surrounding the southeast face. It is located 40 yards uphill and west from the Boxcar Boulder.

◻ 1. **V3** ★
The left arête on the southeast face.

◻ 2. **V4** ★★★
One of the classic problems in Unaweep Canyon! If you make only one trip definitely do this line. Start off the hueco then move left to a sidepull and a big throw. The top holds should be climbed on lightly.

◻ 3. **Invisible Sun V6** ★★
Climb the right-angling seam on positive but minute edges, starting from the good edges with the foot thrown onto the big ledge.

◻ 4. **V3** ★★
Climb the left arête on the southeast face.

◻ 5. **V0**
On the east face are a couple of V0 lines.

Pink Floyd Boulder

From Arête Boulder head northwest 100 yards across an open meadow towards the cliff bands. The boulder faces south and is as obvious as your nose.

◻ 1. **V3**
On the far left side of the south face is a seam that slabs out after the first moves.

◻ 2. **Earthbound Misfit V3** ★★★
On the south face is a superb distinct problem, with a party-trick start, to a pocket then outstanding pulls to the top.

◻ 3. **Comfortably Numb V6** ★★
The hard line right of #2 in the black rock. Start low on crimps then pull to a sharp finger lock, then up. Watch out for the fragile lip holds!

◻ 4. **V0**
On the east face are a couple of uneventful V0 problems.

Liquor Store Boulder

A tall block located 75 yards towards the cliffband from the dirt road, directly across the road from the downhill start of the Grand Valley Overlook pullout.

◻ 1. **V6** ★★
A long left to right traverse along the north face. The top-out is dicey.

◻ 2. **Latin Heat V5** ★
Up the left side of the north face starting from decent flat holds along the traverse to a bad right-hand sloper, then to good pockets. Ends on the same hold as #3. An easier V1 is to the left.

◻ 3. **V3** ★
The problem just right of Latin Heat. Climb straight up.

◻ 4. **V3**
An arête problem on the adjacent boulder to the right of Liquor Store.

ADDITIONAL AREAS

Scott Blunk on Via the Hote One V9   Photog by John Sherman

ADDITIONAL AREAS

BLUE MESA RESERVOIR

Numerous boulders line US 50 west of the reservoir.

IRON DOLLAR-COTOPAXI

A novel set of striking granite boulders quarried for use in places as far away as Chicago. This State Trust Land requires a permit for rocks but none for rock climbing. What this small area offers is unsurpassed obscurity, stellar rock, and memorable lines with a panoramic view of the Sangre de Cristo range.

This area is NOT a summer area, as the southern exposure will melt flesh. Best visited in late fall and winter. Bring a lot of pads!

Directions: From Cotopaxi (located on US Route 50 approximately 40 minutes west of Cañon City/22 miles from Salida) head south on 1A Road (at the gas station/grocery store) for 3.0 miles to a left at 37 Road (McCoy Gulch). Take this easy dirt road for 1.3 miles past the right hand road leading downhill (stay left) and continue to a quarried area and parking spot alongside the road. A steep, 4x4 road leads to the left for a very short distance and the first quarried rock is on the road's left side with V0 to V6). Walk up the dirt road for 10-odd minutes (approximately 900 yards) past some intermittent blocks. You will know when you have arrived when a set of huge, white, quarried boulders lead up the hill on the right and the mountains are visible to the left (south). Expect to bushwhack!

FUSION WALL

The name will be all too evident once you are standing in front of this spray painted block. Don't be too discouraged, as the warm-ups are nice and the top-out views are unsurpassed. On the back side of the first monster quarried blocks (40 yards up the hill). Skirt around the right quarried boulder or scramble between the blocks. Problems listed from left to right:

❑ **1. E's A V1**
On the separate block left of the Fusion Wall is a nice, shorter arête just left of the chimney between the boulders.

❑ **2. V2** 🌐 ⚙
The tallest problem up the far left side and above the offset horizontal crack.

❑ **3. Furry Flake V0** ⚙
Climbs the thin flake to huge jugs at the top (17 feet). Probably the best downclimb.

❑ **4. V2** ⚙
Right of Furry Flake, up not so good rock.

❑ **5. V1**
Middle of the wall.

❑ **6. V2**
The shorter right side of the wall has a crimper problem with two long moves. A number of contrived traverses and straight-up problems round out the warm-up.

BACK-DOOR BOULDER

Immediately uphill from the Fusion Wall is a white boulder with a shorter uphill side and taller downhill side.

❑ **1. Uphill Affair V0** ⚙
The corner and ramp on the uphill side of the block.

❑ **2. South Face V?** ⚙
Undone due to the fear factor.

DEAD MAN ARÊTES

Again, just uphill a couple of yards from Back-Door Boulder are two extremely tall arêtes with pretty good landings, although you would do best never to fall from the 25-foot lips.

❑ **1. V?** 🌐 ⚙
The left laser-cut arête with little on the righthand face. Just a 90-degree vertical arête for 25 feet.

❑ **2. V?** 🌐 ⚙
The arête right of the corner crack. Climbs straight up the face or venture out on the arête.

UPPER BLOCKS

Two boulders are at the top of the ridgeline and can be reached by following the faint trail (drainage) right (east) of the monster quarried blocks (do not try and scramble around the boulders with a pad unless you like frustration and bushwhacking). Start from Fusion Wall and go uphill past the Dead Man Arêtes staying to the right (east) and hop over a couple of boulders until reaching the drainage, then walk a couple of minutes uphill to the ridgeline.

THE RIPPER BOULDER

The boulder closest the trail/drainage with a distinct east facing crack. The downclimb ventures across the west face above an ankle-breaking boulder.

❑ **1. East Side Crack (aka American or Americant) V6** 🌐 ⚙
Scary as you reach up high for the insecure hand jams. A darn good problem worth lugging five pads up the hill.

❑ **2. Mexican or Mexicant V2** 🌐 ⚙
The classic line on the northeast corner that starts with a little jump start. V7 sds.

❏ 3. The Ripper V5 😊
Climb up the north face from a good edge and bad undercling to a long reach for the ripper edge. A harder variation starts the same but moves left from the jug to slopers then the right-facing layback and more slopers.

THE PIT BOULDER
To the west of The Ripper is another huge, quarried boulder with au natural problems on the north side and quarried lines on the south side. Best downclimb is above The Pit.

❏ 1. Traverse V? 😊
On the northeast face is a left-to-right lip traverse above a terrible landing zone.

❏ 2. The Pit Crack V1 😊
Just right of Traverse is a deep, dark pit with a splitter crack.

❏ 3. North Arête V1 😊
A couple of moves on the north arête.

❏ 4. The Arête V8 😊
The steep, south-facing arête on the left side of a block touching The Pit Boulder's southwest side.

Coal Creek Boulders Overview

COAL CREEK BOULDERS
Located west of Redstone. Drive west past the coke ovens to a large talus slope on the right side of the road. Plenty of parking just after the cattle guard. Problems range from V0-V8.

COTTONWOOD LAKE (BUENA VISTA)
Take Cottonwood Pass Road (CC 306) to a left on CC 344 (sign for Cottonwood Lake) and drive 2.5 miles to parking on the left. Walk up the road 100 yards and a large block sits in the woods on the left.

CRESTONE (NORTH CRESTONE CAMPGROUND)
Take Road T east into Crestone (not the Baca Grande) following Golden Road to Alder Street (go left) to Mica following brown National Forest signs to the campground. Total mileage from CO 17 and Road T is 14.1 miles. A few fun boulders are littered throughout the campground with developed problems from V0-V7.

CAMPGROUND 7 BOULDER V0-V6
An awesome block sits in the woods next to the creek with problems all over the boulder! If you can get this campsite or #6 you will have the boulder to yourself.

CAMPGROUND 5 V0-V6
Across the road from the campground is a boulder sitting next to the road with a couple of decent lines. Another boulder sits up the hillside with good V0 slabs and a tough little V3 on the west face.

Phillip Benningfield on Campground V5

Campground #5

Trailside Boulder

TRAILSIDE BOULDER V1-V7
Located at the end of the road at the parking for the trail. Short, steep problems exemplify this high quality granite block.

EAST HAGERMAN PASS (LEADVILLE)

This alpine bouldering area has a few quality lines (V0-V9) dispersed between many exfoliating piles and lichen covered blocks.

Directions: From the stop light at Safeway in Leadville head west following signs for Turquoise Lake. Pass the lake and continue west to a left turn on a dirt road for Hagerman Pass. Continue on this well-maintained road past the trailhead parking at the tunnel to the second large pullout across the road from the Centennial Midland sign.

Pullout boulders can be found by walking through the woods north (or up the road) approximately 100 yards. The V3 Crack is located here as well as other lines from V0-V5.

YOU PEOPLE/POWER SURGE

From the parking area cross the road and walk up the Centennial Midland trail and cross the first drainage/trail on a FAINT trail headed uphill. Continue approximately 150 yards to a set of boulders in an open area (You People V5 and the classic V3 can be found here). Power Surge is another couple hundred yards uphill at the cliffband within a talus field.

James Wilde on Power Surge V5

Pete Zoller on You People V5

East Elk Creek Boulders- New Castle

Continue past the New Castle Boulders on a rough dirt road to the end of the road. The first boulder is at the parking. Continue up the trail to a few blocks (visible from the trail and on the other side of the creek). Blocks are found on both sides of the creek.

Kelsey Campground (South Platte) V1-V4

A couple of tall crack lines exist near this campground, if you like committing, old-school cracks with numerous undeveloped (although pebbly, sharp Pikes Peak granite).

Park at the campground gate and follow a climber's trail towards the cliff. Walk past newly-established trails (two total) for approximately 250 yards. Go southwest on the second trail for 30 yards to the first boulder with highball crack...a couple other boulders are directly uphill a few yards. Along the trail another 30 yards is the second highball affair.

Lightner Creek (Durango)

Directions: Head west from Durango on highway 160 then turn right on CR 208 and follow national forest signs for Dry Creek. Boulders are located off the road before the trailhead. All rock on the east side of the road is closed for wildlife. Public access is prohibited east of La Plata Co. Rd. 208 and north of US 160 from April 1 through July 15. Public access is prohibited from the last day of the established deer and elk seasons through March 31.

Chris Schulte on Scimitar V10 (Lightner Creek)

Mike Freischlag on a V3 at Lime Kiln

Lime Kiln

Directions: From the intersection of highway 160/285) in Monte Vista, go south on CO 15 then turn right on Lariat Rd. just after the fire house. Follow the road for about 4 miles; it turns to dirt at 2 miles. Before the road makes a 90-degree left turn, take a right onto a smaller dirt road; follow it for approximately 4 miles; it will cross a dry creek bed at 1.5 miles and then head due west. At the four-way intersection, take the left road that heads south. This section of the road has some dips and mudholes that can be rough for low clearance vehicles. Follow this road for one mile, past the first cliff, with a handful of bolted routes, to the main cliff 1/4 mile farther. Park at the main cliff (Promised Land) with dozens of bolted climbs.

Hike right/east along the base of the cliff until you can pick your way up the hill aiming for the big ponderosa pine to the right. Once you've made it through the next band of rock head left (west) across the slabs to find Sabra and Shatila shelter.

Lonely Stoners (Witches Canyon)

If the extensive cornucopia of problems in Witches isn't enough simply put on your hiking boots and take a 20 minute stroll up and southwest from Witches You Bitches Wall following intermittent cairns (DO NOT THINK THERE IS A CAIRN EVERY FIVE FEET) and you will come across a distant and quiet zone with high quality problems ranging from simple V0s to tweaky V7s to super highball V2s.

McCoy Gulch (Cortez)

This gulch runs through parts of Cortez and has decent sandstone but sees little traffic. Be aware of snakes in the warm months.

Trixie T on V3

OIL WELL FLAT ROAD (CAÑON CITY)

Take Field Avenue north to Fremont County Road 9 (Red Canyon and Shelf Road). Drive 3.3 miles just past the bridge over Fourmile Creek. Take a right on an unsigned dirt road (marked after first switchback as Oil Flat Road). Boulders can be found throughout the area to the south. Follow dirt roads to the terminus in the far south reaches of the area.

OURAY

A few boulders line the highway on the left as one enters town.

RIFLE MOUNTAIN PARK

Rifle Mountain Park is a sport climber's dream with spraying crowds and excellent limestone. As an added bonus, the bases of the cliffs provide some good boulder problems. This is certainly not a destination spot for the wise boulderer, rather it's a good change of rock and the opportunity to brush shoulders with egomaniacal sport climbers.

Directions: Coming from Denver on I-70, take the New Castle exit (#105) and drive through town to 7th Street (CR 245). Take a right and follow this road for 12.3 miles. Make sure not to turn right or left on the occasional side road. Of note is that CR 245 turns to CR 226 (Grass Valley Road) before eventually intersecting with State Route 325. Go right on Hwy. 325 until it enters Rifle Mountain Park. Location of crags is given in mileage from the RMP entrance sign.

THE WASTELAND is located at a pullout on the left side of the road after 0.4 mile. The crag is directly across the road. The Lower Tier has a two-car dirt pullout at 0.5 mile. Walk the trail to the cliff then go right.

THE BAUHAUS WALL has a pullout on the right at 0.8 mile. Cross the creek (on a wooden bridge) then go right then take a left after approximately 40 yards on a faint trail leading to the cliff. The problems are at the far left (highest) end of the cliff.

ANTI-PHIL has a picnic area pullout on the left at 1.1 miles. Cross the creek on a log downstream then go right and follow the trail to the cliff (go right when the trail hits the cliff). The problems are in the clearing with the picnic table and beyond before reaching the small dirt knoll.

FIRING CHAMBER has a large parking area on the left at 1.3 miles. The crag is across the creek.

SAGUACHE (CO 114)

West of Saguache at the intersection of Conejos Pass Road (41G) many cliffbands line the south side of the highway.

SHELF ROAD

The limestone boulders of at Shelf Road's dry creekbeds and wooded hillsides are a diamond in the rough. The pocketed and edge-filled boulders are sharp, occasionally fragile, and mostly covered in pine needles and grass. A few of the problems are worn smooth as butter from the once-active creek. These afford kind pockets and smooth slopers. Shaded boulders, with various orientations, allows bouldering to be a nearly year-round activity. Best of all, the boulders are well away from the blabbering dressed-to-kill sport climbers.

Directions: In Cañon City locate Field Avenue (on the frontage road between Burger King and Pepsi Cola). Drive north on Field, which turns into Fremont County Road 9. Mileage to reach the camping and bouldering areas is given from the frontage road and Field Avenue.

SAND GULCH CAMPGROUND is located at 12.7 miles on the left of Fremont County Road 9. Sand Gulch Boulders are located by following the marked trail from the Sand Gulch Campground. Go down the hill and follow the creek bed into the canyon. The boulders begin at the trail headed up to the Contest Wall and continue past the northern trail connecting the Freeform Wall and the Contest Wall.

DARK SIDE BOULDERS are reached from the marked trail, past The Bank campground. Park in the day-use lot and walk down The Bank road to a sign directing climbers to the Dark Side/Cactus Cliff.

HEAVEN BOULDERS are located at 16.3 miles. The parking is at 16.6 miles on the left. Do not park on the road below the boulders. A short walk, approximately 300 yards back up the road (east) brings one to the blocks. For obscure bouldering continue up the drainage for 20 minutes to a ponderosa hillside, shade, and cooler temperatures and quiet UNDEVELOPED bouldering.

A V3 at The Quarry

STEALTH BLOCKS-BUENA VISTA

Across the Arkansas River from the Numbers boating put-in on US 24 north of Buena Vista. Park in a large pullout on the river side of the highway just south of mile marker 198. Access requires crossing the river at low water above the put in...BE VERY CAREFUL! Problems range from cruiser V0s to classic V9.

THE QUARRY (DEL NORTE)

A large area similar to the Penitente area developed by highly motivated youths from the San Luis Valley. The entire area includes numerous canyons and draws to develop new lines as well as repeat some very fine ryholite faces. To date, the developed problems range from casual vertical routes to steep, pocketed, and huecoed lines.

THE SPOILS

Same directions as Sand Gulch in Howard but continue up the road/drainage a total of 2.3 miles on Sand Gulch Road and park (at 2.4 miles the road splits and you have gone too far). Follow a small drainage on the west side of road and follow cairns to a high ridgeline littered with cobbly rock. Problem range from V0-V?.

US HIGHWAY 50

(PARKDALE TO COTOPAXI)

Numerous areas are roadside from Parkdale to Cotopaxi. Easy parking and the largest conglomeration of problems ranging from V0-V6. Although this set of boulders lies in spitting distance of the highway, the Arkansas River drowns out almost all the road noise. A pleasant setting with high quality problems, fly fishing, and cold water to keep beers chilled and soak swollen fingers.

WOLF CREEK PASS

All along US 50 from South Fork west, boulders and cliffs can be found...do not trespass!

Beaver Creek Recreation Area has a few obscure boulders that see little traffic. Turn right off US 50 west of South Fork 1.4 miles and drive 1.1 miles to a large pullout on the right. Cross the road after 40 yards, going north.

MM 263

The Spoils project

SUMMIT COUNTY

Summit County doesn't lack boulderering stone. With three main areas to choose from—each differing in quantity, level of development, and rock type—the hungry boulderer will be satiated. The alpine environment is a great place to escape the blistering heat of the lowlands and huge crowds. Only the Frisco Boulder leaves something to be desired, as it sits directly above Interstate 70 and constantly echoes the drum of diesel engines.

Directions: All areas listed are reached via Interstate 70.

MONTEZUMA is reached by taking the Dillon exit (exit 205-Keystone Ski Resort) and driving on US Route 6 east, almost past Keystone Ski Resort. Take a right on Montezuma Road (the last turn into Keystone) and drive to two areas located at 1.1 miles and 1.8 miles. Both areas are located on the left side of the road.

SWAN MOUNTAIN BOULDERS are reached by taking Highway 6 east towards Keystone. The mileage is 3.3 miles to Swan Mountain Road from the light at Dillon Town Center. Turn right on Swan Mountain Road and drive 1.9 miles to a right turn into Swan Mountain Recreation Area. Park immediately on the right and walk a dirt road (on the right) that begins just past the entrance gate. The road heads north, but at approximately 150 yards a trail heads northwest from the left side of the dirt road. Reach the ridge and drop down to the boulders.

FRISCO BOULDERS are found by taking the Main Street exit for Frisco (exit 201). Park on the north side of the interstate and walk the westbound entrance ramp until almost even with the last light pole. Scramble up the hill to the right. The boulder appears on a tier above the entrance ramp.

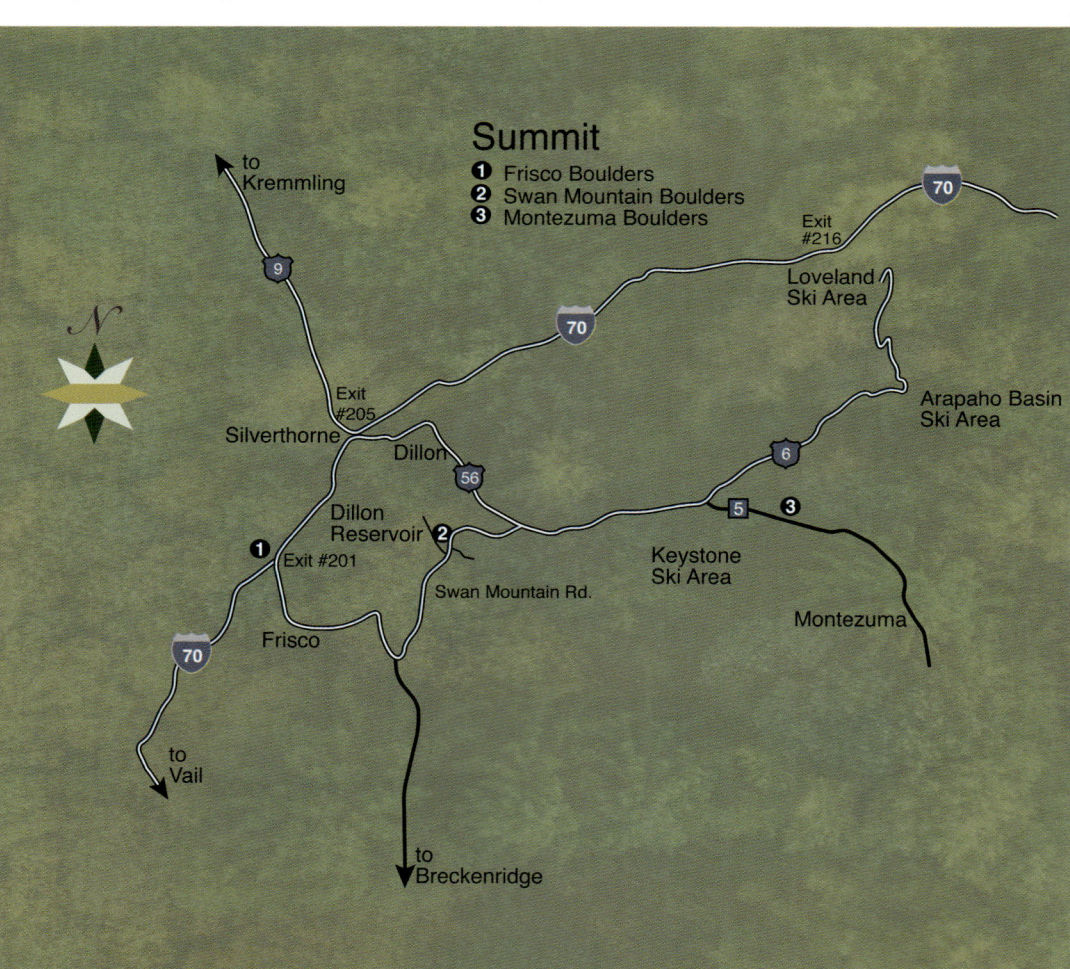

MONTEZUMA

The granite boulders on Montezuma Road are rarely climbed and the chance to find new blocks is ever-present. A few of the holds are dusted with faint chalk marks, but even these may disappear as new development threatens the bouldering. Because of these future access problems, comprehensive information is not given. The first area is located on the left side of Montezuma Road at 1.1 miles (just past the Ski Tip Lodge) and is easily visible through the trees. The other area is found at 1.8 miles. Park in a pullout on the left side of the road and follow a trail from the right of the pullout into the woods. A couple of small boulders appear after approximately 50 yards and sit within spitting distance of the road.

SWAN MOUNTAIN BOULDERS

A long ridge of sandstone with many tall problems as well as two smaller boulders sitting on the hillside below the ridge. An excellent area for beginner and intermediate bouldering. Problems are listed from The Pillar to the Slab Wall then the smaller separate boulders.

THE PILLAR

The distinct pillar that is broken off from the ridge-line at the far north end of the area.

❐ 1. **V0** ★★★
A jug haul on the west face. Beware the loose blocks with chalk Xs.

❐ 2. **V3** ★★
A traverse of The Pillar from the west face crack around right to the east face. Bad footholds and sloping edges on the east face.

❐ 3. **V1** ★★
The southeast arête has a committing problem above talus that feature small crimps on the right side of the arête and flat jugs on the left.

TALL OVERHANG AREA

Just right of The Pillar is a section of the ridge with blocky overlaps above ankle-breaking talus.

❐ 4. **V0** ★
The wide crack set back in a small alcove with good handholds surrounding the crack. Left of the main overlaps.

❐ 5. **V0**
The problem just right of #4.

❐ 6. **V1** ★
A low traverse under the overlaps can be done from right to left.

❐ 7. **V1** ★★
On the right side of the overlaps is a committing problem. Another problem appears to pull out the middle of the overlaps and is substantially scarier.

SLAB WALL

The tall slab stretching from the right of the overlaps to the trail on the far right. Many decent lines with a multitude of variations exist on this wall.

❐ 1. **V0s** ★
Many easy problems on the short left side of the wall.

❐ 2. **V0** ★
A 19-foot-tall crack right of the shortest left side of the wall with jugs surrounding the crack. The face just left is V1.

SOUTH PLATTE

The immensity of the Platte region provides a near-endless supply of bouldering possibilities, although many of the boulders, on closer inspection, are nothing short of piles. A handful of areas, namely Turkey Rock, Sheep's Nose, Sphinx Rock and Glen Elk have easy access and occasionally really prime granite—never underestimate the potential for new problems—nor, for that matter, old forgotten gems from the days of yesteryear.

SPHINX ROCK

From Denver: Take US Route 285 past Conifer to Pine Junction. Go left (headed south) on Road 126 (Pine Valley Road) for 6.5 miles to Pine. Turn left on Jefferson County Road 83. Drive 0.4 mile to parking on the left or right of road. Sphinx Rock (the cliff band on the right that houses the famous overhanging splitter Sphinx Crack) is a two-minute hike to the east and easy to see.

From South Colorado: Take State Route 67 from Woodland Park to Deckers then continue north on Jefferson County Road 126 to Pine and follow directions above.

GLEN ELK BOULDER

From Pine, drive east on Jefferson County Road 83 (past the ever-popular Bucksnort Inn) to a lone boulder next to the road (with an adjacent one-car pullout) before entering the small enclave of Glen Elk. The block sits next to Elk Creek. From US Route 285 at Conifer, you can also continue west to a left on South Elk Creek Road. Drive south through Glen Elk and just after passing through town, the block is on your right, by the creek and visible from the road

TURKEY ROCKS-SOUTH SIDE BOULDERS

A massive area overflowing with hundreds of boulders: some chossy, some scrumptious. A few of the developed blocks are listed below.

Directions: From Campsite #3 take the closed dirt road to the south and continue approximately 150 yards to the silver gate. The boulders are past the gate to the northwest.

☐ 1. **Crack Boulder Problem V?** ★★★
This boulder sits 75 yards past the silver gate and 60 yards up the hillside to the west. A classic line that couldn't be more obvious as one jams the off-hands right-leaning crack. This is, more than likely, a toprope.

☐ 2. **V1**
Obvious little cracked boulder 35 yards behind and to the west from Crack Boulder.

☐ 3. **V2**
Crumbly arête on the boulder adjacent to the V1 crack.

LITTLE ARÊTES AREA

These little blocks are small and safe: a nice respite from the highball affairs. Continue down the dirt road past the silver gate to a haggard old barbed-wire fence. Then walk west up the fence-line to the first Little Arête.

☐ 1. **Fence Arête V4** ★ 🌙
The arête problem next to the fence, with a weird start to a double arête.

LITTLE LEFT ARÊTE

This block is next door to the Little Right Arête and located 20 yards south from the Fence Arête; the boulder rises a mere 10 feet tall.

☐ 1. **V3**
Climb the overhanging east face from a hard start to a mantel on the slab.

☐ 2. **V0**
The right-leaning arête on the northwest face.

LITTLE RIGHT ARÊTE

The boulder sitting next to Little Left Arête.

☐ 1. **V0**
A couple of easy lines on the south and west faces.

☐ 2. **V0**
The right side of the south face.

NORTH ARÊTE BLOCK

This singular boulder sits 30 yards to the north of the Little Arêtes.

☐ 1. **Running Fart V2** ★
A ridiculous running start problem on the left side of the south face to bad little slopers and a flop finish.

☐ 2. **Brain Fart V1**
Crumbling mass on the southwest arête.

TURKEY TAIL - NORTH SIDE BOULDERS

From campsite #8 walk up the only trail (10-15 minutes) headed to the north face of Turkey Tail and the gap to reach the south face of Turkey Perch.

ARCH ENEMY SLAB

A spectacular slab tooth sitting on the north face of Turkey Tail and next to the trail. Two boulders to the east offer more problems in the V-easy range.

☐ 1. **V2** ★★
Climb up the huge northwest slab from the left to reach the high seam.

☐ 2. **V1** ★★
The right arête on the northwest face to the high seam.

☐ 3. **V0** ★★ 😈
Climb the double arête on the south face—this is also the downclimb.

TURKEY PERCH BOULDERS

These boulders can be reached from the south side by walking through the jumbled masses below Rooster Tail and Turkey Tail and by some houses (a faint trail leads across the south side and intermittently joins with an old washed-out road). The boulders are also reached from the north side from campsite #8 or the Turkey Rock access trail. Walk through the gap between Turkey Perch and Turkey Tail's north face.

QUIVERING QUILL BLOCKS

These boulders sit in clear sight of the classic Quivering Quill 5.10d crack (faces north). Problems range from V0 to V2.

ADDITIONAL TURKEY PERCH BLOCKS

There is a huge boulderfield below the ultra-popular cracks on the south face of Turkey Perch. Problems range from V0 (with real bad landings) to V2 (with not-so-bad landings).

BOTTOM OF THE HEAP BLOCKS

These boulders are the lowest boulders on the hillside below the south face of Turkey Perch. Scattered throughout the boulderfield are a handful of higher quality lines, with plenty of potential for new problems.

BLOOD BOULDER

This is one of the lowest blocks in the boulderfield, with a view of an old tan trailer to the south. A roadbed is 60 yards to the south before the trailer. The problems are on the south face.

❏ 1. **V0**
Climb the left arête on the south face.

❏ 2. **V6**
Right of #1 in a left-facing dihedral with an atrocious finish. The rock is fragile at the lip.

FUN GOTTI BOULDER

Directly behind the Blood Boulder five yards to the north. To the north of Fun Gotti is a beautiful, thin, vertical face that spits off all attempts—well, mine anyway.

❏ 1. **V0**
Climb the north slab.

❏ 2. **V2**
Climb the overhanging south face to a knife-edge arête and finishing slab. A traverse can be done from the right.

STEAMBOAT SPRINGS

The bouldering in and around Steamboat may have nothing on the excellent skiing, mountain biking and rafting, but what bouldering exists is pretty good. If you need a fix, and your fingers are not soft mush from sitting in the hot springs, two areas can be reached very easily 10 minutes from the town's main drag.

Fish Creek Falls

The definition of a quick-fix bouldering session, offering problems in a range of grades. The base of the crag offers a few fun problems. A couple of boulders near the cliff can be exploited for a decent pump. The views from this boulderfield are incredible!

Directions: From Lincoln Avenue turn right on 3rd Street then right on Fish Creek Falls Road. Drive 2.9 miles to the parking area on the left. Additional parking is just up the road a short distance. From the first parking area walk up the paved sidewalk next to the road (towards the other parking area). Take the rocky path on the left (heading north) and walk for a few minutes staying on the main trail. The trail hits the obvious crag and surrounding mini-blocks. The crag has a few bolted lines and a great view of Fish Creek Falls.

West Rabbit Ears Pass

A quiet boulderfield just off the turmoil of US 40. A few years ago a handful of problems were developed, but neglect over the past couple of years have left them devoid of chalk and flesh. A motivated climber could easily get a substantial pump and possible first ascents. The completed problems are hard to discern as spider webs and lichen have taken hold once again. Problems range from V0 short slabs to V8.

Directions: From Steamboat drive up US 40 towards Rabbit Ears Pass 7.8 miles from the junction of Highway 131 and US 40. A long pullout is on the right with a sign indicating a $1370 fine for shooting moose. The pullout is between mile markers 144 and 145. From Rabbit Ears Pass summit the pullout is 9.8 miles. From the middle of the pullout walk down the hillside 75 yards on a faint trail past a large cliff to the boulders.

SOUTHWEST RABBIT EAR BOULDER

The main block, down the hillside from the cliffs nearest the highway. The boulder is discernible by a large flat top that is easy to gain with a mere hop. A small cave is on the northeast side. Some wooden pallets are strewn below the boulder to add a white-trash feel to the area.

❏ 1. **Show Me V5** ★★
The problem starting inside the small cave on the left side. The small block to the left is off.

❏ 2. **Weather Report V5** ★
On the left side of the taller east face. Start low below the small block then move up and right to the top. A V6 traverses in from the left and finishes on Weather Report.

❏ 3. **Munjal Traverse V4** ★
Start low on the south face (left of #2) and traverse up and left on good holds to finish on a scary top-out.

❏ 4. **V0**
To the left of #3 is a straight-up problem on the far left face.

Down the hillside to the south is a reported V8 called Six Shooter. Tons more bouldering is within spitting distance.

Rabbit Ears Pass

Fish Creek Falls

Mark Wilford on The Couch   Photo by Sherman

NATURITA

The boulders of this region aren't frequently visited due to obscurity and limited climbing community. Years ago many problems were done by Mark Wilford, and more recently by Charlie Fowler and others. The quality of the stone varies from absolute choss to solid sandstone, while the problems consist of vertical faces, overhangs, and lip traverses. Year-round bouldering is possible in this mild environment. The remoteness and views of the La Sal and San Juans mountains make up for any bad rock and ascent failures.

Directions: From Naturita head west on State Route 141 to State Route 90 (1.9 miles from the Uravan 15 miles sign leaving town). From the intersection of Hwy. 141/90, follow Hwy. 90 and drive 5.2 miles to EE 22 (a dirt road). Take a right and drive another 1.7 miles to a dirt turn-off on the right (Antenna Crag can be seen to the north). Take the dirt road, staying to the right when it splits. A half-mile up the dirt road is a split. From this point the areas are visible and are as follows:

Antenna Crag (west with the antenna on top). No problems are listed for this area but the potential looks good. The first plateau east of Antenna Crag has nothing; the second plateau east is Lost World (some rock worth fiddling on) and behind it is Pebble Beach (no problems listed); the third plateau is The Ozone Layer (good rock) and the fourth long plateau is the Sawtooth Ridge (no problems listed as rock is low quality). From the split go straight to the Lost World Boulders. It is nearly impossible to reach the boulders in a car, so park before the washed-out culvert and walk about 200 yards to the east side of the small plateau. To reach The Ozone Layer go right at the split in the dirt road for 0.6 mile to another dirt road going left. Take the left road for less than a 100 yards and park. Walk a short distance (85 yards) to the brown boulders lining the western hillside. Sawtooth Ridge is east 0.3 mile after The Ozone Layer. The road is definitely four wheel drive and best taken on foot.

The Brain Area is located at 4.1 miles due east from the mine ruin (directions with The Garden Area) and below the ridge.

The Garden Area is 4.3 miles from the turn-off for EE 22, past an old mine ruin on the left. Turn right on BLM Road 4044 and drive to the top of the hill (0.3 mile). Park and walk 300 yards up the faint 4x4 road to the north ridge and skirt the north ridges base past a large detached block (approximately 80 yards) to The Couch.

Atomic Energy Boulders are located 5.8 miles from the turn off of Hwy. 90 on EE 22. A distinct dirt road is on the right with a large boulder sitting on the left side of EE 22. The boulders are approximately 150 yards from EE 22 on the righthand road. Problems range from V0 to V3 on numerous softer blocks!

Note: These problems are rarely done. Be cautious at all times for fragile holds, gritty exits, and exploding pebbles. With time and enough traffic many of the lower quality problems will clean up nicely.

Waves Boulder

Uphill (north) from Cut and Dry, approximately 40 yards, is a block with a wavy west face and near-horizontal overhang on its north side.

❏ **1. Retribution V4** ★★
The overhanging north traverse starting as low as possible and following the rail system to an easy top-out.

❏ **2. V0** ★
The left side of the west face. Exit up and left on a good rail.

❏ **3. V0** ★
The middle of the west face. A tenuous top-out on loose holds.

❏ **4. V0s**
On the adjacent boulder to the north of the Waves Boulder.

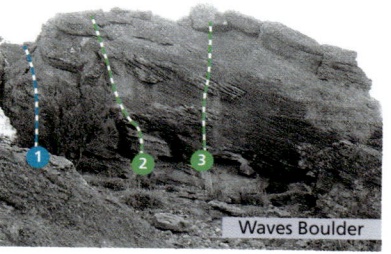

Waves Boulder

Single Minded Boulder

Located 10 yards to the west of the Waves Boulder.

❏ **1. V1**
The scoop on the south face behind the juniper.

❏ **2. Lout V2** ★
A sds in an overhanging scoop on the east face. A tad dirty.

Single Minded

Lip Boulder

Just uphill (north) from Single Minded is a short block with an overhanging southwest face. Not pictured.

❏ **1. White Lipped V4** ★★
A left to right traverse across the southwest face. Ends on the east face.

Cracked Block

Located about 15 yards to the southeast of the Waves Boulder. It has an overhanging north face with a wide crack filled with bones and debris. Not pictured.

❏ **1. Ridiculous Man V2**
A lip traverse starting low on the northeast arête.

❏ **2. A Single Moment V2** ★
A one-move dynamic problem right of the crack.

The Brain Area

This area, east of the mine ruin on EE 22, is found in the extensive boulderfields below the ridge. Expect problems on good stone.

The Garden Area

A pristine area with pine needle landings and plenty of shade. Numerous boulders line the north slope and offer hueco-covered blocks, slopers, and tall slabs. The listed boulder has the most prominent problems. Other boulders that have seen traffic are across BLM 4044 from the parking for The Couch.

The Couch

A beautiful block set just off the north ridge. A few splendid hueco problems climb up the east and northeast faces. Down-climb the south face. Top-outs are very loose and covered in pine needles.

❏ **1. V3** ★★
Start on a good left-hand pocket then up to a sloping edge then left. A V1 dihedral is just left and gritty!

❏ **2. V2** ★★
Just right of #1 is a tall problem that climbs big huecos.

❏ **3. V2** ★★
Just right of the east arête and up a gray lichen face. Filthy on top.

The Brain

❏ **4. V4** ★
Right again on the tan and gold face. Fragile undercling crux.

❏ **5. V5** ★
A traverse on the northeast face from right to left staying on the low huecos and ending on the east arête.

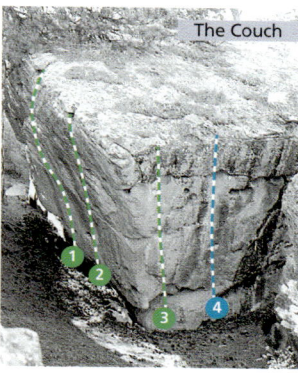

The Couch

RAMPART RESERVOIR

The Rampart Reservoir Recreation Area is home to granite boulders and spires. Every parking area within the Promontory Picnic Area affords first ascent possibilities. The texture is considerably different from the nearby Woodland Park Boulders. In general, the boulders are also lacking in quality. A great view of the reservoir, as well as Pikes Peak to the south, can be seen from some of the summits.

Note: A $4.00 fee is required to climb on the fragile and relatively low quality stone. No photos or problems are listed due to the low quality rock.

Directions: Take US Route 24 to Woodland Park from Colorado Springs. Turn right on FR 393 (Baldwin Street) and follow it to the intersection of Rampart Range Road and Rampart Range (Loy Creek Road). Turn right to Rampart Reservoir and drive 1.5 miles to FR 300. Turn right following the sign for Rampart Reservoir for 3.9 miles to FR 306. Another 1.3 miles brings one to the Promontory Picnic Ground Entrance. Go left and past the entrance kiosk to three pull-outs with boulders in them.

LEFT PICNIC AREA BOULDERS

A few slab problems on the block just over the left side of the fence surrounding the parking area.

RESERVOIR BOULDERS

The boulders sitting next to the outhouse in the last parking area of Promontory Picnic Area and down the hillside offer some decent problems. The problems are thin, painful slabs on sharp granite. Be well aware of fragile rock, lichen and pine needle covered top-outs.

WOODLAND PARK

Lining the hillsides above Rampart Range Road are beautiful lichen-covered blocks, nestled at an altitude of 8700'. One drawback, however, is that the texture of this Pike's Peak Granite produces a sensation akin to pulling on razor blades. If, however, your tips are prepared for some serious abuse, the perfect vertical faces and awesome cracks of Woodland Park are the ticket. The adventurous will appreciate the fact that for every boulder with developed problems there are at least that many waiting to be climbed.

Directions: Take US Route 24 from Colorado Springs to Woodland Park. Turn right on FR 393 (Baldwin Street, a McDonald's is at the intersection). The mileage is given from the intersection of Highway 24 and FR 393. Baldwin Street changes to Rampart Range Road on the way to the boulders. Do not turn right when Rampart Range Road heads right to Rampart Reservoir.

The Corridor and Disc area is located 3.6 miles from the intersection of Highway 24/FR 393 just off the left side of the road. Parking is found below the Disc. To reach The Corridor walk west up a well-beaten path from the Disc for approximately 80 yards.

DISC BOULDER

A novelty block as it rests on top of other boulders and is about as thick as a Big Mac. The V1 traverse across its lip is fun although rather painful. The boulder supporting The Disc has a few casual V0 slabs.

THE CORRIDOR

Uphill from the Disc Boulder is a group of tall blocks forming a tight gap. Problems are within and outside the gap on nice slabs.

CORRIDOR BLOCK

The first boulder on the right side of The Corridor.

❏ 1. **V0** ★★
Climb the flake just left of the left crack ending in the right crack.

❏ 2. **V1** ★★
The left crack is climbed by using finger and hand jams.

❏ 3. **V0**
The right (first) crack as one enters The Corridor that goes straight up.

GARGOYLE ROCK

Just opposite Corridor Block. There is no easy way off the block. Downclimb or downjump.

❏ 4. **V4** ★
Climbs the northeast arête up a set of laybacks to small pebbles.

❏ 1. **V2** ★★
A slabby face at the end of The Corridor before it turns right and exits.

The next three boulders are not pictured. These blocks make up the left side of The Corridor.

TRIATHLON BLOCK

A large block that has a nasty crack on the left side of the south face. A V2 follows the crack. Downclimb the easiest line or exit on suspect pebbles.

PILLAR ROCK

Just west of Triathlon, this makes up the left side of the V2 crack. Downclimb or summit via scary pebbles.

❏ 1. **V1** ★
The recently fern-filled (now clean) crack that angles slightly right.

HENGE BLOCK

The next boulder west of Pillar Rock. The left boulder making up the awful offwidth of Pillar Rock (#1). A tall V2 climbs the west face. It begins on good edges that get progressively worse. Downclimb or do the highball exit. Two crack problems are left of Henge Block. One is a V1 and climbs the south-facing hand crack. A V2 crack that faces Henge Block pulls through a roof crack with a bad landing, and is just left of a massive load of bat guano.

Disc Boulder

The Corridor

Howard/Sand Gulch

The near endless rock in this dry canyon has many manifestations: nice solid pockets to mungy lichen edges. Developed rock tends towards the better stone, but a demented mind has landscaped tall slabs. Although fairly limited, the main area makes for excellent sessions. The Spoils is currently being developed. **A hunting license must be in one's possession while bouldering here.**

Directions: From US Highway 50 in Salida (intersection of Highway 50 and Oak Street [CO Highway 291]) drive east to Howard. Take a left on Fremont County 4 and drive 0.5 mile across the Arkansas and go right at the T staying right on the dirt road FC 44 at the next intersection. Go 0.7 mile to a left on a rough dirt road (Sand Gulch). Drive 1.4 miles to a pullout on the left. Park and follow cairns west (toward a solar panel and stock tank) down 50 yards and across a wash to a distant second dry creekbed 150 yards (more cairns). Walk up this dry creek bed 440 yards staying in the right drainage until you run smack dab into the Mariposa Boulder.

Justin Douty on Mariposa V5

Mariposa Boulder

The first and largest boulder as one walks up the dry drainage. A wide-open corner is met as one approaches the southeast face. Over a dozen problems can be done on this higher quality boulder.

South Face

☐ 1. **V6** ★
Climbs through the left overhang on the southeast face starting on painful pockets to a big reach over the bulge.

☐ 2. **Mariposa V5** ★★★
A classic stand-up in the open corner. Finish straight up or move left into the high hole for a tad easier variation. A lower start off the lowest left-hand undercling makes a tough V7.

☐ 3. **V1** ★
The right-facing corner just right of Mariposa. A low start from under the roof boosts the grade to V8.

East Face

☐ 4. **V2** ★★
Immediately around the corner from the V1 corner is a committing and sloping slab. Use the arête for an easier variation.

☐ 5. **V2**
The next slab right starting off the ground-level block. A start from the ground is the same grade.

☐ 6. **V2** ★
The thin pocketed face on the northeast blunt arête.

☐ 7. **V0**
A short, fun warm-up on the left side of the north face.

☐ 8. **Downclimb V0**
The right-facing corner/ramp littered with big huecos and pockets. A great V0 climbs up the face right of the downclimb.

West Face

This wide expanse of pockets with a small overlap in the middle has problems from V1 (left), two V2s through the small overlap, to a V4 (far right-side bulge). A traverse can be done from right to left under the overlap finishing up on Wing.

☐ 9. **Wing V1** ★★★
The beautiful, highest pocketed face on the left side of the west face.

Miscellaneous Boulders

Continue up the drainage and a number of boulders are encountered with problems (V0-V4) including sit down starts, a pocketed arête, tall slabs, and innocuous lines.

Mariposa Boulder South Face

Mariposa Boulder East Face

Mariposa Boulder West Face

POCKET BOULDER

Walk a few minutes up the drainage to a fine, pocketed block sitting on an exposed, flat ledge. Excellent winter sunny exposure with a slew of short boulders in the vicinity with lines from V0 to V9.

South Face

❏ 1. **The Pocket Line V5/V9** ★★★

Straight up the south face on thin pockets and slots. A lowball start off the hueco jug catapults the grade to V9.

❏ 2. **V2**

The right face utilizing the big right-hand layback. Not very good stone.

❏ 3. **V0**

Around the corner on the east face is a low angle slab starting on a right-hand layback. Another V0 is just right.

North Face

The dark, short undercut side.

❏ 4. **V3**

The center problem starting off a good left-hand pocket to good edges.

❏ 5. **V2**

The right problem on the north face.

❏ 6. **V3**

On the left side of the west face above the tree landing. Starts off a sinker pocket and sloper next to the low corner.

❏ 7. **Red Line V5/V9**

The southwest arête starting from a high left pocket and small right-hand crimp. A low start off an undercling pocket and low sloper makes a solid, crimpy V9.

Pocket Boulder

Justin Douty in action on The Pocket Line

Symbols
10 Cents Short of a Dime V1 191
16 Horsepower V4 ★ 164
20 Percent V2 142
80 Percent V3 143

A
Abolish Monday Mornings V3 186
Above the Corridor Arête V3 23
A Brief History V3 193
Abyss V2 63
Ace of Spades V4 88
Addicted to Material Goods V5 187
Adventure Bouldering Part One V5 22
Adventure Land V1 130
Affinity V2 63
Afternoon Monsoon V5 184
Agent Orange V9 189
Agnes Vaille Boulder 120
Air Boulder V4 ★★★★ 19
Aircraft Carrier 64
Airing of Grievances V2 116
Alarm Clock Awakening V6 39
Allesandrina V1 153
Alley, The 190
All Hands on Deck V5 ★★★ 164
All Time Crack V6 128
Al Montana V10 185
Amber Waves V3 ★★ 81
American Hero V4 ★★ 96
Amitabha V6 36
Amphitheatre, The 30
Anaphylactic Shock V6 ★ 56
Anchor Boulder 205
Anchors Away V2 ★ 164
Apocalypse Area, The 168
Arch Enemy Slab 224
Arête Boulder 214
Arêtestein V7 ★★ 69
Arête, The V3 18
Arête, The V6 ★★★ 69
Artifact Boulder 211
ASAP V4 ★ 20
Aspen Arête V7 ★★★ 92
Aspen Boulder 92
Assault on a Minor V9 83
Assorted Stein V2-V7 ★★★ 69
Atari aka Double Dike Spider Arêtes V4 ★★★ 39
Atomic aka Tick Fever V7 166
Atrocity Exhibition V5 ★ 170
Authority, The V4 189
Average Ale V1 ★ 170
Average Arête V0 ★★ 167

B
B3PO V10 ★ 35
Back Boulder 75
Back Door Boulder 216
Back Stab V8 114
Backtalk V4 142
Badmouth V8 ★★★ 23
Bandits V1 106
Barnacle Boulder, The 72
Barracks V2 92
Bat Cave 204
Battleship, The 164
BB Shot aka Bob's Dyno V3 170
B.C.'s Western Boulders 211
Bear Creek Boulder 177
Bear Trap V7 38
Beastie Boulder 81
Beckon the Call V8 193
Belly V5 108
Bernholtz's Arête V6 166
Bessie V10 49
Best Boulder Problem in Colorado V8, The ★★★ 76
Best Boulder Problem in Unaweep, The V7 203
Best Buddy, The 203
Beyond Matters V8 50
Big Air V3 ★★★★ 19
Big Ass Boulder 189
Big Black 211
Big East 194
Big Easy, The 69
Big Easy Traverse V1 ★★ 69

Big League V8 or V9/ Growler V10 ★ 106
Big Luther V2 145
Big Mouth Boulder 134
Big NB 133
Big Nose Boulder 83
Big Picture, The V12? 135
Big Red Boulder 212
Big V4 ★★★ 163
Big West 193
Bird Hole Left V6 194
Black Arête V7 189
Black Beard V3 ★★★ 91
Black Block 152
Black Caesar Boulder 88
Black Corner V2 ★ 30
Blacked-Out Boulder 213
Black Mariah V3 ★★★ 22
Black Wall 140
Black Wave 212
Black Wave Area 212
Brain Area, The 212
Blade, The V4 23
Bleeding Lip Boulder 185
Bleeding Lip Traverse V6 185
Bleed V6 ★ 98
Blinded by the Light V1 131
Bliss Boulder 94
Blood Boulder 224
Blunt Arête V2 108
Blunt Boy V1 ★★★ 163
Blunt Pinch V1 81
Bob's Wall V5 ★ 30
Body Count V2 ★★ 95
Bolt Flake V2 20
Bone Boulder 109
Bone Park 209
Bone, The V5 109
Bonzai Boulder 168
Bonzai Left V6 168
Bonzai Right V5 168
Bonzai Straight Up V9 168
Bottom of the Heap Blocks 224
Boulder A Number One 74
Boulder, The (Campsite 5) 91
Boxcar Boulder 183, 214
Brain Area, The 227
Brain Fart V1 224
Brain, The aka Dr. Seuss Cave 212
Breakfast Boulder 148
Brilliant Wings V11 ★ 35
Broken Boulder 208
Bucket Cave 212
Bucket List Boulders 143
Bucket List V0 143
Buena Vista Boulder 112
Bulb, The V1 ★★★ 18
Burned at the Stake V11 41
Burning Bridges V6 144
Butch V6 116
Butter Boulders, The 71
Butter Hole V3 ★★ 167
Buzz Cockman V3 145

C
Camp 5 Boulders 91
Campground 5 V0-V? 217
Campground 7 Boulder V0-V6 217
Campsite 1 Boulder 31
Campsite 2 Boulder 32
Campsite 22 Boulders 74
Cancel Christmas Block 206
Cancel Christmas V6 206
Canine Boulder 74
Captain EO V3 ★ 163
Captain Kid V6 ★ 91
Cardboard Dog V6 115
Casual Comer V1 166
Caught in the Web V4 ★ 171
Cauliflower Traverse V7 108
Cave Area, The 170
Cave Lap V7 ★ 170
Celebrated Summer V7 171
Center El Skyland V4 ★★★ 166
Center El Turtle V6 193
Center Lincoln V1 ★★ 200
Centerline V2 109
Chained Heat V6 ★★ 112

Chapman Reservoir 74
Chasm Block 124
Cheeky Monkey V1 ★ 166
Che it Loud V8 ★ 100
Cherry Pie V6 115
Chick Climb V2 ★ 96
Child of Darkness V9 86
Chinese Algebra Boulder 213
Chinese Algebra V6 213
Chiseled Arête 207
Chuckler V2 115
Chucks' Roof 132
CIAOB V8 134
Cigarette Boulder 190
Cigarette Problem V4 190
Classicnessitude Arête V3 185
Cliché V4 156
Coal Creek Boulders 217
Cock Fighting V4 120
Code Name V5 189
Collage V4 100
Colored Boulder 209
Comfortably Numb V6 214
Compression Matters V7 50
Cool Arête, The V7 ★★★ 64
Corkscrew Boulder 68
Corkscrew V5 - V6 ★★★ 68
Corner Problem V1 145
Corridor Block 205
Corridors, The 136
Cottonwood Lake (Buena Vista) 217
Couch, The 227
Count Clovis V8 97
Country Cardio V4 189
Crack Boulder Problem V? ★★★ 223
Cracked Block 227
Cracked Boulder 110
Crack, The V10 ★ 72
Crack Traverse V2 ★ 30
Crack Wall 140
Crazy Horse V5 45
Creamtime V4 ★★ 81
Created by God V0 156
Crescent, The V4 82
Crested Butte 161
Crestone (North Crestone Campground) 217
Crimping Matters V10 50
Crotchety Arête, The V4 117
Cube, The 89
Cubism Area 89

D
Daisies and Butterflies V2 203
Dance of the Caucasian V 116
Dark Horse V10 45
Darkness to Light V1 185
Dawnella V1 145
Dawn till Dusk Wall 136
Dawn V4 136
Dead Man Arêtes 216
Death Slab aka Loose Bowel V2 129
Deception Rock 208
Deep Six Holiday V6 87
Dennika Marie V2 145
Dependent Boulders 99
Desert Rain V5 189
Desert Sun V3 185
Diagonal Seam Block 152
Diamond Block, The 195
Diaper Man V3 143
Dihedral Boulder aka Stompin 92
Directs V3 ★★ 94
Disagreement Man V3 142
Dog's Eye V3 ★
Don't Look Ma V3 173
Don't Stop Believing V5 114
Downclimb, The V0 18
Downclimb V0 114
Downhill Slide V1 143
Dragon's Head 32
Drunken Bumbler Arêtes, The 136
Due East V2 ★
Due West Boulder 75
Dugout Cave, The 135
DYC V3 156
Dynamic Plan Blocks 98

evo
ROCK + FITNESS

E

Earthbound Misfit V3 214
Earthmover Boulder 128
Earthmover V5 128
East Elk Creek Boulders-
New Castle 219
Eastern Block 194
Eastern Line V3 ★
East Face V3 46
East Hagerman Pass (Leadville) 218
East Scoop Block 151
Eco-conscious V4 189
Egg Boulder 89
Eldo Contingent's Area, The 158
Electric Hoedown V5 ★★ 164
Elephant Rocks/Shawsprings and Sideshow
Canyon 147
Ellen's Arête V8 190
Ellen's Boulder 190
El Vere V4 100
End of the Day V1 137
End of the Line 137
Envy V3 131
Envy Wall, The 131
Eric's Arête V5 158
Eric's Vicous Sloper Problem V4 172
Erratic Arête V2 90
Escape Hatch V2 ★ 163
Eukanuba Boulder 200
Euro Boulder 187
Explosive Man V3 147
Extra Stout V2 ★ 170

F

Faces Boulder 207
Fade Away V4 193
Faded V9 91
Fairie Grotto 132
Fall V6 123
Far East Boulders 101
Fat Bottom 171
Fat Bottom Hippie Chicks V3 ★★ 171
Fear and Chaos V8 187
Feared by Satan V5 156
Feats of Strength V0 116
Felix V6 ★★ 86
Fence Arête V4 223
Fence Arête V4 ★ 223
Fifth Boulder 22
Figure 8 Boulder 189
Figure 8 Traverse V3 189
Figure It Out V4 ★ 99
Fine Arête, The V7 142
Finger on the Steel V7 36
Fin, The V6 194
Fin V4 ★ 20
Fire Pit Area, The 16
Fireside Boulder 151
Fire the Still V8 128
First Boulder 94
First West Boulder 212
Fissure Boulder, The 123
Fissure, The V2 123
FITB Boulder 108
Flesh Taken V4 142
Flight of the Thresherman V5 130
Flyer V6 106
Flying High V6 ★ 170
Forever and Sunsmell V7 130
Fossil Boulder 209
Frankenstein V8 ★★ 69
Freakshow Boulders 147
Friday the 13th V7 ★★★ 39
Front Traverse V6 69
F Stop V5 ★★ 81
Fucker V4 115
Fun Gotti Boulder 224
Funky President V4 ★★ 95
Fun with Fatty V5 ★★ 35
Furry Flake V0 216
Fusion Wall 216

G

Gang of Three V4 190
Garden Area, The 227
Gash Rock 208
Geiman in a Blender V6 40

Gertrudestein V9 69
Get on the Good Foot V5 95
Get on Up V7 95
Get that Jug V3 116
Giant Steps Boulder 75
Giant Steps V4 ★★ 75
Gift of the Valkyrie V4 190
Girl Boulder 189
Glacial Erratics 90
Global Warming V8 185
Gloomy V3 ★ 167
Glory Arête V9 187
Glory Digger V5 ★ 171
Goal Post Area 84
Goal Post, The V4 84
Golden Arête V8 189
Golden Arm Traverse V11 187
Golden Dihedral V4 ★★ 20
Golden Face Block 158
Golden Overhang V2 ★ 20
Grand Valley Overlook Area 213
Great Gumby, The V8 42
Great White Boulder 108
Green Boulder 76
Green Dream, The V2 142
Grinch, The V3 206
Grisseltwist V10 ★ 69
Grit Spitter, The V2 147
Groove Boulder 173
Groove, The V1 173
Groovy V3 137
Grotto Wall Boulders
aka The World of Hurt 86
Gunnison 161
Guns and Roses V6 ★★ 68
Gutter, The 168

H

Hammer V5 128
Hand Jive Boulder 101
Hard Mantel Boulder 173
Hard Mantel V5 173
Hartman's Rocks 172
Heart Boulder 150
Hecla Heckler V4 115
Hell's Ditch V2 ★ 161
Here Comes the Skinny Man V3 147
Hernando's Hideaway 82
Hick Rocks 164
Hidden Arête V5 117
Hidden Grottos 141
High Times 166
High Wire V4 ★★ 90
Historical Conquests V5 190
Hold on to that Feeling V4 114
Hole in One Boulder 210
Holloway Boulder aka Poor Man's Bleau 200
Hone Stone 166
Honeycomb, The V1 157
Horizontal Crack Boulder 205
Hornsilver Campground 62
Hornsilver Day Use Area 62
Hot Dog V4 130
Hot Pants V3 ★★ 95
How Old are You Boys? V3 132
Hueco Area, The 154
Hueco Boulder, The 155
Hueco Warm-ups 157
Husky Boulder 87
Husky V3 ★★★★ 106

I

ICBJ aka Pass Walls Boulders 82
Ice Cream Blow Job V6 ★★★ 82
Ice V1 ★★★ 81
Ichi Ban V6 63
Ilium Boulders 178
Immersion Boulder 68
Immortality V7 ★★★ 56
Ineditable Boulder 86
Ineditable, The V6 86
Instances of Silence V7 134
In the Nick of Time V2 136
Intimidating Traverse V7 ★★ 198
Intimidator Boulder 198
Intimidator V2 198
Intimidator V2 ★ 198
Into the Woods V3 ★★★ 82

Into Thin Air V8 ★★ 19
Intruders V4 ★★★ 90
Invisible Sun V6 214
Iron Dollar-Cotopaxi 216
It's a Man's World V5 ★★ 95
It's a Wash V1 ★ 22

J

Jacques Cousteau V11 ★ 42
Jagged V0 ★ 162
James Brown Boulder 95
James Brown Boulders 94
Jamrock Part 1 V7 97
Jaws Boulder 80
JB Left 96
J Crack, The V5 166
Jealousy V3 131
Jeremy's Problem V4 ★ 198
Joint Rock 163
Journey of Foreigner V5 184
Jugga Mugga V2 116
Jumping Jack V7 187
Junior Cave 204

K

Kama V4 135
Kelsey Campground 219
Keystone Cave Boulder 190
Kia V4 154
Killing Moon, The V5 129
Kluttergarden, The 52, 59
Know it All V3 144

L

Lard Ass V6 170
Laser V4 184
Last Boulder 124
Last Stop, The 171
Last Stop V0 171
Last Tango in Durango V6 186
Latin Heat V5 214
Left Arête V6 ★★ 71
Left Block 106
Left Bullet V5 120
Left El Skyland V3 ★★★ 166
Left Gonad 210
Left Lincoln V4 ★★ 200
Left of Corkscrew V5 ★★ 68
Legacy of the Kid Boulder 186
Legacy of the Kid V9 186
Leroy V4 115
Lesoterica V5 ★★ 84
Less than Desirable Boulder 157
Let it Grow V2 130
Let The Chips Fall Where They May V0 212
Lichen Project V4 143
Lichenstein V6 ★ 69
Lightning Bolt Boulder 99
Lightning Bolt Crack V0 ★ 99
Lightning Foot Jones V3 ★★ 200
Light Sentence V3 ★★ 112
Lilly Boulders 174
Lime Kiln 219
Lincoln Creek Boulders 90
Linkenstein V5 ★★★ 69
Lip Boulder 227
Lippy V0 200
Liquor Store Boulder 214
Little Air V3 ★ 19
Little Arêtes Area 223
Little Left Arête 224
Little NB aka The Piano 132
Little Neighbor Blocks 140
Little Sandy Boulders 184
Little Visor V3 128
Livin' on a Prayer V8 36
Lolita V4 154
Lone Boulders 27
Lonely Stoners (Witches Canyon) 219
Lone Pine Campground 169
Loner Stone 99
Long NB 134
Look Ma V2 173
Loose Liver V2 129
Lorax, The V7 190
Lost Canyon 170
Lout V2 ★ 227
Loved by All V3 156

Love Matters V7 50
Lowball V1 109
Lower Ned 158
Low Linkenstein V10 69
Low Traverse V10 69
Lump, The V1 90
Luther's Boulder 145
Luther V2 145

M

M7 aka Green Iguana V7 40
Machine Head V5 ★★ 166
Magic Potion V5 187
Magister's Terrace V10 36
Mahone V5 ★★ 161
Main Boulder 90
Main Hang, The 171
Main Squeeze V6 ★★ 68
Main Treeline Boulder 82
Manginalogues V4 106
Man in the Moon V3 150
Mann's Warm Down V1 137
Mariposa Boulder 231
Mariposa V5 231
McCoy Gulch (Cortez) 219
Meadow, The 129
Meat Wallet V10 41
Meet Your Maker V1 143
Megalodon V7 ★★★ 40
Melonstein V6 ★★★ 69
Merotica V2 ★ 84
Mexican or Mexicant V2 216
Micro V1 ★ 161
Middle Arête V2 ★★ 71
Midnight Rider V3 195
Mike's Arête V2 ★★ 92
Mike's Face V1 131
Mike's Prow V2 ★★ 99
Mike's Slabs 134
Mikodin Cocktail V3 132
Milligan's Way V1
Mind Matters V12 50
Mine Boulder 177
Minor Thing V1 116
Mirror Pond Area 83
Mister Twister V2 ★★ 163
MM10 Boulder 169
Mojo Risen V7 41
Mulder V3 186
Monika V6 155
Monkey Boy V4 114
Monkey Hang V4 193
Monster, The 106
Montezuma 223
Moon Tide V1 96
Morning Wood 80
Morning Wood Mantel V2 ★ 80
Mortirner V1 171
Motze V7 88
Munjal Traverse V4 225
Murray Boulders 28
Murray Right V5 ★★ 28
Mutiny V3 116
My Turn V5 132
My Two Cents V1 191

N

Nail V6 128
Nameless Boulder 172
Names Boulders 144
Nasty Downclimb, The V0 154
Naturita 226
NBA Pro Jams V11 40
Ned's Highball aka Cyclops V3 130
Ned's Highball Arena 130
Ned's Pocket Wall 158
Ned's Wonderland of Rock 158
Neighbor Boulder 123
Neighbors Boulders 120
Never End V6 108
New Castle 198
New Freedom V7 ★★★ 23
Newman V2 116
Nickness Right, The V11 35
Nickness, The V10 35
Nimbly Bimblies 132
Nipple Ripper Traverse V5 186
North Back Breaker V4 108

North Block 191
North Face aka The Scoop V1 ★★★ 18
North Side Boulders 224
No Traffic V3 186
Nuerobashing V3 ★ 170
Nuthin' Beats Cope V7 ★★ 106

O

Off Ramp V0 ★★ 166
Oil Flat Road (Canon City) 220
Old Guard V8 ★★★ 41
Old Timer Arête V0 ★★ 171
Once-ler V1 190
One Mile Boulder 109
One V5 198
On the Fence V2 141
Orange Crush Rock 208
Orange Crush V1 ★★ 106
Orange Face Boulder 83
Orange Face V3 86
Other Warm Up Boulder, The 98
Ouray 220
Outhouse Wall 90
Out of Bounds V1 ★ 167
Overlooked Boulder 100

P

Panacea V2 137
Panama Red V5 115
Panorama Boulder 108
Pappy Boulder 100
Pappy V1 ★ 100
Park Boulder 104
Parking Lot Block V4 86
Pass Boulders, The 100
Passion, The V9 40
Pass, The V? 100
Patrol Boulder 80
Paw Me V0 81
P Boulder 81
Peace Arête V4 131
Penitente Canyon 138
Penny Boulder 191
Penny Candy V1 191
Perfect 10 V3 150
Percent, A V0 142
Pete's Wicked Traverse V5 ★ 170
Petra V4 153
Petrified Arête V3 185
Petrified Boulder 185
Petrified Prow V5 185
Picnic Area 138
Pillar, The 168, 223
Pillar, The V2 20
Pinapple Express V5 ★★★ 36
Pinchenstein V4 ★★ 69
Pink Floyd Boulder 214
Pipe Dream V2 133
Piranha Boulder 80
Pit Boulder, The 217
Pit Crack, The V1 217
Pit Full of Patchouli V4 ★ 171
Plethora Boulder aka Right Gonad 210
Pocket Boulders 129
Pocket Change V3 189
Pocket Line, The V5/V9 232
Pocket Line V2 143
Pocket Route V1 ★★ 71
Pockets of Perception V3 189
Pointed Pain V4 123
Pole Rock 209
Portrait of an Artist Boulder 161
Portrait of an Artist V5 161
Precision V6 140
Press Test V3 109
Pretentious Vendor of Invention V10 42
Prow, The V7 71
Prow V6 94
Psycho Boy V6 212
Pumpkin Chucking V6 129
Pyramid, The , 31
Pyramid, The V0 91

Q

Quaking V5 140
Quality Granite Block
Quarry, The (Del Norte) 221
Queen Ann's Revenge V5 ★★ 91

Quimby Boulder 63
Quimby V2 63
Quivering Quill Blocks 224

R

Racing the Sun V2 214
Raindrops to Waterfalls V2 203
Rank V5 171
Raptor Boulders 131
Reanimator V8 87
Rebekah V5 150
Recession or Depression V7 190
Red Boulder 59
Red Line V5/V9 232
Red Sky Boulder 162
Red Sky V6 162
Redstone 66
Renga V2 132
Retribution V4 227
Retribution V4 ★★ 227
Reverend, The 156
Reverse Population Growth V6 187
Rhythm of the Saints V8 ★ 64
Rib, The V5 185
Richard Simmons Total Body Workout V3 187
Riders on the Storm V3 ★★ 41
Ridiculous Man V2 227
Rifle Mountain Park 220
Right Arête V1 ★ 71
Right Block 106
Right Bullet V6 120
Right El Skyland V2 ★★★ 166
Right Guard V7 41
Right to Your Left V2 109
Ripper Boulder, The 216
Ripper, The V5 217
River Pirate V0 116
Road Block 153
Road Boulder 191
Robinson's Rail V9 91
Rock Garden 207
Rock Garden Boulders 129
Rock Shop 204
Roller Girl Boulder 81
Roller Girl V2 ★★ 81
Romeo V6 ★★ 64
Roof Area 141
Roof Boulder 74
Root Canal, The 154
Root Down V5 ★★★ 81
Root of an Unfocus V9 132
Running Fart V2 ★ 224
Ryan's Frightmare (Big Jim) V2 137

S

Sacred Traverse V10 187
Safety First V3 ★★★ 23
Sailing Hawks 184
Sanctuary, The aka The Room 190
Saquache (CO 114) 220
Scary V6 ★ 19
Scoop, The V2 71
Scott's Arête aka Assboss V8 ★ 200
Scott's Arête aka Assboss V8 200
S Crack Block 214
S Crack V1 214
Seam V? ★★ 81
Second Boulder 22
Second West Boulder 212
Seem V0 131
Separate Wall V3 94
Setting Sun V4 83
Sex After 50/51 V8 ★★ 72
Sex Machine V4 ★ 95
Shack, The V2 124
Shadow, The V4 ★★★ 22
Shady Character 198
Shapes Boulder 140
SHAW SPRINGS 147
Sheep's Nose 14
Shelf Road 220
Shield, The 166
Ship's Prow V2 195
Short Change V1 15
Shortie V0 109
Show Me V5 225
Sideshow Boulder 147
Sidewinder Canyon/Balloon Ranch Boulders 147

Sign Boulder 60
Simplestein V0-V2 69
Single Minded Boulder 227
Single Moment, A V2 ★ 227
Sing the Sorrow V7 ★ 36
Singular Affair V3 ★★ 35
Sit Down V2 31
Skully 186
Skully Direct V3 186
Skyland 161
Slabber V1 133
Slab du Jour 129
Slab du Jour V2 129
Slab Happy V2 ★ 163
Slab Masters of the Universe V2 ★★ 162
Slab Rock 101
Slabs Kick Ass V2 ★★ 162
Slabs Rule V2 ★★ 167
Slabular Block 211
Slab V3 ★ 41
Slab Wall 223
Slam Dunk V3 96
Slap Happy V4 133
Slinky Plus Escalator V11 135
Slippery Serpent V3 129
Slippery Slope V1 143
Sliver V7 ★ 91
Slope Boulder 90
Slopenstein V6 69
Sloping Matters V8 50
Slot Block, The 168
Slot Minimalist V? 134
Slot Problems 140
Slum, The 204
Small Boulder 148
Smashing Boulder 22
Smile Happy Crack V2 136
Snug Slot V4 ★★ 168
Society Turn 177
Solar Collector, The 106
So Many Times V7 137
Something for Nothing V4 ★★★ 23
Something Must Break V4 ★ 168
Something Shitty V2 143
Something Wicked this Way Comes V4 184
Sound of Wind, The V5 129
Southern Block 212
South Face Rock 86
South Face V1 46
South Face V2 46
South Platte 223
South Side Boulders 223
South Slabbers V0-V1 40
South Slabs V1 - V3 ★★ 68
Southwest Rabbit Ear Boulder 225
Spades V6 88
Spice Rock 161
Spider Monkey V2 ★ 171
Spill Some Wine V2 133
Split V7 131
Spoils, The 221
Spooookie V2 ★★ 39
Sprung V5 92
Squat 108
Squeeze Box V6 117
Squeeze Job V2 17
S Seam V3 214
Stand and Deliver V5 190
Star Crossed Lovers V5 ★★★ 64
Stealth Blocks-Buena Vista 221
Steamboat Springs 225
Steep Arête V3 117
Stein Boulder, The 69
Stemming Matters V6 50
Sticky Fingers V5 ★★ 56
Still Feel Gone V4 ★ 164
Stinkin' Lincoln V5 200
Stinkin' Lincoln V5 ★★★ 200
Stinkin' Linkage V7 ★★★ 200
Stinky V5 ★ 171
Stompin V7 92
Storm Boulder 94
Straight Up Pocket Problem V2 ★ 69
Striped Rock 209
Sub Boulders 180
Substantial Slab Boulder 151

Sugar Cube, The 167
SUMMIT COUNTY 222
Sunday Driver V3 186
Sunday Stroll Boulder 186
Sunday Stroll V6 186
Sunset Boulder 88
Sunset Cruise V8 88
Sunshine Boulder 76
Supernatural Boulder 164
Supernatural V10 164
Swan Mountain Boulders 223

T
Tall Overhang Area 223
Target Practice V4 88
Tasty V2 114
Taylor Canyon 167
Teepee Boulder 195
Telephone Boulder 198
Tempt Fate V7 ★★ 106
Texas Boulders 204
Thing, The V3 99
Three Barrel High V7 ★ 40
Three Slices V5 189
Three V7 198
Throw Me a Stick V0 145
Tied-Up Boulders 138
Tier Boulders 128
Till Dusk V3 136
Tojo Risen V6 ★ 41
Tonsils Boulder 22
Too Big for Britches V5 144
Too Good to Be True V2 114
Top-out or Tapout V4 63
Total Immersion V2 ★★ 68
TR #3 (Vegetarian's Delight) V6 ★★★ 20
Trabaharder V9 200
Trabaharder V9 ★★★ 200
Tragedy Resides in You V6 56
Trail Rocks 138
Transient Filament, A V5 108
Treasure Chest, The 91
Tree Hugger V2 97
Treeline Area 82
Trees on Rock V4 134
Triage V2 154
Triangle Boulder 184
Triangle Stone 141
Tributation V7 ★★★ 108
Triple Decker V4 ★★ 101
Triplet V1 ★★ 31
Trite Bologna V2 75
Tropic of Capricorn V7 ★★ 164
Tsunami Boulder 184
Tsunami Relief Arête V7 184
Tsunami V3 184
Tunnel Boulders 104
Turd Boulder 32
Turkey Perch Boulders 224
Turkey Rock Area 223
Turkey Rocks - South Side Boulders 223
Turkey Tail 224
Turkey Tail - North Side Boulders 224
Turtle Lake Boulders 191
Twang V4 134
Tweak Wall 171
Twisted Tree V2 132
Two Smoking Klems V3 203
Two V6 198

U
UFO, The 167
Ultimate Sideshow Boulders 147
Unaweep Canyon 202
Unbeaten Path Boulders 101
Uncivilized V8 ★★ 41
Under the Sea V6 189
Underwear Direct V3 ★
Ungenius Wall 144
Unknown Pleasures V4 ★ 170
Uphill Affair V0 216
Upper Blocks 216
Upper Boulderfield 211
Upper Boulderfield aka Bulldog Boulders 98
Upper Ned 158
Up Side of Down, The V7 114
Urango V8 187

Urinary Tract Wall 90
US Highway 50 (Parkdale to Cotopaxi) 221

V
V0 Block 59
V0s Slab 20
Vaporizer, The V3 117
Victoria's Secret 209
Virgin Boulder, The 138
Visor Boulder 128
Voltaire V8 89

W
Waffler, The V3 ★ 19
Walden V5 82
Walk Softly Sit Start V11 36
Walk Softly V9 ★ 36
Warm Up Boulder, The 98
Warm Up Rock 161
Warm-up Slab 152
Washout Boulder 22
Wash Your Mouth Out V4 22
Waterfall Project, The V10 41
Wave Corridor 137
Waves Boulder 227
Wave, The 162
Wave V5 185
Weather Report V5 225
Web V1 ★★ 171
Web Wall, The 171
Wedge, The 163
Weider Boulder 72
West Block 172
West Bulge V2 109
Western One V4 ★ 193
West Face V2 46
West Virgin Boulder 138
Whatever Boulder 145
Whatever Dom Wants V5 174
Whatever V2 145
Whirlpool Area 82
Whirlpool Arête aka The Battle Royale
V7/V10 sds ★★★ 82
White Boulder Area 87
White Corner V7 ★★ 17
White Dike V0 115
White Face V11 87
White Grease Streak V0HH 167
White Guilt V4 155
White Lipped V4 227
White Power V1 ★★★ 108
White Right Boulder 59
White Rock 187
Why V4 132
Wilder Arête, The V10 164
Wild Rock Project Wall 97
Wild Rocks Boulders 96
William Shatner V12 ★★★ 35
Will's Left Line V5 ★★ 23
Wing V1 231
Witches Canyon 139
Witches You Bitches V2 140
Wolf Creek Pass 221
Wonder, The V4 193
World's Smallest Problem V0 ★ 200
Worm Area, The 173
Worm Drive V4 ★★ 68
Worm, The V0 173

Y
Yardstick, The V9 96
Yasmine's Arête V5 156
Yasmine's Boulder 156
You People/Power Surge 218
You're Not that Special Boulder 132

Z
Zach's Campground 167

ONE MOVE TOO MANY

By Volker Schoeffl, Thomas Hochholzer
& Editor Sam Lightner, Jr.

For those of us who've made one move too many, esteemed German sports medicine doctors Dr. Volker Schoeffl and Dr. Thomas Hochholzer provide an in-depth examination of common climbing injuries, treatments, and prevention. From the mildest case of belayer's neck to a complete finger pulley rupture, get the information you need to avoid injury or to get back on the rocks as soon as possible.